More acclaim for MARY

"An intelligent, trenchant puzzling over the details of history and culture, as well as a reclamation project . . . a tremendous accomplishment."—*Seattle Times*

"*Mary* has the starch of real history to it . . . [Hazleton's] writing flows like wine and readers of fiction as well as history will enjoy it . . . Those who revere Mary needn't worry that this book will de-mystify one of the world's great religious figures. Instead, Hazleton adds a layer to the Mary story that actually makes her more remarkable than ever."—*Santa Cruz Sentinel*

"Although Hazleton's research is scholarly, her prose is anything but academic. Instead her words like beat like a human heart, warm and strong and full of possibility. In fact, this book may remind readers of Anita Diamant's *The Red Tent*, for both offer lush you-are-there descriptions and a passionate female perspective . . . Absorbing reading . . . difficult to put down."—*Oakland Tribune*

"Hazleton not only helps readers to see who this Mary might have been but also places her in a social and religious context, shows how she absorbed the goddess myths, and does it all in language that is thoughtful, evocative, and eminently readable . . . Hazleton's musings on the Resurrection and on the meaning of Mary's virginity are dazzling to read and weighty to ponder."—*Booklist* **(starred review)**

"The book weaves an amazing tapestry of the threads of Maryam's skills, experiences and actions, all plausible . . . Hazleton provides fascinating details of Galilean women's common knowledge of herbs, healing and midwifery/abortion . . . She convinces readers by the end of the book to reject—or at least reconsider—the traditional image of Mary as quiet, humble and self-denying."—*Charlotte Observer*

"A knowledgeable journalist profiles history's most renowned Jewish mother . . . This Mary isn't the blue-robed icon painted by Fra Angelico or the young mother carved by Michelangelo, but throughout it all, Maryam remains full of grace."—*Kirkus Reviews*

"At last! A real, flesh-and-blood Mary. Recent scholarship about Jesus, situating him in the social and political milieu of first-century Palestine, now extends to his mother, Mary. Far from robbing us of faith, this grounding of Mary's life as a brown-skinned, struggling peasant girl invites us deeper into the sheer, paradoxical mystery of faith."
—**Sister Helen Prejean, author of** *Dead Man Walking*

"Here is the Mary we've been searching for, the strong, courageous, wise woman we always knew had to exist. Lesley Hazleton's riveting biography will resonate deeply with contemporary women worldwide. Powerful and empowering, inspired and inspiring, this is a book that will move you to tears."—**Naomi Wolf, author of** *The Beauty Myth*, **cofounder of the Woodhull Institute for Ethical Leadership**

"Drawing on a wide range of sources including the sometimes suppressed history of the feminine in ancient religions, Hazleton paints a convincing picture of Mary, the mother of Jesus. Both scholars and nonspecialists are bound to enjoy this highly readable intellectual and spiritual treat."—**Harvey Cox, Hollis Professor of Divinity, Harvard University, and author of** *Common Prayers*

"With all the biographies of Jesus, we finally have a study of the most important person in his life: his mother, Mary. Lesley Hazleton gives us a rich, provocative, suggestive, and enormously insightful exploration of one of the most influential yet neglected women in world history."—**Susannah Heschel, Eli Black Professor of Jewish Studies, Dartmouth College**

"By far the most exciting treatment of Mary I have ever encountered. Hazleton's historical and literary imagining is deeply grounded in thorough research into the conditions of life in ancient Galilee and Judea. She summons her most powerful prose for treatment of the most sensitive issues—Mary's impregnation and her experience of her son's gruesome death by crucifixion—and brings her trauma and struggles to life like no other recent writer."—**Richard A. Horsley, Distinguished Professor of Liberal Arts and the Study of Religion, University of Massachusetts Boston, and author of** *Jesus and Empire*

MARY

A FLESH-AND-BLOOD BIOGRAPHY
OF THE VIRGIN MOTHER

LESLEY HAZLETON

BLOOMSBURY

Excerpts from "Thunder, Perfect Mind," on pp. 205–6, taken from pp. 297, 301–302 in *The Nag Hammadi Library in English*, 3rd, Completely Revised Edition, James M. Robinson, General Editor. Copyright © 1978, 1988 by E. J. Brill, Leiden, The Netherlands. Reprinted by permission of HarperCollins Publishers Inc.

Published by Bloomsbury Publishing, New York and London
Distributed to the trade by Holtzbrinck Publishers

The Library of Congress has cataloged the hardcover edition as follows:

Hazleton, Lesley, 1945–
Mary : a flesh-and-blood biography of the Virgin Mother / Lesley Hazleton.—1st U.S. ed.
p. cm.
Includes bibliographical references and index.
ISBN 1-58234-236-9
1. Mary, Blessed Virgin, Saint—Biography. I. Title.
BT605.3.H39 2004
232.91—dc22
2003017403

Paperback ISBN 1-58234-475-2
ISBN-13 9781582344751

First published in hardcover by Bloomsbury Publishing in 2004
This paperback edition published in 2005

1 3 5 7 9 10 8 6 4 2

Typeset by Hewer Text Ltd, Edinburgh

All papers used by Bloomsbury Publishing are natural, recyclable products made from wood grown in well-managed forests. The manufacturing processes conform to the environmental regulations of the country of origin.

Printed in the United States of America by Quebecor World Fairfield

For Gloria Loomis

CONTENTS

INTRODUCTION

She is thirteen. Short and wiry, with dark olive skin. The trace of a mustache on her upper lip, soft black down on her arms and legs. The muscles are hard knots in her arms, solid lines in her calves.

Her hair is almost black, and has been folded into a single braid down her back for as long as she can remember. The weight of it raises her chin and makes her walk tall, as she has learned to do when carrying jars of water or bundles of kindling on her head. You don't bend under the burden. You root into the ground and grow out of it, reaching up and becoming taller. The greater the weight, the taller you become: the peasant woman's secret of making the burden light.

Her thin linen shift is torn from snagging on rocks and thorns. Even the patches are torn, and the original black has long since faded into gray. When there's a village feast—a wedding or a circumcision—she begs a few threads of brightly colored wool from the old women, the ones too infirm to do anything but sit and weave, passing stories and shuttles back and forth in the sun-baked courtyards. Then she and her girl cousins huddle together, giggling as they work the threads into each others' braids. They have two colors: red from madder juice, yellow from kaolin clay. They've never seen blue wool. Only the rich can afford indigo, and in this village, as in all the Galilee villages, everyone is poor.

The shift hides the gentle bulge in her belly. She is unmarried, and pregnant. Sometimes, when she's sure nobody else is around, she'll fold her hands just below the curve, feeling how much it has grown.

1

Her grandmother once told her you could know a child's sex before it is born by where you put your hands: above the belly means a girl, below the belly, a boy. Or is it the other way around? She can't remember, and it doesn't really matter. Like every pregnant woman, she hopes for ten fingers, ten toes, a hungry mouth, and a lusty yell—a healthy baby, despite the odds.

She knows how long those odds are. All the young women do. They've heard the stories the old women tell down by the spring, washing themselves once they've spread the laundry to dry on the rocks, and then lingering to gossip. Horror stories told by women splendid and terrifying in their brief nakedness as they raise their shifts to pour water over creased bellies and drooping breasts.

Yes, you can die in childbirth. Many do. The first time especially. You can howl for hours, even days, until it takes three women to hold you down as the midwife kneels between your legs, her hands covered in your blood. She presses her head hard into your belly, trying to force the child out, until the pain is so bad that you beg and pray to Isis, to Artemis, to any and every god, to help you, forgive you, spare you. Every god, that is, but Yahweh, the god of all gods, too grand and too remote to hear a peasant woman's pleas. You hear yourself begging to die, cursing the child that is struggling inside you, cursing even the name of your husband and all his issue, for doing this to you.

Yet this girl is not afraid.

Her name is Maryam. A name so common in her time and place that if you call out "Maryam," one out of every three women is likely to answer. The Latin version of her name, Maria, will come into common usage only four centuries after her death, once the universal Catholic church has been established with its base in Rome. Later still, in what will become the English-speaking world—for this is some two thousand years ago, and English does not yet exist as a language—she will be known as Mary.

Even in her own time, her name gets lost in translation. In Hebrew, the formal, ritual language of her people, she is Miriam, after the sister of Moses, the great priestess who led the Israelites in song after they crossed the Red Sea in their exodus from Egypt. In Greek, the administrative language of the Roman Empire throughout the eastern Mediterranean, she is Mariamne—the name of King Herod's most beloved wife, the Hasmonean he married to bolster his claim to Jewishness, then fell obsessively in love with, and so, in the end, murdered. In Coptic, the Egyptian language in which many of the second- and third-century gnostic gospels will be written, her name is Mariham. And in Arabic, in which she will be honored in the eighth century in the only sura in the whole of the Koran to be named after and devoted to a woman, her name is Maryam. The same name as the one she goes by, but in a different language.

The language she speaks is Aramaic—the language of the Assyrians, from the region of Aram, near Damascus, whose empire dominated the whole of the Middle East eight hundred years before she was born. This is the language that displaced the Israelite Hebrew and countless other local tongues to become the lingua franca of the eastern Mediterranean for well over a millennium, in a wide arc from what is now Iran all the way to North Africa. It is both the language of trade and the peasant language, spoken by those who live by whatever meager crops they can coax from desert and dust, rocks and thorns. Its multiple dialects bind Judeans and Galileans, Syrians and Persians, Egyptians and Arabs, Nabateans and Idumeans—all the peoples, tribes, and nations living under the far-flung rule of the eastern Roman Empire.

The Aramaic name is important—the Middle Eastern name—for Maryam's is a Middle Eastern story. Where Mary floats to us on a cloud of incense, a delicate European draped in silk, Maryam carries the scent of heat and dust clinging to her skin and her thin linen shift. One is the legend; the other, the real woman. And if we are to reach beyond the legend, we must surely start with the most basic gesture of respect. Let us do Mary the honor, then, of calling her by her real name,

Maryam—the name she recognized and responded to, the name she thought of as hers.

Some two thousand years have passed since Maryam was thirteen, and yet the date she gave birth is deeply embedded in our consciousness. We number years by A.D. and B.C. (Anno Domini, and Before Christ) a system conceived by the Scythian bishop Dionysius Exiguus in the sixth century, formulated by Isidore of Seville in the seventh, popularized by the Venerable Bede in the eighth, and now universal. Whether in Jewish or Arab Jerusalem, in Cairo or Damascus, in New York or London or Paris or Tokyo, we measure time this way. We do it so easily, so automatically, that we rarely if ever pause to ask where it began. The twenty-first century since what? The year 1776 or 2010 since when?

No matter what faith we profess—or abjure—we date our checks, invoices, e-mails, newspapers, newscasts, history books, birthdays, anniversaries by this one event that took place in the Middle East two thousand years ago. That year in Maryam's life is seamlessly integrated into everyday twenty-first-century life. It makes no difference if we substitute the political correctness of C.E. and B.C.E. (Common Era and Before the Common Era), since the "common era" dates from that same moment. Maryam gave birth, and even the strongest atheist cannot conceive of time without acknowledging her.

How, then, can we know so little about her?

She lived in Nazareth, that we know. And she had a son. Beyond these bare facts, she is given mere cameo appearances in the New Testament gospels: anxious at the temple and at the wedding at Cana, and in only the last one, John, grieving at the foot of the cross. Even then she is nameless, simply "his mother." And Paul? In all his voluminous letters, he never even mentions her.

Everything else we think we know—even who her parents were—is legend accrued over the centuries, far removed from her in both time and place. And though these legends are magnificent, they work as perhaps all legends do: they obscure any idea of who the real person was. Each successive image of Mary has taken her progressively further from the reality of Maryam. She has been used, as all those who are venerated are inevitably used, to further individual, social, theological, even political causes. She has been garbed in silver and pearls, crowned with gold and girded with angels. And in the process, she has disappeared. She has become all image and no reality: a virtual Mary. Or rather, an infinite number of virtual Marys.

Many Christians do not even care to entertain the fact that she was a Jew. And Jews tend to respond in kind. In Israel, she is called *Maria hakedusha*: "the holy Maria." The use of the Latin Maria instead of the Hebrew Miriam is a means of distancing her, keeping her at arm's length as though to say, "No, not one of ours." Another way, that is, of stripping her reality from her.

What was that reality, then? Who was she? Who must she have been? Who could she have been?

Just asking the questions is exciting. We are so used to the image that the very idea of the real person sets the eyes alight, the mind to wondering. And yet precisely because we are all, one way or another, deeply involved with her, there is also a great sense of trepidation.

Virginia Woolf's biographer Hermione Lee wrote that readers of Woolf's journals "will feel an extraordinary sense of intimacy . . . They will want to call her Virginia, and talk proprietorially about her life. She seems extremely near, contemporary, timeless. But she is also evasive and obscure."

How odd to read this about someone who left a vast trove of written material, let alone the mounds of writings about Woolf by those who knew her—someone we can see in photographs, who existed in living memory—as I was researching the life of a woman who left no written material and about whom we have nothing at all written by her contemporaries. No eyewitness accounts, no recollections of those who knew her, not even a record of birth or death. It is as though the most famous and revered woman in the world never existed in the flesh.

The proprietoriness and protectiveness that Lee notes about Woolf exist a hundredfold, if not a thousandfold, when we come to Maryam. And this is daunting. In the four years it took to research and write this book, I've fielded innumerable intrigued questions from friends and acquaintances who knew what I was working on and were eager to know what I had found out. Yet I sensed that more than answers, what they wanted was reassurance. There was a certain discomfort, maybe even embarrassment, at the very idea of Maryam the flesh-and-blood woman. A feeling, perhaps, that this is one figure we shouldn't touch. That we'd be better off to leave her alone, to surrender her to myth and legend, accede to the established church image of her.

I suspect the source of this unease is a fear that she may emerge from any biographical exploration as less than we would wish for. If we strip away the aura, we fear standing there bereft. And this fear seems almost Freudian. The image of her as the ultimate mother—a symbol of maternity whose physicality has been transformed into the metaphysical—reaches deep into even the most agnostic heart. We quake at the idea of getting too close, at the prospect of the sacred revealed as human.

The "official" biography of Maryam has survived and flourished over two millennia for a very good reason: it works. Yes, it is impossible for a virgin to give birth. And yes, that is precisely why the story works. It is a mystery tale: a mystery both in the modern, detective sense and in the far older, religious sense, touching on things mysterious and unknown to mere mortals. The crux of her story—the virginal mother—is the perfect paradox. The sound of one hand clapping pales by comparison.

How dare I, then?

This is the question that haunted me as I began this book. How dare I even think of a biography of someone so intimate, so integral a part of our culture, and yet simultaneously so remote? How dare I seek the flesh-and-blood woman behind the legend?

I knew that the simplicity of asking who she was and who she must have been was deceptive. Such questions lead straight into a minefield of deeply held beliefs, unwitting preconceptions, cultural assumptions, even vested interests. Yet once I had asked them, they couldn't be unasked. I wanted to know. There was no way to go but forward. And though I didn't start out with a detailed map, I had at least a clear idea of the lay of the land.

I lived in Jerusalem for thirteen years, working first as a psychologist and then as a political and cultural journalist. Those years gave me fluency in Hebrew, a rough grasp of Arabic, and the ability to decipher more Aramaic than I'd thought. More important, however, they gave me a strong Middle Eastern sense of both place and time.

In most of the modern world, two thousand years ago seems an eternity. In the United States, twelfth-century Anasazi ruins are called prehistoric; a foreign visitor has to do a double take and remember that history is relative—that this is the "New World" and that so far as most Americans are concerned, their history only began in the fifteenth century.

Not so in the Middle East, where what happened two thousand years ago has a tangible presence: cultural, religious, and above all, political.

There are other places with ancient pasts, to be sure. But in Europe, say, Greek and Roman ruins have shed their religious and political significance. Tourists can admire a temple of Apollo with carefree ease; nobody believes in Apollo any more. In the Middle East, however, nothing ever seems to shed religious and political significance. What is prehistory in the States and archeology in Europe—magnificent ruins ensuring a continuous flow of tourist revenue—is everyday political reality in this part of the world.

Those years in Jerusalem either warped or strengthened my sense of time, depending on your point of view. Events of two thousand years ago seem close, familiar. You live with history, just a short walk from the giant ashlar stones of the retaining walls of Herod's temple in Jerusalem, his pride and joy and the cause of as much trouble two thousand years ago as today.

How not have the long view of the present, reaching deep into the past, when a single olive tree can be a thousand years old or more? How not be aware of what happened in this land two millennia ago when the very place names—Nazareth, Bethlehem, Jerusalem, Capernaum, Galilee, the Jordan River—are familiar to you from childhood, when you know them from Bible stories, from Christmas carols, from the Koran, from the Passover Haggadah, from hymns, folk songs, and spirituals.

You'd think that when you live here, everyday familiarity would dull the aura of these places. Not so. Instead, you incorporate them into your sense of time. You leap millennia in a sentence, even in a thought. The Via Dolorosa is where Jesus carried the cross and where there's this blue-fronted antique store full of old postcards and poor man's icons made of tin. The Mount of Beatitudes, overlooking the Sea of Galilee, is where Jesus gave the Sermon on the Mount and a perfect place to spend the night in the convent guest house. The Temple Mount is the site of both the first and second temples of Yahweh, but it's the two Islamic domes—the Dome of the Rock and the El-Aksa Mosque, gold and silver—that create its grace and majesty today. The flagstone floors, subterranean flights of stairs, and grim-faced Eastern Orthodox nuns in the Church of the Holy Sepulchre, built over the site of the crucifixion, make a film buff think of the classic movies of Sergei Eisenstein from the 1920s and 1930s.

Everything is anachronism, not in the usual sense of being out-of-date, but in the more precise sense of being out of its place in time. Or rather, in two times at once: simultaneously past and present.

Sometimes, in fact, it seems there is no such thing as the past at all. In this history-soaked part of the world, you could well argue that history does not even exist.

Nothing is ever done with. Nothing ever past. Stones and slingshots, the weapons of biblical tales, were the weapons of the Palestinian Intifada in the late 1980s. For years, the most popular Israeli sandals—basically just strips of leather on a leather sole—were called *tanachiot,* "biblicals." Jewish settlers' claims to the land are based on Hebrew texts that originated 2,500 years ago. The hatred and violence on both sides are of epic Old Testament dimensions. And in Nazareth, the most bitter source of tension in the past few years, pitting Moslems and Christians against each other, has been the attempt to move the shrine of a nephew of Salah ed-Din, known as Saladdin to westerners. The nephew was mortally wounded on July 4, 1187, when Salah ed-Din's forces decidedly defeated the Crusaders at the battle of the Horns of Hittin, and he was brought back to Nazareth to die. The idea of moving his modest shrine would be insult enough to Moslems; adding insult to the injury is that the move was planned in order to create more parking space for the marbled Basilica of the Annunciation nearby.

This is the way of the Middle East. The past reverberates through the present; the present cannot shake off the past. There is none of the distance usually required for the historical view. Yet for me, this compression of time seemed to help rather than hinder.

When I began to think about who Mary really was, I could see her reflection all around me. Not in plaster statues and gold-flecked holy cards, nor in the richly decorated icons of the Eastern churches, nor even the masterpieces of Renaissance art. These were the Mary of devout imagination: a figure divorced from her time and her place, stripped of individuality and personality, of background and identity, of her language and even of her real name.

But Maryam was very close. I could see her face everywhere I looked. It was in the olive-skinned and dark-eyed faces of Sephardic Jewish women of Yemenite or Iraqi or Syrian or Egyptian descent. It was in the faces of Palestinian Arab women in the small peasant villages of the West Bank—the ancient areas of Judea and Samaria. It was in the worn faces of Beduin women herding flocks out in the hills of Galilee and Judea and the Negev. These were Middle Eastern faces, belonging to people speaking two languages very similar to the one Maryam spoke: Hebrew and Arabic, sister languages of Aramaic.

Two thousand years may have passed, but Maryam was still very much alive in this land.

Knowing the lay of the land was only the start. I began to read deeply in history, anthropology, archeology, biblical studies. And the more I read, the more I was amazed that no such biography as this already exists. Because though it is true that few of the usual biographer's tools are available, that does not mean there is no way to reach Maryam. We have a wealth of knowledge about the societies, cultures, religions, and politics of the Middle East in the first centuries B.C. and A.D., all of it serving to open up our ideas of who Maryam was.

The great British historian R. G. Collingwood maintained that writing history requires both empathy and imagination. He did not mean spinning tales out of thin air—far more than enough of that has already been done in the case of Mary, both by those who worship her and those who seek to tear her down—but taking what can be known and examining it, following the strands of the story until they begin to intertwine and establish a thick braid of reality.

The story begins, then, in Part One, with what Maryam saw, heard, and experienced in her day-to-day life as a peasant Galilean living under foreign rule. It grounds her in her physical, social, and political context—in her real culture—and so allows us to see the world, as it were, through her eyes.

Part Two looks at all the issues to do with her pregnancy, starting with how much was known at the time by village midwives and healers, including Maryam herself. It explores the meaning of virginity and its relationship to fertility. And of course it examines the paradoxical possibilities as to the father of Maryam's child, whether human, divine, or even both.

Part Three focuses on Maryam as a mother, but far beyond the classic image of Madonna and child. Starting with the crucifixion of her son—how does a mother bear such a thing?—it looks at her role in the burial and resurrection, where loss is transformed into renewal, and then follows her into active and productive later life.

The picture that develops is of another woman altogether from the one I grew up with, surrounded as I was by images of her in the English convent school I attended for twelve years: statues in the corridors, portraits of her on "holy cards," the ever present rosaries, hymns, invocations . . . I grew up, that is, with an anodyne, alabaster image. She was always in the same pose, standing with arms slightly outstretched, eyes downcast, mantle falling from head to shoulders to wrists. A modest Mary, never shown pregnant, let alone nursing her child. So modest that in what now seems a cruel stroke of irony, the convent—Saint Joseph's—was named not for her, but for her husband.

I took her for granted, as children do. She was simply there. To be sure, I heard stories of her appearing to children at Lourdes and other places. I even sneaked into the convent chapel to see if the life-size statue of her there would talk to me, though I realized instantly that it wouldn't. Not to me, "the Hebrew girl."

It didn't occur to me then that she too was a Hebrew girl.

This may be the answer to the question "How dare I?" Perhaps my own biography is what gives me license: as a Jew who once seriously considered becoming a rabbi, as a former convent schoolgirl who daydreamed about being a nun, as an agnostic with a deep sense of religious mystery though no affinity for organized religion. Or perhaps I take my license as a woman for whom there is no heroism in "meek and mild," or as a psychologist seeking understanding, or as a journalist seeking out the real story. But if I had to point to one single motivating factor, it would be the old kabbalistic ideal of *tikkun olam,* "repairing the world."

This is what I want: To repair the world of Mary, and weave it anew into whole cloth. To give her back to herself, starting with her real name. To restore her strength and her intelligence, and see her as the multifaceted human being she was before she became an icon: a peasant, a healer, a nationalist, a mother, a teacher, a leader—and yes, a virgin, though in a sense we have long forgotten.

It occurs to me now that perhaps this book is my way of finding that Mary did speak to me after all—not the gilded image in the convent school, but the wiry, dark-skinned, hard-muscled Maryam, barely out of adolescence when she gave birth, her face lined by hard work and harder experience, etched deep by violence and struggle, survival and loss, determination and courage.

There is nothing meek and mild about Maryam. She is neither pale nor passive. She emerges as far more than we have yet accepted her as being: a strong woman of ability and wisdom who actively chose her role in history, and lived it to the fullest.

PART ONE

HER WORLD

I

Maryam wakes with the rustle of the pre-dawn breeze, sharp and cold. Grabs a bite of sheep's cheese and flat bread dipped in *za'atar*, the crushed wild oregano that is the spice of peasant life in the Middle East. Fills a small goatskin with water from the clay jar set into the hard-packed dirt floor just inside the door to the house.

The air is fresh outside. A coating of dew makes everything sparkle in the half-light. She pauses a moment to breathe deep, automatically checking the sky. The direction of the wind, the color of the sunrise, mist down in the valley or clouds on the horizon—any or all of these will determine which way she takes the herd. The decision is hers. It's her job to find good grazing among the thorns, to get the animals into shade on the hottest days, and in the late afternoon to bring them back to the village for milking and then to the spring, where she'll haul up pail after pail, pouring the water into a stone trough as thirsty snouts jostle each other for position.

She moves lightly, with the ease of healthy youth. Her thin sandals aren't much protection against sharp rocks and thorns, but she doesn't even notice cuts and scratches. They'll heal. The sheep nuzzle her thighs while the goats hang back, and she urges them on with a short, guttural "krrrr," a switch of acacia in her right hand to help keep stragglers in line. Once she's gained distance from the village, she'll tie a piece of rope around her waist and hike up her shift, giving her legs freedom to move so that she can run after strays or climb down into a ravine to retrieve a trapped lamb.

15

It feels good out here in the open, away from the jumble of stone-walled houses built one onto the other, threaded through with courtyards and narrow stepped alleyways. The tiny, dark rooms have only small openings high in the walls for ventilation, and the air inside is thick with the musty closeness of old straw and sweat, of dry dung piled up near the hive-shaped oven for fuel, and of dust. Always the dust.

At night the floor is thick with bodies. Grandparents, parents, children, cousins, uncles, aunts, all lie one next to the other on thin straw pallets. At least in summer they can take their beds and sleep on the roof, under the reed canopy where herbs and raisins are laid out to dry. The air is better there, and you can hear the whole village on nearby roofs. You know who snores, who moans in sex, who tosses and turns, who has nightmares, whose child is ailing, who sits up through the night unable to sleep, listening to the howling of wolves and jackals, the donkeys braying in alarm, the sheep and goats shifting uneasily in their pens.

During harvest times they leave the village completely. Take their pallets and move to the fields far below in the valley for barley and wheat, or out along the hillside on the stone-walled terraces for grapes and olives. That's when the night world opens up. The full moon shines so strong that you can play with your own shadow. A woman can stitch her embroidery by that light. A boy can hit a rabbit with his slingshot. A shepherd girl spot a mountain lion, or a watchman in the vineyards a wolf hankering for ripened grapes.

Such nights, it seems as though someone has sprinkled silver dust over the whole landscape—a sky goddess, perhaps, opening her hands and laughing as she watches it drift on down. Not Yahweh, for he is beyond imagining. Not for him something so playful as sprinkling silver dust over the hills of Galilee.

New moon, when there is no moonlight at all, is just as good in its own way. Then the whole sky is almost solid with stars, and Maryam gets to play the celestial magician: she stands as tall as she can and spreads her arms wide, so that the whole of the Milky Way seem to stream from one upturned palm into the other.

Her grandmother tells her that if you know astrology, as the priests do in the great temple far to the south in Jerusalem, you can read all manner of secrets in the stars. Auspicious times, omens, the future. But to Maryam there seems little point in that. If the fates are already cast, you can only accept your lot, and that's that. If they are not . . . Ah, if they are not . . .

She knows this is no way for a peasant girl to think, yet these open-air nights of harvest moon and starlight give her a sense that much more is possible. That there can be more to life than sitting and waiting for what will happen anyway. "That's the way things are," the old men say when she asks why her mother had to die in childbirth, or why her cousin has crooked legs and has to crawl instead of walk. "It's written," they say, gesturing in a wide arc above their heads, "written in the sky." They speak with the respect of those who cannot read for the totemic power of writing. And with a shrug of helplessness in the face of such power: "What can we do?"

She isn't sure yet, but something in her resists accepting the inevitable. She learns from her grandmother, the village healer. She gathers herbs for her out in the hills, watches as she grinds them and soaks them in oil, goes with her as she tends to a sick child or makes a splint for a broken bone. Not that the old woman is always successful, but still, Maryam senses that you don't have to die early, and you don't have to live crippled. That there are things humans can do. Actions they can take. That not everything is fate, even in a small, insignificant village like Nazareth.

Nestled into a fold in the southernmost hills of the Galilee, Nazareth seemed to blend into its landscape so well that you'd never know it was there unless you looked for it. Few people did. It wasn't a world-famous place as it is now; it hadn't yet become the home of Jesus. In fact it was so insignificant to all except the two or three hundred people who lived there that it never even merited a mention in the Hebrew bible.

The literal meaning of its name is "small fort," and it probably began that way, thanks to its commanding view over the broad Jezreel Valley far below. You could look down and see camel and mule caravans moving slowly along the valley floor, for this was an extension of the famed Silk Road, and served as the main east-west route from the Jordan River to the city of Caesarea on the Mediterranean coast. The caravans carried precious cargoes like silk and saffron, luxuries the peasant villagers had never experienced. They came from another world in the east, and went to yet another one in the west. If the Nazarenes thought of them at all, it was in the same way they thought of the spring migration of storks flying overhead. They could be seen but not touched. They were just passing through.

Nazareth's stone-walled houses clustered together so tightly they seemed to be clinging to each other for shelter. As in the scores of other small villages dotted around the hills of Galilee, they were set high above the valley floor for one very good reason: that was where the water was, two thirds of the way up the hillside. Wherever there was a spring, there was a village—wherever, in a water-starved land, there was any amount of water emerging from the rock. Like Nain across the valley to the south, which you could glimpse at night—if your eyes were healthy and not infected—by the glimmer of an oil lamp through an open doorway, the flame guttering even in the still night air. Or Bethlehem, just five miles along the ridge to the west. Not the Judean Bethlehem, near Jerusalem, but the Galilean one, larger and older than its southern namesake.

All these villages were off the beaten track below—literally beaten, for tracks were worn into the earth by usage; the Romans wouldn't lay the first paved roads in the region until more than a hundred years later. True, Nazareth was "only" some seventy miles north of Jerusalem as the crow flies, but humans aren't crows. In Maryam's time, those seventy miles were more like seven thousand today. Jerusalem, with its magnificent temple, was another country. Even another world.

The track up from the valley was a narrow, foot-worn path following the contours of the hillside, snaking this way and that in a long series of hairpin turns. Mules and donkeys negotiated it easily. Humans too, so long as they had strong legs and ankles. Stones and thorns etched deep scratches into their feet, but they never noticed unless one of the thorns embedded itself and festered. They'd have been amused if they could have seen a health-club buffed modern visitor panting for air and water, making a big deal out of the climb. Amazed at the special hiking shoes, the high-tech trekking pole. The children would have gathered around to stare and giggle. After all, an hour or two up a steep hill was nothing unusual. Many of the villagers did it every day, going down to the fields in the valley to tend the wheat and barley, then up again as the light began to fade. They knew how to let their stomachs and thighs do the work, keeping a slow, steady pace as their legs moved smoothly from the hips in a fluid stride. Knew to hold a pebble on the tongue to keep the lips closed and the saliva flowing.

The track led straight to the spring, where the women gathered in the heat of the afternoon. They'd glide down the rock-hewn steps with large clay jars balanced on their heads and often an infant slung in a cloth hammock across their backs. This was the heart of the village, the place to linger and chat; it was where they could imagine for a while that there was not a whole world of tasks still to be done before sunset. But even this small luxury waned as the summer drew on. Anxiety began to crease the women's eyes as they watched the flow of water slow, decrease to a trickle, and in drought years, stop. Then they could only hope there'd be enough stale rainwater from the past winter collected in the village cisterns. Enough at least to drink, if nothing else.

In this climate, where from April through September the earth dries, parches, cracks, goes bone hard and brittle, moisture was everything.

The very language was determined by it—the consonants guttural, in the back of the throat, the vowels soft and deep, issued through a mouth half-closed. To be a Palestinian peasant was to be an expert in conserving moisture.

These were people who knew what it was to be without water, to look on helplessly as crops browned and shriveled. They had to haul the water they drank, and their backs and shoulders knew exactly how much it weighed. They ladled it carefully out of the tall, narrow-necked jars at the entry to each house, then savored every mouthful, swirling it around in their mouths.

Nothing was wasted, nothing thrown away. Water used to wash hands and feet was poured onto vegetable plots or sprinkled onto dirt floors and roofs to keep the dust down. The residue of the olives after the last press was used as fertilizer. What remained of the wheat after threshing was packed into sleeping pallets and bolsters. Even animal dung was valued: the hard-packed fibrous pellets burned slow and even, an ideal fuel for cooking.

Like all peasant peoples, the Galileans lived lean, and you could see that leanness in them. They were thin and wiry, with the dust of the land in their nostrils, their mouths, even their skin. Etched deep into their pores, the dust traced spidery diamond-shaped patterns on the backs of their hands and on their feet.

It was hard living on a hard land. Even if you survived birth and infancy, you grew old quickly in such a place. And so you gave birth early.

Pregnancy at thirteen sounds scandalously early to the modern ear. It brings to mind stories of inner-city girls who have sex in desperation for love and attention, then treat their newborns as though they were living toys—barely out of adolescence, children bearing children.

It can't be, says the western mind, "not Mary." Except for the collective mind of the Vatican, which retains a less sentimental and—ironically—more realistic view of human physiology. The official Roman Catholic celebration of Mary's two thousandth birthday was in 1987, thirteen years before that of her son.

Never mind for now that the Vatican reckoning is off, since calendars have become more precise through the intervening centuries. Whether you reckon the year of Jesus' birth at the academically agreed if peculiar date of 4 B.C.—Christ born four years before Christ—or at the simpler and popularly accepted stroke of midnight between 1 B.C. and 1 A.D., or, as we shall see, at the more likely date of 6 A.D., one fact remains: Maryam was thirteen.

Why should we be shocked at the idea? In much of the world today, girls are still married off at puberty. And Maryam lived seventeen centuries before what Philippe Ariès would call "the invention of childhood" in the west. Children were seen simply as small adults. Their ages were figured not by numbers, but by what they could do: "the age of chasing stray sheep" or "plant gatherer" or "plower."

This is how things still were in many small Palestinian villages as late as the 1960s. There was no electricity. No running water. No indoor plumbing. No plastics, no batteries, no cars, no phones. It was still possible to sit under an olive tree and gaze out over terraced hillsides, watching a peasant farmer urge on a mule pulling a single-prong wooden plow over the parched, rocky ground. You could think romantically—and for once, the romantic view corresponded with the facts—that what you were seeing was like a scene straight out of biblical times. Even down to the deceptive peacefulness of it all.

Young girls shepherded goats and sheep with sticks and the occasional throaty yell floating up into the dry, dusty air. Barefoot or in thin leather sandals, they picked their way over the rocks and thorns with an agility learned from their wards. By the very fact that they were out there herding the flocks, you knew that they were adolescents, just shy of puberty. Because at puberty, they would be married.

This too was biblical. As in the life of a peasant girl in the twentieth

21

century, so too two thousand years ago, marriage came early. It had to. When life is short, you need to grab at every opportunity to reproduce it. And life two thousand years ago was very short.

True, there is the biblical reckoning of a long life, still echoed in Israel with the birthday toast "to a hundred and twenty." But nobody does live to a hundred and twenty, not today and not in biblical times either. Long before records of births and deaths were kept, it was an idealized lifespan, an image of being a patriarch or matriarch looking on in satisfaction at four or five generations of offspring, the visible proof of having been fruitful and multiplied. And it rolls as resplendently off the tongue in English as in ancient Aramaic and Hebrew: not just the abrupt ending of "a hundred," but the fullsome continuity of "a hundred and twenty"—the plenitude of a hundred, and then some.

To see just how idealized this biblical number was, you don't even have to go back two thousand years. You need only look at almost any peasant population today—in Afghanistan, in Somalia, in all those countries that many westerners barely register as even existing, let alone recognize on a map of the world, until some form of military intervention suddenly brings them into the brief and fickle spotlight of world attention.

The numbers are chilling. One stillborn per five live births. One in ten of those born, dead in the first year of life. A third dead by age five. Less than half of those born make it to puberty. And even for the survivors, life expectancy in many parts of Asia and Africa is under fifty.

Not that the western world is far removed from such lifespans. Go back a mere couple of centuries to eighteenth-century London, and records show well over half of those born dying by age sixteen. Only ten percent made it beyond age forty-five—the same number as in ancient Rome. In nineteenth-century Massachusetts, more than a third of all women died by age twenty. It wasn't until the twentieth century, once the germ theory of disease had been accepted, and especially with the introduction of penicillin and vaccination, that lifespans began to increase to what we now take for granted in the west.

In the ancient Middle East, as many as half of all children died before age five. Infant mortality was so high that Aristotle noted in his *Historia Animalium* that newborns were not named until a week after birth because many wouldn't live that long.

Childbirth was almost as dangerous for the mothers. Miscarriage was common, usually due to malnutrition or disease. Of those who carried an infant to term, about one out of three died in childbirth from uterine hemorrhage or infection, often with their first delivery. Five or six live births would be high for any one mother, and since so many died in infancy or early childhood, the effective birthrate was lower than it is today in the industrialized world.

This is why the number of siblings given for Jesus in Matthew—four brothers and an unstated number of sisters—sounds peculiarly high. To preserve the doctrine of Mary's perpetual virginity, the Vatican maintains that Matthew refers to cousins, not biological brothers and sisters. And it may well be right, if for the wrong reasons. Peasant families of the time were not nuclear but extended families. First cousins considered themselves brothers and sisters, and distant cousins were as first cousins are today. Whatever the state of Mary's hymen—a question we will come to later, where the answer is by no means as obvious as either the faithful or the cynics might suppose—it would certainly have been quite normal for any woman to have only one child survive into adulthood.

The other famed biblical lifespan, three score years and ten, was the sole preserve of the fraction of one percent who were wealthy and sheltered, and even then of very few of them. The second-century philosopher-emperor Marcus Aurelius, raised by his grandfather after his parents died when he was young, saw nine of his twelve children die in infancy or childhood, and that was with the best hygiene, nutrition, and medical attention available in Rome.

Such figures applied only to "normal" times, when death was caused by disease, or by the kind of gross accident familiar to farmers worldwide, or by infection; even a cut or a rotten tooth could kill you. Death by human violence shortened lifespans still further. Political upheavals sent foreign armies roaming and killing at will, with no distinction between military and civilian targets, while internecine conflicts spiraled out of hand as they still do two millennia later (think of Hutus and Tutsis, Serbs and Bosnians, Irish Catholics and Protestants, to name just a few literally mortal conflicts). At such times, death rates surge beyond predictability with, depending on the place and the century, firing squads, "disappeared" people, massacre by machete, torched villages, mass crucifixions, marketplace bombs, unmarked common graves.

Imagine, then, the idealism with which one could even conceive of someone living to three score and ten, let alone a hundred and twenty. Imagine the power of the biblical command to be fruitful and multiply when being fruitful and multiplying was so rife with risk, the odds so loaded against success. Who needs such a command, after all, except those for whom it is in doubt?

When life is so short, there is no such thing as "youth." In a sense, there were no teenagers two thousand years ago, as there are none in many parts of the world today. To be thirteen when the average lifespan is so short is equivalent to being a young adult in modern western society. Westerners are shocked at thirteen-year-olds toting Kalashnikovs and shoulder missiles in African and Middle Eastern warfare, but that is because we take for granted the idea of childhood, and of the teen years as a kind of older childhood, a slow adaptation to adulthood. We forget that to be a teenager is a luxury afforded only those with good nutrition and health care. For nearly the whole world two thousand years ago, there was no such luxury. And so a social economics of demography took place. Together with the short lifespan, the high risk of maternal and infant death in childbirth made early marriage and pregnancy essential to survival of both families and peoples.

A thirteen-year-old girl was considered a woman. Menstruation had begun. She was fertile, and fertility meant maturity. What we now celebrate only as ritual—the passing into adulthood marked by rites such as confirmation or bat-mitzvah—was fact two thousand years ago. A thirteen-year-old would be a mother. A woman of forty would be a great-grandmother. By her fifties, if the survival odds worked in her favor and left at least one surviving child in each generation, she would be a great-great-grandmother. She would be truly ancient.

Most of the Galilee villages of Maryam's time would not survive much longer than their inhabitants. Any that sheltered rebels against Roman rule would be reduced to rubble within a few decades, when the Romans suppressed all opposition with ruthless efficiency. Their remaining walls crumbled and filled in with wind-blown topsoil and dust, and are now so overgrown with two thousand years of thorns and shrub oak that you'd have no idea anything was ever there unless you happened to trip on a hidden hand-hewn stone or to catch your ankle in the top of a collapsed cistern. You need to literally stumble over them.

The few villages that have been excavated do not attract attention as do the far more impressive ruins of Sepphoris, the garrison town a few miles north of Nazareth that would grow into a thriving city in the fourth and fifth centuries. There, you can sit in the amphitheater, tour elaborate mosaic-floored mansions, stroll marbled walkways. As always, the buildings of the wealthy are the ones that last through the centuries; peasant homes disappear back into the land.

At least Nazareth survived, though not in any form Maryam would recognize. As it emerged from insignificance with the spread of Christianity, it was built over, again and again, and whatever remained of the village that once existed sank deeper and deeper into the ground.

A small city now spreads out from where the village once was. Some sixty thousand people, an uneasy mix of Christian and Moslem Arabs, live under the shadow of a newer Jewish city, Upper Nazareth, built along the top of the ridge. Arab Nazareth's economy is based almost entirely on pilgrim tourism; tour buses park by the dozen near the Basilica of the Annunciation, an unmistakably 1950s edifice with echoing marbled walls built over the excavated remains of what was purportedly Maryam's house.

Pilgrims tend to go quiet when they descend to the basement of the basilica and peer down into the darkness. They move back upstairs so quickly that their silence seems due not to awe, but to disappointment. There's not much there, after all. Just a few excavation ditches revealing crude stone walls and the outlines of a couple of small, cramped rooms. It is nothing at all like the Italianate palaces in Renaissance paintings of the Annunciation. In fact it looks more like a hovel.

But to focus on the physical remains of a house, let alone one that may or may not be as old as claimed, is to misconstrue the essence of Maryam's life. She was a peasant villager, deeply bound to the land. The very word "peasant" comes from the French *paysan*, meaning "of the land." And this peasant identity was central not only to her life and her son's, but also to his teachings. There is no real understanding the philosophy of the New Testament gospels— "the salt of the earth" raised up to inherit the kingdom—without understanding the depth and breadth of the peasant bond between people and place.

Maryam would certainly have been puzzled at the idea that anyone would think of calling stone walls a house. In her world, a house was not stones, but people. It was what is still called in modern Arabic the *hamula*: the extended family and everything it owned, including land, livestock, and produce. Just as the Hebrew Bible talks of the House of David or the British refer to the royal family as the House of Windsor, so too peasant villagers thought of a house as something far larger and far more lasting than a dwelling.

There were no "single-family houses" since there were no single, nuclear families. Children were raised communally, by kin. Aunts and grandmothers acted as mothers, while the one they called father—

abba—was the patriarch, the oldest man to whom all the others were related either by blood or marriage.

Of course we have no record of who Maryam's immediate parents were, and the New Testament gospels never mention them. They may well have died when she was young; her mother may even have died in childbirth, and Maryam may never have known her. This was common enough. What we do know is that the legend of the infertile Anna and the priest Joachim came into being only some three hundred years later, nurtured by a spate of novelistic "infancy gospels." These apocryphal accounts filled in the vast gaps in the earlier gospels of Matthew and Luke with vivid imagination. They became immensely popular, and helped transform Maryam into the sacred image of Mary.

If you had told the Nazarene girl that she would be given not only a mother old enough to be her great-grandmother, but a miraculous conception of her own, a priestly background, and a privileged childhood, she'd have collapsed in giggles. Or perhaps simply taken pity on you as a fabulist. This wealth of later fictional detail was calculated to appeal to newly converted Christians in the urban centers of Turkey, Greece, and Rome, far removed from the reality of peasant life in Galilee. In that reality, you were defined not by your individual parents, but by your *hamula*, your village, your people. You were, in short, where you came from.

This bond between land and people persisted through the centuries, to the extent that Maryam and her son are often cited by modern Palestinians as "famous Palestinians in history"—a claim that is, as most points made for political purposes, both right and wrong.

Though the use of the name Palestine today is highly charged, emotionally and politically, there was no such problem two millennia ago. By the first century, the name was in regular use for the whole area between the Jordan River in the east and the Mediterranean Sea in the west—the area now covered by the State of Israel and by the Palestinian Authority, which in principle covers the West Bank and the Gaza Strip. Aristotle, Ovid, and Herodotus all used the name this way. So too did the first-century Jewish philosopher Philo of Alexandria, and the Judean general turned Roman historian Josephus, a.k.a. Joseph ben-Matthias. By the time the emperor Hadrian suppressed the last gasp of Judean revolt in 135 A.D. and declared the province Syria Palaestina, he was merely ratifying existing usage. Among the conquerors, that is. Not among the people who actually lived there. Maryam certainly did not think of herself as Palestinian. The name itself was foreign. It was the one used by the rulers, by the Greeks and then the Romans. It rode roughshod over local distinctions between Judea, Samaria, Idumea, and Galilee, with their separate histories and ethnic backgrounds. It bound them together as Palestine for the administrative convenience of empire.

She might be considered a Palestinian hundreds of miles away in Athens and Rome, but in her own world she was a Galilean and an Israelite, a daughter of Israel. She was a descendant of the great Kingdom of Israel that existed some eight hundred years before she was born, and that was for a time greater, richer, and more powerful than its southern neighbor, the Kingdom of Judea. And though she could neither read nor write, she knew the history of her land as well as she knew the sound of her own heart.

On long winter evenings, Maryam hears that history. Wedding and nativity feasts always take place in the winter months, when the harvests are all done and there's time to celebrate, and the story-telling at the end of the feast is as essential a part of the celebration as the food.

Most of the year, the villagers are sparse vegetarians. Not out of principle, but out of necessity. The sheep and goats are needed for milk and wool. Meat is a rare treat. One of the boys might get lucky with his slingshot and bring down a rabbit or a pair of migrating quail. Or occasionally, if someone has walked the fifteen miles down to Magdala on the Sea of Galilee—and another fifteen miles back uphill—there'll be dried fish, tough and salty, with the stink of the town it comes from.

Maryam won't taste fresh fish until years later, when her son joins the fishermen, and then she'll laugh at the moist softness of it, and learn to crunch the tastiest parts: the head and tail and fins. Not the eyes, though. Fishermen never touch the eyes, lest the evil eye descend on them.

But to roast a whole sheep or a goat? That's the mark of a big event. The whole village feasts. And as the darkness closes in, they gather close around the fire. Bellies sated with the unfamiliar richness of animal fat, with cakes drenched in grape syrup and rough new wine made palatable by cutting with water, they give themselves over to the chanting of the story-teller.

Branches of pruned olive wood burn in the open fire, scenting the night air. In the flickering light of the flames, their minds soothed by the familiar lines and rhythms, the listeners can forget the thorns and the rocks and the relentless summer dust. The broken limbs and blinded eyes and wasted bodies of the sick. The deformities of children born to die young. The families dispossessed from their land. The men working as day laborers in the garrison of Sepphoris over the ridge, or for months or even years at a time in Jerusalem or Caesarea, so that children grow up with only a vague memory of their fathers, as Palestinian children still do, their fathers away working in the oil-rich Gulf states, sending home remittances.

For the space of the evening, they are proud and independent again.

The children huddle together under heavy blankets, the weave rough against bare skin, scratchy and comforting at the same time. Wide-eyed to fight off sleep, they absorb the story of how the Galileans rose in rebellion against the upstart King David. And rose again against his son Solomon, who tried to force Galilean men into labor on his temple in Jerusalem and destroyed the northern temples in Shechem and Beit-El. They rose up and separated, and created a true, Israelite monarchy, the royal house of Omri, with a great capital of its own and a temple built in ivory.

Children and adults alike nod in recognition, knowing what comes

29

next, for kings and priests are never to be trusted. Always, they'll betray the people of the land, the peasants. And so arose Elijah, the great prophet of the north, from the wild, ultra-austere sect of Rechabites. Elijah, who came from the poor and spoke for the poor. Who lived by the Jordan River and was fed by ravens. Who wore animal skins and fed on carobs—the fruit of the honey locust tree. Who bested the priests of Baal on Mount Carmel and brought down rain. Who heard the voice of God on top of the sacred mountain:

"And behold, the Lord passed by," chants the story-teller. "And a great wind rent the mountains and broke in pieces the rocks before the Lord."

And together, they respond: "But the Lord was not in the wind."

"And after the wind an earthquake."

"But the Lord was not in the earthquake," they reply.

"And after the earthquake a fire."

"But the Lord was not in the fire."

And then a pause before the softly spoken final line they all know is coming, the one they mouth silently along with the teller: "And after the fire a still small voice."

There is never any tiring of tales of Elijah. How he multiplied the wheat and oil. Raised children from the dead. Cured leprosy and blindness. Foretold the future. Smote the waters of the Jordan River with his sacred mantle and parted them, just as Moses parted the waters of the Red Sea. And at the end of his life was swept up in a whirlwind and mounted to heaven in a chariot of fire, leaving behind his mantle for his successor, Elisha, to wear.

Open-mouthed children slip into sleep, comforted by the familiar stories as children still are comforted by stories they know well, insisting on the same words, the same inflections, the same pauses, the same places where they can join in—always wanting the stories to be told anew even though they know them by heart, word for word.

And among the adults, many stare into the fire and wonder not if, but when there will be another Elijah, another prophet living in the desert in rags, eating the fruit of the honey locust tree. Another to whom God will talk, who will create food where there is none and make the crippled walk and raise the dead. Another who will ascend in glory to heaven.

This is how the biblical stories were told in Maryam's world, long before they were committed to papyrus or parchment, and longer still before the invention of printing. There was no distinction between entertainment, history, identity, and faith; the stories fulfilled all these needs simultaneously. And they were recited out loud because only a fraction of the elite could read, let alone write. In the villages of Galilee, nobody could.

Maryam was illiterate, as was everyone she knew. Illiterate, but not ignorant. As Claude Lévi-Strauss has pointed out, in a culture such as ours that tends to equate the two, it would be more accurate to say "without writing."

Without writing, then, but with powers of memory that we have all but forgotten are possible. It seems ironic that the more literate we become, the more memory fades. Our dependence on the written word means that once something is committed to writing, we no longer need to know it by heart. We can refer back to it, look it up, read it. Essentially, writing replaces memory.

"Recite!" the angel commanded Mohammed at the start of the Koran. And Mohammed recited what the angel told him. He had to, since he didn't know how to write. The Koran—qur'an, meaning "recitation"—would not be transcribed until after his death. His followers learned the Koran by heart, as students still do in Islamic seminaries, and that phrase "by heart" is appropriate: they took it into their hearts.

Four centuries earlier, the central text of rabbinic Judaism began the same way. Mishna means "repeat," for this is how its texts were learned, even after they were committed to writing. Manuscripts were icons rather than books, too cumbersome and too precious to actually read. Like Mohammed's early followers, so too early rabbinical students relied largely on memory. And people still do so in many parts of the world, where what anthropologists call "the oral tradition" is alive and well.

Some years ago, I spent a starlit night in the sand dunes of the northern Sinai munching on giant olives and listening to Beduin elders recite long narrative poems about the stars and their legends. They had learned these poems—"stories," they called them—from their own elders, who had learned them from theirs, through the generations. The tellers competed genially with one another, and the listeners were part of the performance, reciting a line here, nodding in appreciation there, rather like jazz fans listening to a particularly inspired improvisation on a well-known theme.

But what was most striking was how biblical these Beduin elders sounded. At the end of the twentieth century, rhythms, images, indeed whole phrases echoed across thousands of years, defying the multiple religious and nationalist rifts in Middle East culture. "Those who have ears to hear, let them hear," Jesus says many times, a phrase I first heard in Arabic from a Beduin telling the legend of Saint Onuphrios, the fourth-century hermit who heard the voice of God echoing through the mountains of Sinai.

For these traditional Beduin, the heard word was as alive and fertile as it was two thousand years ago. They would have understood the legend that has Mary conceiving through the ear, or John writing that "the word was made flesh . . . full of grace and truth." In the oral tradition, words are heard, not read, and the hearing itself gives them a mythic power.

In a literate society, it is easy to forget the imaginative connection that comes with the spoken word. And yet we do still recognize it. When we hear the kaddish prayer for the dead or the call of the muezzin or an African American spiritual, we respond to the rhythm of the voice. We know that to fully appreciate the power of "I have a dream," you need to hear the voice of Martin Luther King Jr., as well as the voices of those listening to him rising in assent. Words come to life in the hearing.

This is why we still speak of great story-tellers, not great story-writers. The tellers are the ones who carry the story. Indeed, there were no single authors of the stories we now know as the Bible, no copy-righted, fixed texts. As linguist William Whallon says, "they were all part of the once undifferentiated collection we now know as psalm, proverb and prophecy. They belonged to the culture as a whole." And until they were written down, they changed not only with each teller, but also with each telling.

The Bible came into being "from your lips to God's ears," as the old Jewish saying has it. What was heard from human lips would even-tually become holy writ. But in Maryam's time, the contents were still fluid. Which books were in or out, which stories, which language, all depended on who was doing the telling.

Some might consider this a painful way to think of our holy books. For others, like myself, it's a liberating way. We can see them anew as living traditions instead of canonized documents. Stories alive in the mouth and in the ear found new life with each telling. They tumbled and danced through the joint lives of tellers and listeners, binding them together.

Biblical stories are still told like this, as I found out one fine spring day on the northwest shore of the Sea of Galilee.

I had been trying to find a way into the remains of a sixth-century Byzantine monastery built over the ruins of Magdala, home of the "other" Maryam. A high stone wall enclosed the compound, but there seemed to be no gate. Fierce barking from the other side of the wall put paid to any notion of climbing over, so I followed the wall down toward the lakeshore, bushwhacking through tall reeds until I came to a section that was only shoulder-high. In the center of it was a chained gate. I yelled hello, and a man appeared behind the wall, the first person I'd seen all morning.

He was sixtyish, wearing a *keffiya*, and all three large dogs behind him were growling ferociously, hurling themselves against chains that were far too long and looked like they would break under the strain at any moment.

I greeted him in Hebrew-accented Arabic and he returned the greeting in Arabic-accented Hebrew, but before I could utter another word, he said, "You can't come in. Nobody can come in. Those are my orders."

"From whom?"

"From the Latins. The ones in Capernaum."

"The Franciscans?"

"Those ones."

A scent of mint came toward me on the breeze, and I saw that the whole compound was overgrown with the stuff, run wild and rampant. "What is this place?" I asked, just to keep talking.

He shrugged. "They say it was where this rich woman once lived. A long time ago. They say her name was Maria Magdalena. But that's all I know."

I gave him a quizzical look. He stared blandly back, not giving anything away. And so we introduced ourselves, he on his side of the wall, me on mine. His name was Khiyr, and he was the caretaker. And after we'd talked for a while about what it was like for a Moslem to work for "the Latins," he said, "If you like, I can tell you something else about Maria Magdalena."

"Please," I replied.

"She had this man friend, and one day he heard a very wise man speaking. This man's name was Jesu. You've heard of him?"

I nodded, and reassured, Khiyr continued.

"This man friend, he liked what he heard Jesu saying, so he left Maria Magdalena and went to follow him. Now she was very sad because her man friend had left her. So she went to the man called Jesu and said, 'How can you take my man friend away from me and leave me alone like this?' And Jesu looked at her and said, 'Come join us too.' And she did. And that's all I know."

That last phrase alone said there was more to come, but that I'd need to be patient to hear it. So over the shoulder-high wall, we went on talking about other things—how all Khiyr's children had grown up and left, how things had changed in the nineteen years he'd been here. His wife came out of the caretaker's shack to hang some washing on the line, smiled bashfully, then disappeared again. The dogs had long calmed down and were lying peacefully in the shade. And finally Khiyr offered to tell me more about Maria Magdalena.

"You remember I told you Jesu said she could come join him and his followers? Well, the other followers were not very pleased with this, because she wasn't"—he paused to find the right words—"a *good* woman, if you know what I mean?"

He looked at me carefully to see if I understood, and to make sure he hadn't offended me. Satisfied that it was all right, he continued:

"So the other followers said, 'How can you let a woman like this join us?' And do you know what Jesu did?"

He waited for me to shake my head, and then went on.

"He picked up a stone off the ground"—and here Khiyr bent down as though to pick up a particularly heavy stone—"and he said, 'Let any of you who has never done something bad in his life take a stone and hit me with it.'" And Khiyr struck the side of his head with his empty hand to make the point, and with the hand still to his head, looked at me searchingly.

"And nobody did hit him," he continued, "because you know, we've all done something bad at least once in our lives, every one of us. Haven't we?"

Under those searching eyes, even as part of me was stunned and delighted by the twist he'd given the familiar tale of the adulterous woman and "He who is without sin let him cast the first stone," another part of me thought of the bad I had done, and I blushed and said, "It's true, we have."

Somehow, in that moment, we forgave each other with no need to know what we were forgiving. A Moslem had told a Jew an ancient Christian story, and now that it had been gratefully accepted in the spirit in which it was told, he smiled and said, "Maybe, if you don't tell anyone, it will be all right if I open the gate and let you in . . ."

II

Maryam has never been to the great temple in Jerusalem. True, there will later be stories that she was raised from age three inside the temple, but for now, it is safe to assume that she has never been farther than fifteen miles east of Nazareth, down through the narrow defile of the Arbel gorge to the Sea of Galilee.

The old men are the ones who go, the ones too bent with age to do the hard work of the fields. They fulfill the vow to make the pilgrimage once in their lifetime, as Moslems still do today to Mecca. And they're honored afterwards as the Moslem hadji is still honored today.

They are travelers returned from an exotic land, bringing back stories and news. Things seen with their own eyes, heard with their own ears. The villagers gather around them late into the night, dazzled at their descriptions. Walls so high that they touch the sky! Marble so white that it blinds the eye! Gold flashing like fire in the midday sun!

But it's the water that impresses the Nazarenes most: the very idea that water can be wantonly, flamboyantly, wasted—a sign of riches far beyond gold and silver.

"Water everywhere!" the old men exclaim, withered hands moving expansively as though the dry hills and dusty landscape around them were running with moisture. Huge pools of water for pilgrims to wash in, purifying themselves before entering the temple courtyards. Water running in gutters along the flagstone floors. Tall trees of water in the courtyards of the king's palace—for how else explain fountains to those who have never seen them? And exotic trees that do nothing but give shade: no fruit, just shade!

Maryam, like all the villagers, is stunned at the very idea of so much water that you can immerse your whole self in it. True, in wet winters, pools form where there's a depression in the hills, and she'll rush into them fully clothed with the other children, laughing and splashing through the goats and sheep lined up at the edges. But they know that the water will disappear in a week or two, and the depression revert back to caked earth and dust.

And as for the idea of running waters . . . She gasps as the old men describe the aqueduct bringing water to the temple from miles away. Water running high through the air on columns and arches of stone? Impossible, surely, yet the old men swear on all that is sacred that they have seen it with their own eyes. Huge man-made pools collect winter rainwater from the surrounding hills, they say, and then the aqueduct funnels it to the great temple. There, it runs through gutters and sluices to wash down the altar, supply the immersion pools, feed the fountains and trees of the king's palace, and fill the giant cisterns beneath the temple.

"No spring, like ours?" someone asks, and the old men laugh. Jerusalem has a spring, to be sure—the Silwan spring, at the lower reaches of the city—but that's not for drinking. That's reserved for healing, as befits a holy city. The sick and crippled are borne on litters down narrow steep-stepped alleys to the covered gallery over the spring, with the center of the roof open to the sky. Here, the old men say, the water washes away what ails you. Carries it off and bears it back down into the earth. And they swear by their fathers' houses to the miracles they have seen at Silwan: a man who got up from his litter and walked, a girl whose eyes cleared and could suddenly see, a leper whose skin became clear and soft.

"Miracle water," the old men call it, and villagers for whom water itself is often close to a miracle nod in agreement.

*   *   *

For peasant villagers, to offer water was a sign of respect. You washed the feet of an honored visitor when he entered your home, for instance. Moslems today still wash their feet before they enter a mosque. And pilgrims still kiss the stone at the Church of the Holy Sepulchre where Mary Magdalene washed the feet of Jesus. So what if the woman in the gospels of Luke and John was not the Magdalene, and it was not in Jerusalem? A peasant custom has been elevated into sacred image, and the dry-land respect for water has been preserved.

Nazarenes could only be stunned by Herod's aquatic lavishness. No matter that the water in those ritual pools in Jerusalem was filthy from all the dust and grime of the bathers. Only the faintest ripple disturbed the surface as fresh water from the aqueduct trickled in, but this was enough to make it "living water"—running water—as the temple required. Its purpose was ritual, not hygienic, and this was what impressed the villagers more than anything: that water could be used for no human purpose at all, only for a godly one. The water itself was a sacrifice to Yahweh.

But the truth is that all that water in the Jerusalem temple was not just for ritual purification. Or to satisfy the thirst of the thousands of civil servants and cultic personnel who served and serviced the temple. Or even to be displayed in lavish abundance in palaces and gardens, impressing peasant rubes from the north. It was needed for the most practical of purposes: to wash away the blood.

Sacrifice is a messy business. The temple air was thick not only with incense, but with the stink of drying blood, the acrid smoke of burning animal flesh, and the stench of rotting entrails. The cries of animals being slaughtered—frightened birds, lambs and calves bleating and bellowing in alarm—rang through the colonnades. The priests were filthy, their robes spattered with blood spurting from slashed throats and stained with fat spitting from the eternal fire on the altar. They were flushed and sweaty with heat and exertion. In the midst of all the noise and commotion, they went about their work in grim-faced silence, their movements as coordinated as a meat-packing line.

Horrifying as the idea may be to a modern sensibility, the temple was a slaughterhouse. As in all temples of its time, the center of its ritual was sacrifice, and sacrifice meant blood. In Hebrew, the altar is the *mizbe'ach*—literally, the place of slaughter—and the temple itself was called Beit HaZebach: the House of Slaughter. Nobody believed in euphemisms in those days.

Sacrifice was an attempt to placate the implacable: the divine. There were no kind gods such as Jesus would become. The Greek gods especially were unpredictable, wrathful, and vengeful. They acted on apparent impulse, toying with humans. There was no appeasing them; you could only offer, and hope.

The Jerusalem priests operated as priests did throughout the Mediterranean at the time. They cut the animals' throats, caught the blood in silver bowls, poured the blood onto the ground around the altar, then pulled out the entrails and set aside choice cuts for their own tables. Doves and other birds were used whole, but only the thigh piece of a lamb or a calf was given to the altar, wrapped in a length of entrail, encased in a double layer of fat, and sprinkled with incense. When it was cast onto the altar fire, the fat and incense sent crackling sparks flying high in loud display. Smoke rose high over the gold leaf and white marble walls, billowing not just from the sacrifice itself, but from the flames that flared up each time the priests added a special salt called *maaleh ashan*—"smoke-raiser"—to make the sacrifice look all the more impressive.

It was unending. There was the *tamid*, the continual offering, or Yahweh's daily food, twice a day; the whole-burnt offering, known in Greek as the holocaust; any number of peace offerings, sin offerings, thanks offerings, guilt offerings, and purification offerings; offerings twice daily for the Roman emperor—a continual insult to purists like the Pharisees and the Essenes; and of course thousands of pilgrims' offerings each day during festival times.

For peasant villagers, these were sacrifices in more than one sense. They were major financial sacrifices as well as ritual ones. A lamb was out of the question; only the rich could afford to purchase a flawless lamb for the altar fire. But even buying an unblemished dove from one of the dove sellers in the temple bazaar cost everything you had. And as though to add insult to the financial injury, what you offered was taken in silence, apart from the crackle of sparks and flames. Prayer was not part of the ritual, since there was nothing personal about it. Yahweh was beyond the personal.

If all this sounds like it belongs to another world, it's worth remembering that ritual sacrifice still continues. Not human sacrifice—the story of Abraham and Isaac was meant to mark the end of that era—but animal sacrifice. In Moslem tradition, a sheep is slaughtered by each family for Id el-Adha, the feast of the sacrifice of Ishmael (for Moslem tradition says that it was Ishmael who was nearly sacrificed by Abraham, not Isaac). Two and a half million sheep, cows, and goats are sacrificed each year for Id el-Adha in Turkey alone, with one third of the meat going to the needy. One visitor described "whole families searching for the perfect sacrificial sheep or cow, much like an American family's outing to select the perfect Christmas tree."

Lest Jews and Christians be inclined to feel somehow superior in this regard, consider that Christianity is based on the last great ritual act of human sacrifice—Jesus—and that Jews still celebrate the Passover seder with the shank bone of the Paschal lamb, whose blood was smeared on their ancestors' doorposts so that the angel of death would "pass over" their houses when it came to strike down the first-born of Egypt. We are much closer than many might think to the Middle East of two and three thousand years ago.

The hushed, dignified places we now call temples, cathedrals, and places of worship only became that way much later. As with sacrifice, so in every other manner, the Jerusalem temple was of its time. The huge compound housed a vast array of activity: local and national government, law courts, beggars, livestock auctions, healers, teachers, scribes, bath-houses, fortune-tellers, amulet writers, astrologists, food stalls, water sellers, tamarindi sellers pouring the pomegranate juice from the big urns on their backs into little silver cups. And soldiers, of course, keeping watch from the rooftops and the Antonia fortress alongside the temple. And money changers to transform whatever form of money you had into the one coin accepted in the temple, the shekel. And as in any Middle Eastern souk today, alleys full of tourist stores, places for fleecing pilgrims of their unaccustomed coins with enticingly colorful kitsch.

Why be surprised at the existence of a bazaar on the temple grounds? Temples then were centers of life rather than worship. Many still are today. Think of a temple complex like the Senso-ji complex in Tokyo, where you thread your way through a long gauntlet of stalls selling not just herbs, amulets, and prayers, but expensive silks, cheap rayon, ivory combs, plastic barrettes, traditional dolls, electronic games, fresh-grilled rice cakes, cold cans of black coffee, leather purses, woven bags, nylon umbrellas, paper parasols, all in every color you could ever imagine and then some, the Japanese love of the tchotchke run riot. Then you suddenly emerge into daylight and there is the temple itself, imposingly graceful. In front of it is a huge grate with gaping maws to catch the coins you are supposed to throw in, and a giant stone incense vat with people crowded around it—young girls in absurdly high platform shoes, somber-suited businessmen, smart women in Prada suits, young men in baseball shirts, old women in the Japanese equivalent of babushkas, all fanning the healing smoke over their heads, shoulders, arms, chests, backs, wherever the ailment is.

There is nothing quiet or hushed about such temples. They teem with life, and the life itself is testament to the vitality of faith.

The old Nazarene men on pilgrimage had seen more people than they'd ever imagined existed. To peasants from a village of two or three hundred people, a crowd of one thousand would have seemed vast, let alone the tens of thousands who thronged the narrow alleys of Jerusalem in festival times. Think of a peasant farmer from northern Afghanistan, one with no access to television or videos, placed suddenly on Fifth Avenue in Manhattan. Who could have imagined buildings that high, or all that traffic, or those strange goods in the stores? The noise, the buzz of the city, its never-ending hum and jostling and sheer peopled-ness? The elegant men and women, like creatures from another planet, with soft hands and unlined faces, plump satiated bellies, garments of silk and impossibly soft wool?

The people thronging the alleys of Jerusalem in pilgrimage time talked in so many dialects of Aramaic that the Nazarenes could barely understand every second word. There were some with skin so dark you could barely see them at night, and others with faces so pale they seemed to light up the night.

The old men tried to explain the strange feel of coins in their hands and the dealings of the money changers, who made incomprehensible calculations as they changed the Roman currency with its graven image of the emperor Augustus, a man who dared to call himself a god, into temple shekels. And the villagers shook their heads in wonder at the very idea of transforming food and herbs into pieces of bronze and silver instead of their simpler, more direct way of barter.

They stared into the firelight, mesmerized, as the elders talked about the nights in Jerusalem. So much light, they said, you couldn't even see the stars. Oil lamps everywhere, as though there were enough olives in the world to banish not just darkness but the night itself. The whole of the temple glowing from within, lit not just with single-flame lamps like the villagers used but with whole candelabra, hundreds of lamps hanging on a single chain.

And with every gasp, every stunned exclamation of awe and disbelief, the villagers were reacting exactly as Herod had intended, for he had rebuilt the Jerusalem temple less as a testament to divine power than as a showcase for his own.

Herod's temple was, as historian and sociologist Richard Horsley puts it, "a monumental institution of religio-political propaganda." One of the most ambitious construction projects in the world at the time, it made the previous temples on the site seem like rustic shrines by comparison. Perhaps in fact they were.

Built in the grand Hellenistic-Roman style, the temple complex—courtyards, cloisters, colonnades—was raised up on a high platform. At the center, towering high above all else, its marble glistening white in the Mideast sun, its gold leaf flashing like fire, was the sanctuary containing the holy of holies, the home of Yahweh. Only the high priest could enter there, through massive cypress doors covered by a giant gold vine with clusters of grapes the size of a man, and then only on the most sacred day of the year, Yom Kippur. Most could venture no further than the courtyard in front of the altar, which was simply a huge limestone slab. This was the original peak of the mountain. It was the same slab of stone where Abraham had laid Isaac/Ishmael for the slaughter, and which nearly seven centuries later would be the point from which Mohammed ascended on his night visit to heaven.

The bottom of the steps leading to the altar was as far as the old men from Nazareth had gotten as they handed over their sacrificial birds to the priests' servants. But that too was part of the grand design. To keep your distance is an indication of awe and respect; approach too close, and a mere mortal can suffer the wrath of a god disturbed.

Even the priests were remote. You could only glimpse them as they went about their grim work on the altar, or as they swept by on their way to the temple from their mansions on the facing hillside, and then what struck you most was the sunlight reflecting off their gem-encrusted breastplates. They lived like kings in those mansions, people said—like Herod himself—with servants and slaves, their own private guards, and the many wives that only the rich could afford. For to be one of the priestly elite was to be an aristocrat. And to be an aristocrat was to "share" in the immense wealth of the temple.

Corruption was endemic to the system, even on the most minor level. The dove-selling concession, for example, was reserved for relatives of the high priest, Annas, whose son-in-law Caiaphas would soon replace him; like most monopolies, it involved graft and extortionate prices. The temple treasury, housed in strongrooms well below ground, was filled with gold given in tribute by foreign kings and statesmen. Much of this ended up in the hands and homes of the high priesthood, and much more was squirreled away out of the country—to relatives in the Judean communities of Alexandria, Antioch, or Babylon—in case the masses ever got so unruly as to force the aristocracy to flee. Swiss banks today fulfill the same purpose.

The high priests and their families were right to be worried. Who knew what could happen during festival times? They were a chance to let off steam. Pilgrims would do what people have always done when far from home in an anonymous setting: they drank, they partied, and sometimes, well-fueled, they rioted.

Not religious behavior? Not by modern western standards, perhaps, but in most other places and times, religious rites and festivals do not come with the kind of pious solemnity we tend to associate with "church." African and Asian traditions have a far earthier sense of celebration. Services are loud and joyful: a feast day is truly a feast, a festival truly festive. And such behavior is truly in the religious tradition.

The ancient Greeks sought ecstasy in drink and drugs, dancing and singing, seeking out the intoxicating joy of encountering the holy. The word "enthusiasm," we forget, comes from the Greek *entheos*: being filled with God, en-Godded. And Jerusalem in festival times was full of such enthusiasts.

Teachers and healers, self-proclaimed messiahs with an inside lock on salvation, magicians and preachers, wise men and madmen, all gathered in the temple's vast Court of the Israelites, which was very like the large open courts of major Mideastern mosques today. This is where teachers met with groups of their students or disciples, sitting in circles and discussing the questions we now differentiate into philosophy and theology, though in those days, the two were essentially the same. Their disciples addressed them as *rav-i*—"my great one" or "my master," an honorific form of address that would imply no specific religious training until centuries later. Eventually, it would become "rabbi" in English.

These were the Pharisees, the precursors of rabbinic Judaism. They were not the villains they would be made out to be later by the gospel writers, but idealists whose philosophy was very close to that of Jesus, to the degree that some scholars assert that Jesus himself was a Pharisee. Certainly his teachings and beliefs mirror those of legendary first-century Pharisee sages like Hillel, sometimes practically word for word.

Such teachers were often strongly opposed to the corruption of the Judean tradition in the Hellenistic temple, as imams in Saudi Arabia might be today to what they see as state corruption of Islamic tradition. Within the temple precincts, they preached against what it had become: the religio-political propaganda machine. This isn't the true temple, they said. This is an ethical travesty, a tribute from the half-Jew Herod to his Roman employers. This is a foreign abomination run by the high priesthood, the Sadducees, in the service of Rome and of Herod, Rome's servant and puppet.

As they talked, crowds gathered, scattering at the first sign of soldiers moving toward them unless there was one preacher who was especially potent, especially filled with God, and then his rapture would fill his listeners and they'd be moved to confrontation. A mêlée could develop into a riot within minutes, and a riot into a minor massacre. The survivors would be dragged off in chains, never to be seen again. Or worse, as happened to forty students and their teachers the year Herod was dying, to be burned alive after they had surged out of the temple court to the main gate of the temple and torn down the huge golden eagle that Herod had ordered placed there as a symbol of Roman dominion.

The Sadducees and the Pharisees were the two main denominations, as it were, of Jewishness at the time, but not the only ones. In Samaria, between Jerusalem and the Galilee, the Samaritans zealously guarded their own separate Yahwistic traditions, while the Essenes, shut away in their desert stronghold beside the Dead Sea, dreamed of apocalypse and planned to reclaim and repurify the temple. Between these and other factions, to be Jewish two thousand years ago was to be even more fractured and politically divided than to be Israeli today.

Maryam was Jewish, of course, but not by any modern definition. She was not, as the curator of an Israeli museum exhibit on ancient goddesses dismissively called her, "a nice Jewish girl." She did not say blessings over candles and challah bread on Friday evenings. She did not sit modestly in the women's gallery in the synagogue while her menfolk bobbed up and down below, wrapped in prayer shawls. All these traditions had still to come into being. Only priests wore prayer shawls. And there were not yet any synagogues in the way we now think of them. The Greek word *synagogue* was used for a village or town meeting place, not a place of worship. In first-century Palestine, Herod's great temple was the only official place for that.

The Judaism we know today, rabbinic Judaism, did not yet exist. In fact, religion itself did not exist as we now understand it. Ask Maryam what religion she was, and she'd have stared at you in incomprehension. There was no such category. What we now think of in the west as the separate spheres of religion, politics, ethnicity, and culture were so deeply intertwined that there was no distinction between them.

A Jew—*Yehudi* in both Aramaic and Hebrew—was literally someone from Judea, *Yehuda*. Judean-ness was an ethnic and national identity, and the Jerusalem temple, with its recognition of Yahweh as the ultimate god, was the cement binding that identity.

Seen from the perspective of today's Middle East, this is quite familiar. In Israel, identity cards have a category for *am*, or ethnic nationality. The word "Jew" is written for Israeli Jews, "Arab" for Israeli Arabs, whether Christian or Moslem. Thanks to the power of the religious political parties, there is no distinction in law between Jewish ethnicity and Jewish religion, making Israel a far more typical Middle Eastern country than most Israelis care to admit. Meanwhile,

Islamic fundamentalists in Egypt and Saudi Arabia maintain that under Islamic law, there can be no separation of religion and state. Their ultra-orthodox interpretation of Islam *is* their politics, and their rhetoric against the ruling House of Saud or against the Egyptian president sounds very like the rhetoric used in Jerusalem two millennia ago against the Sadducee high priesthood and Herod. More perhaps than anywhere else in the world, religion is still inextricably intertwined with nationalism in the Middle East.

Maryam, however, was a Jew neither in the modern sense of Judaism nor in the ancient sense of being a Judean. She was a Galilean, and Judea and Galilee had a long history of mutual antagonism, reaching back over nine hundred years to their existence as separate kingdoms.

The northern kingdom of Israel had covered all of Galilee and was the richer. It had more rainfall and better agricultural land, and was also closer to the main trade routes of the Silk Road, which is doubtless why it fell first to foreign occupation, being conquered by the Assyrians in the eighth century B.C. The southern kingdom of Judea maintained a precarious independence for another two hundred years before falling to the Babylonians. Its prophets blamed the north's downfall on idolatry—and on a woman. As Eve led to the fall from Eden, they claimed, so too Queen Jezebel and her Baalite priests led to the fall of the kingdom of Israel. But in fact the reasons were as geopolitical as they are today. When you live at a crossroads, you can expect to be crossed by many people.

In the twentieth century alone, Palestinians tick off the succession of occupiers on their fingers: Turks, British, Jordanians, Israelis. Ancient Judeans and Galileans counted off a millennium of occupiers: Assyrians, Babylonians, Persians, Greeks, Seleucids, Parthians, and Romans. The Galileans, however, added one more to that list: Judeans.

Galilee was conquered by the Judeans in 128 B.C. Specifically, by Judah the Maccabee's grandson John Hyrcanus, scion of the Asamoneans, known in Greek and subsequently in English as the Hasmoneans. They had seized power in Judea nearly fifty years earlier in a revolt against the Greco-Syrian Seleucid occupiers, claiming that they were restoring Judea to a purer state, free of Hellenic influence. For the first time in more than five hundred years, there was an independent Judean kingdom. But a familiar pattern developed: what began as a praiseworthy freedom movement devolved into a power-hungry land grab.

The Hasmoneans were as ruthless as any foreign rulers. They annexed Galilee by force: pillage, enslavement, and massacre. And like Solomon hundreds of years before, they destroyed the rebuilt northern temples of Yahweh so that the only one remaining would be the Judean one, in Jerusalem.

The peasant farmers of Galilee hunkered down to wait. There is an Arabic word, *samud*, used by Palestinians today, that translates as "steadfast" or "staying put." It expresses a simple resolution: not to budge, not to leave the land. But it also reflects a deep historic sense. Rulers come and rulers go, to be ticked off on one's fingers by the decade or by the century, but if the people stay on the land, the land is theirs, no matter what the powers-that-be care to call it.

The Galileans remained *samud*. The Hasmoneans were just another in the long line of foreign rulers, no matter what they themselves claimed. Sure enough, they were just as short-lived. Weakened by internecine feuding, they were defeated just three generations later by Herod with Rome's blessing.

Galilee stayed officially part of Judea, but its people still did not see themselves as Judeans. As ever, they considered themselves Israelites, the true people of Israel. And many were never more aware of the cultural difference than when they heard the stories about the new Jerusalem temple. The elders may have been awed into submission, and the children dazzled as though by fairy tales. But the younger adults, those whose ideals had not yet been eroded by hard work and infirmity, were more likely to be incensed. Like the purist Essenes down in the desert fastness of the Dead Sea valley, they saw the Judean temple as a corruption of Israelite values and faith. They may have been living "under the laws of the Judeans," as the historian Josephus put it, but then as now, laws could not control minds, especially stubbornly independent minds like those of John the Baptist.

The Sadducees were destined to disappear by the end of the first century. The disastrous rebellion against Rome that began in the late sixties A.D. resulted in the destruction of Herod's temple, the banishment of Judeans from Jerusalem, and the end of Sadducee hegemony. Without the temple, they had no power. Only then would the word *Yehudi*—"Ioudaios" in Greek—begin to mean anyone who venerates Yahweh and observes his laws, instead of a nation or people from Judea. Religion as we know it today was about to come into being.

In the absence of the physical temple, the rabbis of the second and third centuries would inherit the mantle of the Pharisees and began the process of rebuilding the temple in their minds, creating the Mishna. But even before the temple buildings went up in flames—the limestone cement burning so fiercely between the huge stone blocks that the stones cracked, exploded, and collapsed—another temple of the mind was already in the making.

The real revolution of the Jesus movement was that where the temple had once been seen as the center of all power and sacredness, that center could now be found within each person. This idea originally surfaced with the Essenes and the early Judean gnostics, but John the Baptist was the first to bring it to a mass audience, not as an intellectual or a metaphysical concept, but as part of a widespread peasant revolt of the mind and soul. With baptism, each person could become a part of the temple, regardless of class, ethnicity, clan, gender, wealth. The temple was made of people—the community of Israel— not of stone.

This was a radical notion. It was deeply subversive of the existing order of things, since it made no distinction between rich or poor, sinful or innocent, man or woman; everyone could be part of the temple on equal terms. Inevitably, the very idea would become heresy as the Jesus movement developed into institutional Christianity in the second and third centuries. It would re-emerge only a millennium later in mystical Judaism, with the idea that the whole world is imbued with points of divine light, fragments from the vessel of creation.

The kabbalistic story of how these fragments came to be dispersed still seems especially comforting, even endearing, in times of trouble. Essentially, God tripped. The world is the result of a divine mistake, a moment of awesome clumsiness, in which God dropped the vessel containing the light of creation. The vessel broke into shards, scattering the divine light into darkness and chaos, and the world will be made whole again only when these shards of divine light have been rescued from the darkness and reunited. That is the task for which the Messiah will come—the ultimate *tikkun olam*, repairing the world.

In first-century Palestine, that is exactly what John the Baptist was trying to do, as would Jesus after him. And his enemies were quick to realize the revolutionary threat. The temple cult was essentially exclusive; its practices were restricted to the priestly few, and everyone else simply paid for them to officiate. What the Baptist preached was inclusive; every person mattered, registered on the grand scale of things, and made a difference in the world. The temple cult depended on birth, wealth, and influence; the populist one, on faith and commitment.

Each person an expression of the divine? No matter who they were? The very idea was an outrageous challenge to those who claimed a monopoly on God: to the high priests, to the aristocracy, even to the emperor, who had proclaimed himself divine. And this was the real reason the Baptist was killed.

The story of Salome and the seven veils is a tempting one, full of the kind of detail guaranteed to keep a legend alive. Also convenient, in that it places the blame yet again on a woman: Herodias, the mother of the dancing Salome.

The gospel version has it that Herodias was angling for John's head when he criticized her marriage to Herod Antipas, Herod the Great's son and the ruler of Galilee after his father's death in 4 B.C. Since she had formerly been married to Antipas' stepbrother, such a marriage would have been against the laws of Yahweh, and the Pharisees certainly would have criticized it on that account. But in fact it was Herod Antipas himself who wanted John's head, not because of personal criticism, though that may certainly have been an irritant, but because the Baptist represented a threat to his authority. He was killed because Antipas saw him, correctly, as dangerous: the more popular his preaching became, the more he challenged the status quo.

And of course the Baptist was popular. His notion that God was inside you, not inside a temple, was an early manifestation of the democratic spirit. It was, in a way, the democratization of religion. It meant that every person was potentially godlike, created in a divine image. And that every person was a son or daughter of God.

Dangerous teachings in politically dangerous times.

III

The Arbel gorge is a narrow cleft in the hills of southern Galilee, less than an hour's walk from the lake known as the Sea of Galilee. The cliff walls are honeycombed with caves, the perfect refuge for anyone in trouble with the authorities. Tall, steep, unscalable for all but the most agile, they are natural fortifications. Take control of them, and you are just about impregnable. Which is why the Arbel was the headquarters of Galilean armed resistance for well over a hundred years.

The caves are still there: whole complexes of rooms carved into the rock, connected by tunnels and stairways. Getting to most of them is still impossible unless you are an experienced rock climber. Surviving in them, even today, would require assistance: people to provide baskets of food and water that could be hauled up on ropes or let down from the top.

Guerrilla fighters can only succeed if they have popular local support, and that the Arbel fighters had. For these men were not strangers. They were known. They were kinsmen. Sons of the dispossessed, they seethed with rage and resentment, no longer willing to heed the elders' assurances that "This too will pass" or helpless reiterations of "That's the way it is; there's nothing to be done." Unable to stomach the idea of laboring for Herod or on any of the aristocratic estates established on what had once been their families' land, they took to the hills and waged an ongoing guerrilla war against the Herodian regime, attacking soldiers and disrupting whatever they could of the state machinery. They'd swoop down to raid the major caravan routes to the north and east, then funnel the take from these raids back to their home villages. And whenever the military was sent out against them in force, they retreated to their Arbel stronghold.

The powers-that-be—first the Hasmoneans, then the Romans, then the Herodians—called them bandits. Maryam, like most Galilean villagers, called them heroes: brave men resisting the occupiers, fighting for their land.

Guerrillas or thugs? Freedom fighters or thieves? It's a problem every newspaper editor still tussles with today. The way a group is described depends on who is doing the describing, and on who is listening.

Take, for instance, a familiar figure from our memory of the gospels: Barabbas, the thief released by public acclaim in preference to Jesus. What could possess such a people to insist that Pontius Pilate release a good-for-nothing like Barabbas instead of Jesus? The contrast is so stark: good and evil, worthy and unworthy. Clearly a perverse choice on the part of the assembled Jerusalemites. So long, that is, as you insist on calling Barabbas a thief.

Who was he really? As an individual, it's hard to know. His name, Bar-Abbas, means "son of his father"—the Aramaic equivalent of John Doe. An alias, perhaps, or a nom de guerre, like Yassir Arafat's Abu Ammar, "father of the people."

But whatever his real name may have been, Bar-Abbas was no simple thief. Our memories of the gospels are skewed. In Luke, he is wanted for sedition; in Mark, for insurrection. Matthew describes him as "a notable prisoner." Again, one man's resistance fighter is another's terrorist, and a national hero to one group of people—to Israelis or to Palestinians—is a criminal to the one it opposes. Calling Bar-Abbas a thief is a convenient way to demonize him, and so to demonize those who called for his release over that of Jesus.

In fact, Bar-Abbas was both popular and well known in Judea, while Jesus was an unknown from what the Judeans thought of as the boondocks: Galilee. Given the choice between a guerrilla leader who had fought against the authorities for justice, and an unknown from the provinces—yet another preacher who had merely caused a small fracas in the temple—the Jerusalemites loudly chose freedom for the proven hero they knew over the unproven one they did not.

Bar-Abbas was not the only such figure of his time, however. His was just one of many brigand bands roaming Palestine in the populist phenomenon identified by British historian Eric Hobsbawm as "social banditry."

Like the Galileans in the Arbel, these bandits were neighbors and relatives. Many had had their land taken in payment of tax debt. Others had dared to speak, even act, against injustice and so had become wanted men. Some had undoubtedly stolen to feed their families. For all these reasons and more, they had taken to the hills in a kind of pre-political rebellion that quickly gained political dimensions, thanks to the brutal reaction of the powers-that-be. Then as now, totalitarian authorities hunted down resisters so ruthlessly that they turned them into heroic martyrs.

It didn't make much difference whether the authorities were Hasmonean or Herodian, Judean or Roman. This was a matter more of class warfare, peasantry against gentry, than of nationalism. Or at least it began that way. A fugitive from the alien justice of the rich and powerful was seen as an honorable victim. If he turned to active resistance, honor grew into heroism. And the hero, as always, represented hope. He personified the idea that oppression was not inevitable. That justice could be fought for. That there were options.

The famed Pancho Villa in Mexico was such a bandit leader, taking from the rich and giving to the poor in what you could call either criminal theft or a socially conscious redistribution of wealth—or was it simply political savvy?—and evolving with other former "bandits" into a leader of the Mexican revolution of 1910.

Galilee's greatest bandit leader in Maryam's time was Hezekiah, even though by the time she was born, he had been dead for some forty years. He had turned outlaw when he and his followers were evicted from their land by the Hasmoneans after a disastrous two-year famine. Under his leadership in 53 B.C. the lakeshore town of Magdala rose in a mass revolt against the Hasmoneans and the young military governor they'd appointed in the Galilee, an Idumean by the name of Herod. The revolt was quickly and ruthlessly put down. The lake turned red with blood, and it stank for weeks afterward as bloated bodies decomposed in the water. Thousands of survivors were led away in chains to be sold as slaves. Hezekiah himself was killed. But far from suppressing resistance, the brutality of Herod's troops and the bravery of the rebels became legendary—and inspiring.

Hezekiah's name alone was a call to action. His exploits, and those of his sons and grandsons who carried on the resistance after him, became part of the repertoire of the story-tellers who acted as the mass media of the day. If he became braver with each telling, if the odds against him were stacked higher and his fighters held out for longer, those who listened would have it no other way. No matter how many spies and informers a ruling regime might employ, there was no preventing the spirit of rebellion sinking deep into the consciousness of Galileans. And among them, Maryam.

She would have heard the stories many times, so many that they had become part of her, memorized word for word. Some of the elders of Nazareth had been alive then; they'd seen everything as children, if not with their own eyes, then through the eyes of those who had been there. So Maryam would have known the gory details of the massacre at Magdala as though it had happened yesterday, not fifty years before. She could tell how the brave mothers of hundreds of those killed made the long trek to Jerusalem to demand that the high priest have Herod tried for massacring their sons, and so forced him to flee to Rome. And how, just a few years later, Hezekiah's men, now under the leadership of his sons, resisted fiercely when Herod returned to fight his way to the throne in Jerusalem.

The details were vivid: soldiers being lowered on ropes from the top of the Arbel cliffs to toss firebrands into the caves; the fighters in the caves trapped, some burning alive, others choking to death on the smoke; the survivors fleeing for shelter in the villages up in the hills. The largest of them, the Galilee Bethlehem, was less than twenty miles from the Arbel, but it was still a tough trek for a healthy person, let alone for a wounded man. Nazareth was small, but it was five miles closer. Here, despite the risk of savage reprisal if they were discovered, villagers like Maryam's grandmother nursed the men of the Arbel back to health, and buried the ones who didn't make it in communal tombs carved deep into the rock.

If there is one constant throughout history, it is that power-hungry rulers make their people pay. And Herod, who emerged out of the desert backwater of Hebron, the capital of Idumea, was hungrier than most.

He was especially detested in Galilee, for the good reason that the Galileans had longer experience of him than the Judeans, thanks to his years as military governor there. But even in Judea, "his" people never accepted him. Quietly, in whispers, because who knew who might be listening, they sneered at him as "the half-Judean." The other half? A. N. Wilson calls him "an Arab from the southern Palestinian province of Idumea," which is partly true—and in modern hindsight, of course, tantalizing to think that the king of the Jews was an Arab. But the whole truth is, as always, more complex.

The Herodians became Judean only in 104 B.C. when their kingdom of Idumea—the biblical Edom—was conquered by the Hasmoneans under Alexander Janneus. You might say that Janneus was carrying on a family tradition of annexation, since it was his father, John Hyrcanus, who had conquered Galilee twenty-five years earlier. Janneus allowed the Idumean elite to stay in power so long as they accepted the worship of Yahweh and agreed to be circumcised. Since the latter was not an issue—then as now, circumcision was the custom among most peoples of the area—the elite took the required vows to Yahweh, while their people went right on worshipping their own god, Kose.

It seemed an easy victory, but in fact the Hasmoneans would have done far better to forget territorial expansion and leave Idumea alone. Over the next sixty years, the Idumeans would take fitting revenge for their conquest by manipulating internecine fighting among the Hasmoneans. They played them off both against each other and against the Romans until Herod—the scion of the Idumean ruling elite, the grandson of a forcibly converted Judean, and the son of a Nabatean mother—was appointed by Mark Antony in Rome as client king of Judea.

Not that Mark Antony's say-so alone made Herod king. It took him three years to fight his way to Jerusalem, making many new enemies along the way. The Arbel guerrillas were only one of his primary targets. After he'd smoked and burned them out of their caves, he went on to take the garrison of Sepphoris and the rest of the Galilee, then turned south to Jericho, Jaffa, and finally Jerusalem, where he laid siege to the city. The siege ended with his troops sacking the temple courts and priestly mansions, and butchering the aristocratic elite so that he could install his own appointees in their place.

Given the vast rift between rich and poor, this might not have been such a bad move if he'd wanted to establish himself as a populist king. But he didn't. He had far greater ambitions. He wanted to be not just Herod the king, but Herod the Great. So he built. Monumentally.

Rebuilding the Jerusalem temple on a scale grander than anything else in the Hellenic world was the most renowned of his projects, but there were countless others. He built a whole series of palaces from scratch, for instance, including the administrative palace in Jerusalem, on a hill looking down over the temple, and the luxury winter palace in Jericho replete with swimming pools, the largest of which turned out to be perfect for the "accidental death by drowning" of his Hasmonean brother-in-law Aristobulos. Then there were the palaces of Herodion and Massada, the kind of well-fortified desert escape hatches essential to a tyrant in times of mass unrest. And of course the brand new capital city of Caesarea with its huge artificial harbor and breakwater—larger even than Piraeus in Athens—and its ornate complex of marbled, porticoed, and fountained palaces shining white in the Mediterranean sun.

One temple was not enough. He built another in Samaria, dedicated to the divine emperor Augustus, and a third as a sanctuary for the local cult of Abraham in Hebron, the capital of Idumea. Ranging abroad, he rebuilt the temple of Apollo in Rhodes. He was nothing if not catholic in his religious dedication.

And temples were only the beginning. Herod made himself a major benefactor throughout the eastern Mediterranean. He financed important construction projects in Athens, Lycia, Pergamum, and Sparta. He re-walled Byblos, built a forum in Tyre and another in Beirut, an aqueduct in Laodicea, amphitheaters in Sidon and Damascus, gymnasia in Ptolemaïs and Tripoli. He built a two-and-a-half-mile paved colonnade along the main street of Antioch, finished in polished marble.

But perhaps most stunningly from a modern perspective, in 16 B.C. he came to the aid of the ailing Olympic Games, pledging huge sums of money to ensure that they were held regularly and in suitable pomp. Such munificence came with honors, naturally, and he was awarded the title of Life President of the Games.

Life President is exactly the kind of title that tyrants still lay claim to today. And Herod was indeed a tyrant, no doubt about that. Like every other ruler of his day. The very idea of democracy was seventeen hundred years away. This was a time when royalty was often melded with divinity, when kings and queens—Augustus, Cleopatra—declared themselves gods and insisted on being worshipped as gods. Whether their subjects literally saw them as gods is quite another question, but traditions like the healing "royal touch" lasted well into the Middle Ages. Even the realm of the purely divine was called "the kingdom of god." Herod at least was a secular tyrant.

His lack of divinity was not by choice. Like any ruler of the time, he would have claimed it if he could. But he ruled at the pleasure of someone else: the emperor in Rome. He could not declare himself divine, since that would be to challenge the emperor, and that was the one thing he could not afford to do.

Still, he must have longed to be thought of as a god. Divinity at least ensures a certain measure of resignation, if not acceptance; secular tyrants turn out to be hated all the more. Herod lacked that god-given element of divine awe, and the high priests he appointed lacked the authority of god-appointed ones—that is, the traditional hereditary ones. Human fear was all that remained, but he at least knew how to enforce that.

Tyrants the world over and through time turn out to be remarkably alike. Herod's network of spies and informers, like Saddam Hussein's in Iraq, included one branch spying on another. Continual tests of loyalty resulted in instant execution for failure. And again like Saddam Hussein, Herod's megalomania went hand in hand with paranoia. He repeatedly struck out at those closest to him if he suspected treachery. And he suspected it everywhere, most probably justifiably.

One precaution he took was to avoid using Judeans in his army; they could turn against him all to easily. Instead, he cannily used soldiers from Samaria and Idumea—longtime enemies of the Judeans—together with foreign mercenaries from Thrace, Germany, and Gaul.

Yes, Gaul, or what is now France. However much westerners, and of course the French in particular, still think of France as the nexus of civilized culture, two thousand years ago it was the back of beyond. Gaul was the kind of place nobody wanted to live—so much so that when Herod's eldest son Archelaus, the client ruler of Judea after his father's death, was ousted and exiled by the Romans for an extraordinary mix of brutality and ineptitude (the brutality was fine; the ineptitude was not), it was to Vienne, on the Rhone in southeastern France. Thirty-three years later, when his younger brother Antipas was himself deposed and banished by the emperor Caligula in 39 A.D. it was to Lyon, in eastern France.

Force alone was clearly not enough to stay in power. It never is. Guile was needed too, and Herod the Great was a master of it, with a sophisticated understanding of how the world—that is, the Roman Empire—worked.

A client king needs to be able to read the political winds correctly, and to have the right patron at the right time. So Herod always covered his back. He knew how to use what the Romans called *unguentaria*, from the word for healing and fragrant oils. This was "ointment money" used to smooth the way of the ambitious, or in Dickensian parlance, good old palm grease. In short: bribes. Every official, from the most powerful to the pettiest functionary, took them. At the highest levels, they are oddly referred to in most historical accounts as "gifts." They were not. They were well calculated quid pro quos, especially in the hands of a master like Herod, who plundered the accumulated treasures of the Jerusalem temple, much of which found their way into the coffers first of Julius Caesar, then Mark Antony, and then Octavian, who declared himself Augustus Caesar.

Herod's extraordinary balancing act was made easier by a fact of geopolitics that still holds true today. Palestine straddled the land route from Egypt, which provided a third of Rome's annual grain consumption, and it was a buffer between the Roman Empire and its enemies to the east. Palestine, that is, was essential to controlling the eastern Mediterranean. And Herod assured the Romans of continuing control. He was a brilliant choice for client ruler: absolutely loyal to whoever was in power, no danger of him declaring himself divine since he was not fully accepted by his own people, and above all, capable of keeping things quiet in Palestine.

So far as Rome was concerned, it worked perfectly. Once Herod had fought his way to Jerusalem and claimed the throne, the Romans didn't have to send in their own troops until the year he died. They got thirty-five years of obedience and profit at no substantial cost to themselves: the perfect colonial deal.

Except, of course, for the colonialized.

*　　*　　*

Somebody had to pay for Herod's grandiose ambitions. The Olympic Games alone were as outrageously expensive to stage then as they are now. Without television networks to pay broadcasting fees, or commercial sponsors, the burden fell on those who could least afford it: Palestinian peasants.

Not that Herod didn't have considerable personal wealth. Wealth was the chief prerogative of power. He had the income from the crown domains, which included the immensely valuable date plantations and balsam groves of Jericho. Under lease from Augustus, he had half the income of the copper mines of Cyprus. He also had customs and excise taxes from his Mediterranean ports and from points of entry such as Capernaum at the northern end of the Sea of Galilee, where camel and mule trains traveling north from Arabia along the Dead Sea valley would turn west to reach the seaports. On top of all this, he had the interest on huge loans to the Nabateans, whose realm stretched the length of the east side of the Dead Sea valley, and a free hand, if not exactly license, in plundering the temple treasury.

But with ambitions such as his, none of this was enough. The shortfall could only be made up from the land he directly controlled. That is, from taxes.

The tax burden was crippling. As usual, it fell hardest on the poor. First, one third of the crop went straight to Herod, collecting for the Romans—and for himself. Then a further ten percent was due in priestly tithes: first fruits and so on. And then there was the annual half shekel to be paid directly to the temple, levied not per family but per male in the family, which is why whenever a population census was proposed, uprisings were inevitable. In all, almost half of a farmer's produce was taken away immediately in tithes and taxes, often seized right on the threshing floor. And since whatever the tax collector could extract above and beyond the required amount was his to keep in addition to his regular commission, many peasants paid still more.

The moment the tax collectors appeared over the ridge from Sepphoris—always with a military escort—all the chatter and songs, the excitement and bustle of harvest came to a stop. The usual hubbub of people that greeted travelers the moment they set foot in Nazareth was non-existent. Young boys were hushed so that they wouldn't snicker at the sight of grown men riding on mules, when everyone knew that only the sick and the very elderly did that. A sullen silence descended on the village. Even the donkeys dragging the threshing boards over the newly harvested wheat seemed to move sluggishly, as though under a great burden.

The soldiers were unpredictable, the taxmen thuggish. If they weren't presented with what they considered their due, they took it by force, and then some, to make up for the trouble of exerting themselves. Only the family heads gathered to meet them in the center of the village. Women and girls kept their distance, lest the soldiers decide that rape was part of the bargain. Like girls her age throughout the Galilee, Maryam looked on from high up on the olive terraces, witnessing the shame of her menfolk humbled by extortionists.

Those farmers who could afford it could simply bribe the taxmen to understate their tax liability. This could take hours of desperate negotiation as the soldiers supervised the loading of the mules with wheat, barley, olive oil, whatever was in store or in season. Those who couldn't afford the bribes were often forced on the road to dispossession. They had to ask for credit against the following year's crop, either from Herodian officials or from the priestly aristocracy or, worst, from the tax collectors themselves. In a spiral of indebtedness still known to small farmers the world over, they borrowed against future harvests, and so mortgaged the farm.

Once you started on this road, there was little chance of turning back. The loans were risky. Even under the best conditions, productivity was never very high; a peasant family's plots would produce little more than what was needed for subsistence. If the next year was a drought year, the family was already in danger. Two drought years in a row, and they were done for. The collateral for the first year's loan was the harvest; for the second year, it was the land itself.

Men who had owned their land—land that their fathers and grandfathers and great grandfathers had owned, on down into the past for more generations than anyone could count—became tenant farmers in what had been their own fields, or were forced into construction work in Sepphoris or Jerusalem. Family structures were broken up this way. But more, so was the whole basis of peasant life.

Palestinian anthropologist Ali Qleibo points out that in peasant societies, "the bond with the land is very difficult to sever on emotional, social and historical grounds. It is a highly charged symbol in terms of which one's sense of identity is produced." Family survival on the land of your ancestors—on the land planted with olive trees older than the legends told around the fire at night—was, and still is, the supreme value. Dispossession is more than the loss of the house, or even of the land itself; it is the loss of identity.

This is why the long tradition of great prophets was still so alive in Maryam's mind, and why in time she would make sure to pass it on to her son. The prophets were the guardians of identity. One after another, they invoked divine judgment against rulers who exploited the peasantry and appropriated their lands. Isaiah, Jeremiah, Hosea, Amos, Micah, Nehemiah—all weighed in forcefully.

Nehemiah, writing soon after the founding of the second Jerusalem temple in the fifth century B.C., recorded the people's complaints word for word:

> "We are having to pledge our fields, our vineyards, and our houses in order to get grain during the famine . . . We are having to borrow on our fields and vineyards to pay the king's tax . . . We are forcing our sons and daughters to be slaves, and some of our daughters have been ravished. We are powerless, and our fields and vineyards now belong to others."

Yes, slaves. As in Afghanistan and other countries today, children were often sold to help pay off debts. And since the continuity of the family was invested in the sons, especially the eldest one, it was the daughters who were most likely to be traded away in payment of debt. Daughters like Maryam.

It didn't have to be this way. The old Mosaic law, established in Exodus and reiterated in Leviticus and Deuteronomy, dictated a sabbatical release every seventh year from debt and debt-slavery—a forgiveness of debt that many fundamentalists might consider adding to their religious practice today, particularly if they happen to be bankers. But as with most ideals, this forgiveness was observed more in the breach than in the letter. Like the command to monotheism, it was a principle but not a custom.

As the debt crisis worsened, the temple aristocracy invented the *prosbul*, a special legal device to help make credit available in a sabbatical year, when lenders normally wouldn't want to give any credit at all. The intention was worthy, perhaps, but it backfired. In effect, it simply abolished the very idea of a debt sabbatical.

Yet the ideal lived on. Forgiveness of debt was something Jesus would insist on among his followers. He advocated it in what we now know as the Lord's Prayer, an extraordinary text that today resonates mainly as metaphor. In the Palestine of two thousand years ago, however, it focused on everyday reality in the most concrete way. It addressed the two prime concerns of peasant life: "Give us our daily bread" and "Forgive us our debts." When you do not have enough to eat and are being forced off your land, you do not have much time for metaphor; you mean what you say.

This is how the Lord's Prayer started out, at least. The earliest version, in Matthew, reads, "Forgive us our debts, as we forgive our debtors." But by the time Luke was written, the text had lost partial sight of debt, becoming, "Forgive us our sins, for we also forgive every one who is indebted to us." Eventually, that partial blindness would become total, and the official version of the Lord's Prayer would read, "Forgive us our trespasses, as we forgive those who trespass against us."

The change in wording had a certain logic. Luke and later writers were at a further remove from Palestine than the earlier Matthew, both in time and space. They were writing for an audience blissfully unaware of the situation of Galilean and Judean peasants living under Roman and Herodian rule. But the very fact that debts were changed into sins is sobering. It implies a judgment, as though those in debt were at fault, sinning against some higher order. In an ironic instance of what happens when cultural context is lost, the dominant version of the Lord's Prayer runs contrary to everything Jesus stands for in the gospels. By conflating debt with sin and trespass, it takes the side of the lender against the debtor, of the rich against the poor.

Resistance was inevitable. Especially in the Galilee, where the Arbel guerrillas were now led by Hezekiah's grandsons. But though the guerrillas were heroic figures throughout the hill villages like the Galilee Bethlehem and Nazareth, they also had strong urban support. This was centered in the lakeside town of Magdala, the home of Mary the Magdalene, the woman who represents the meeting place of rural peasant and urban laborer.

There is nothing in the gospels of the real Magdala—no indication that this was the only place in Galilee whose population reached into the thousands instead of the hundreds, and would remain the largest town in the province until Herod Antipas started to build Tiberias, a few miles south, in 19 A.D. Nor is there any awareness of its importance as the center of the Galilean fishing industry.

And industry it was. Magdala was, in essence, a fish-processing plant: a quasi-industrial township populated by peasants who had been forced off their land by drought, war, and tax debt. They streamed into "the city," and there they worked for daily or piece wages, lived in crowded hovels, and found themselves little more than slave labor for others. The whole place seethed with anger and resentment, with visions of a world without the Romans, without Herod, without tax collectors and government agents, bribery and corruption. It was, in short, not unlike any number of third-world towns today where people forced off the land congregate, mired in poverty and filth, and where despair builds on despair.

It's easy now to perch on the big rounded stones of the lakeshore on a calm spring day, near the ruins of a Byzantine monastery overgrown with wild mint and guarded by a Moslem caretaker and his dogs, and think of this as a bucolic place. Easier by far not to imagine how it was two thousand years ago, when tons of fish were hauled out onto the piers every day to be gutted and cleaned, then processed—salted, pressed, smoked, fermented, pickled—and finally sealed in heavy clay jars and sent by mule train south to Beit Shean, then east along the Jezreel Valley to the port of Caesarea, where they were shipped to Rome.

Magdala's specialty was a spicy fish extract known as *garum*. This condiment was a treasured delicacy in high-class Roman banqueting halls. It had the added allure of being thought of as a medicinal cure-all, though it quite possibly killed as many people as it cured. Think a very fishy version of Korean kimchi, or nuoc nam, the anchovy sauce used in Thai and Vietnamese cuisine, then think twice as pungent, and you have an idea what *garum* was like. It was made by leaving the salted and spiced entrails of small fish to ferment in the sun for several weeks—yes, weeks—then straining away the residue. Anyone in England horrified by this description, incidentally, might do well to check what's in a bottle of Worcestershire sauce.

As you might expect, Magdala stank. The putrid reek of rotting fish was everywhere: on hands, in nostrils, in hair, in the mud, in the air. It mixed with the stench of open sewers and acrid smoke from the curing towers until the smell hung close in the narrow alleys, filling the air of the dark slum hovels and permeating the clothes of the townspeople. Cormorants and vultures hovered in huge packs on the outskirts of the town, swooping in on the mounds of steaming bones and innards.

The air was utterly stifling in the still, humid days of summer, when so much moisture rose in evaporation from the lake that you could barely see the hills of the Arbel behind you, let alone the far shore or the snow-covered Mount Hermon rising far to the north. At least winters were balmy by contrast, except for the days when sudden storms came up from seemingly nowhere.

These storms were quick and treacherous. The gorges all around the lake funneled the wind, creating furious gusts that whipped the water into foaming, peaked waves, then drove them against the shores. The waves bounced back to collide with incoming ones, water clashing against water, and tranquility turned into turmoil in a matter of minutes. In the turmoil, fishermen in small boats drowned.

Proudly independent fishermen nonetheless? No. The idyllic vision of them spreading their nets at sunset and genially roasting their catch over an open fire is just that: an idyll. In fact the fishing industry was highly regulated, and the fishermen as exploited as the peasant villagers laboring under their tax burden. Fishing rights were controlled by government representatives who sold to the highest bidder—and the highest briber. These were essentially conglomerates; they hired the fishermen as day laborers, leasing the boats at extortionate fees to the men who worked for them.

Read between the lines in the gospel of Matthew, and it's clear that no independent fisherman would have neglected his boats and gone off to follow a preacher, no matter how charismatic. But an indentured fisherman? One whose boat was his only at the grace of the head of the conglomerate and whose livelihood could be taken from him at any moment? He had nothing to lose.

And then, finally, Herod the Great died. Despite innumerable assassination attempts, he had survived well into his sixties; then as now, tyrants seemed to thrive on their abuse of power. At least he had died an excruciatingly painful death, by all accounts from stomach cancer.

Now the decades of waiting were over. As fast as word spread, street riots broke out throughout Palestine. This surely was the moment for the popular leader to arise, the anointed king, the messiah who would rid the land of foreign occupation and lead his people back to dignity and independence.

There were many candidates. In Perea, east of the Jordan, a certain Simon was proclaimed king by his supporters, then led them in a series of lightning raids against Herodian holdings across the river. They ransacked and set fire to several of Herod's palaces, including the infamously luxurious one in Jericho—a particularly satisfying target for Simon, since he had formerly been a slave there. In Judea, a shepherd referred to historically only by the Greek name Athronges was acclaimed a popular king, and together with his brothers, led guerrilla operations against Herodian troops. But neither these nor others had anything like the following of Hezekiah's grandson Judas in the Galilee.

His guerrilla band augmented by villagers, Judas stormed Sepphoris, the Herodian garrison town just over the ridge from Nazareth. With surprise and sheer numbers on their side, they quickly gained control of the garrison. Once inside, their first priority was to break down the door to the archives and destroy all tax and debt records.

Word spread quickly; more villagers came, reveling in the sudden sense of freedom. Their debts forcibly "forgiven," they looted the regional governor's palace, seized weapons, hauled sacks of grain—their own grain, taken by force as taxes—back home.

It couldn't last, of course. Reprisal, in the classical Roman style, was quick, brutal, and heavy-handed. The Roman general Varus swept down with his legions from his headquarters to the north in Syria. As usual with the Romans, only the commanders were actually from Rome; the soldiers themselves were mercenaries, mainly from Syria and farther east. No honor in arms here; no fine distinctions between combatant and non-combatant. As with all warfare of the time, it was total. Olive groves and fruit orchards were torn up. Wheat fields burned. Women and girls raped and killed. Houses destroyed, sometimes even whole villages, for sheltering fugitives. In Perea, Simon was hunted down and beheaded. Thousands of followers of Athronges, the shepherd-messiah, were massacred, and Athronges himself disappeared. Magdala saw bloody hand-to-hand fighting, and long lines of Magdalenes were led away in chains to be sold as slaves. But the fiercest fighting—and the fiercest reprisal—came in Sepphoris.

The garrison was razed, the leaders of the occupying rebels crucified, and their followers captured and sold as slaves. Nobody knows how many Nazarenes were among them, but certainly any survivors would have headed for Nazareth, just over the ridge to the south. Some of the braver villagers would have gone up to the top of the ridge to watch as the smoke from the burning town drifted across to them. Others, braver still, would have gone down the far side of the ridge to help guide any surviving rebels to safety, first in Nazareth, and then in other, more remote villages.

They'd have been close enough to watch as the soldiers prepared to crucify the resistance leaders—the Roman punishment of choice for slaves, rebels, and traitors. There was nothing they could do but look on helplessly as the crossbeams were raised into place on the Sepphoris hillside, then keep silent, distant vigil as the soldiers jeered at the tortured men nailed to the crosses, day after agonizing day. And when the men died at last, and the soldiers tossed their bodies into a nearby ravine, the villagers had to leave them there, to be polished to the bone by jackals and vultures.

Maryam kept vigil with them. How could she not? There is no question that she was involved in the resistance of her time. The only question is how she could possibly be anything but involved. Like any West Bank villager or Gaza refugee camp dweller today, she was caught up in the political turmoil around her because it reached deep into every village, every clan, every family.

Her own kinsmen were almost certainly among those crucified at Sepphoris, and that scene of crucifixion would sear itself into her brain, brand itself into her consciousness. These men were dying for her, for her neighbors, for all of them. To risk the cross was a sign of courage; to die on it, a hero's death. To abandon the struggle for fear of such a death would be to betray not just everything these men had fought for, but also everything she herself believed in and had worked for.

In any struggle of popular resistance, girls are as valuable as seasoned fighters. Even before Herod's death and Varus' savage reprisal, who better than a shepherd girl in her loose linen shift to smuggle food to the Arbel caves? Who knew the goat tracks better than she did the ones used by men, and knew them as well by starlight as by sunlight? The goats and sheep had taught her every cave, every tree capable of offering shade, every overhang where you could hide from the scorching midday sun, or from soldiers. Maryam was the perfect guide for a wounded fighter seeking safety.

It would never have occurred to her to do anything less. This was not just the idealism of youth, for the principle of resistance was set deep in her mind. It was part of her culture and her history as a Galilean. Repression merely strengthened her determination instead of sapping it. Just as steadfastness became the motto of Arab Palestinians during the Intifada—the uprising against Israeli rule that began in 1987—so too it could have served as the motto of Jewish Palestinians of Maryam's time.

Many of the methods used by the Romans sound jarringly familiar in today's Middle East: mass imprisonment, execution, deportation, collective punishment in the form of homes and villages razed, olive trees and fruit orchards uprooted. Anyone reading a newspaper over the past few years can't help but sense the echoes bouncing across time between the Roman occupation of Palestine and the Israeli one of the West Bank and Gaza.

As in the rebellions against Herod and the Romans, the Intifada was the result of a social and political upheaval within Palestinian society. It combined nationalist warfare with class warfare. The traditional aristocratic families who had protected their assets under both Jordanian and Israeli rule were now threatened, much as the Judean aristocratic elite was threatened by popular uprisings two thousand years ago. Like the high priesthood, the old-guard Fatah leaders were seen as culturally and morally corrupt—"whiskey drinkers" was one of the milder epithets for them—and the rise of the fundamentalist Hamas movement offered a seductive alternative, fueling the revolt with religious revival. As political journalists Ze'ev Schiff and Ehud Ya'ari noted, political activism "now combined patriotism with moral purity, and social action with the promise of divine grace."

The greater the repression of the Intifada, the more widespread its support. Most significantly, perhaps, it involved everybody: women and men, old and young. Grandmothers brought baskets full of stones to children aiming slingshots at tanks. Women organized tax strikes and social services. A new tactic developed reminiscent of the Sicarii, the dagger men, who operated in the middle of the first century: assassination of suspected collaborators. By the year 2001, even long-standing concepts of honor had been turned around, with teenage girls gaining instant martyrdom by becoming suicide bombers.

What applies today, applied also two thousand years ago. Repression may have been effective in the short term, but it was counter-effective in the longer term. The Roman intention was to force the Palestinians into accepting their fate; instead, the Palestinians understood that they could alter and affect it—a revolutionary concept for peasants at any time in any place, and a firebrand one when mixed with religion.

No matter how many crucifixions there were—and there were thousands—no matter how many homes and olive trees were destroyed or people taken into slavery, Varus and his troops couldn't touch the sense that something new was about to come into being. Today we'd call such a sense millennial, though then there was no millennium. It was the year 3761 in the Jerusalem temple, and the year 753 Ab Urbe Condita, since the founding of the city of Rome. But no Galilee villager cared how the years were numbered. All that mattered was that the old tyrant was dead. Steadfastness and patience would now be rewarded. Simon and Athronges had been false messiahs, but if there was ever a time for the true anointed king to appear and lead his people to freedom and independence, it was surely now.

This was Palestine just over two thousand years ago—the world in which Maryam lived, and in which, at age thirteen, she became pregnant and gave birth.

It was the year we now know as 4 B.C.

PART TWO

HER WOMB

IV

Maryam learned early about childbirth. Since she was young, her grandmother has taken her along whenever there's a delivery. The old woman is in her fifties, but as alert and sharp as any shepherd girl; like all village wise women, she seems to defy age. Her name? The same as the midwife of apocryphal legend: Salome. It's a name that can mean either woman of peace, or woman of wholeness. Perhaps the two are the same thing.

At first, Salome just had Maryam carry her box of herbs and oils, but gradually, without the child even realizing that she was learning, she taught her how to help: pull here, apply pressure there, mix these herbs for an infusion, those for a poultice. And Salome knows now that she's chosen her successor well. The girl is quick to learn, with strong hands that can be firm or gentle according to need. Gifted hands, Salome calls them.

When word comes—a boy arriving breathless at the door, often in the middle of the night—the two women, old and young, make their way through the alleys to find the kinswomen of the household huddled around the moaning mother. The men sit in silence on the roof, keeping their distance; this is women's work. Salome checks that everything is in place: a stone on the floor for her to sit between the mother's open legs, a fire to heat water and oils, soil scattered in front of the midwife's stone to soak up the blood.

Maryam hangs the holding rope from a beam, so that the mother can cling to it as she pushes in labor. Salome directs the kinswomen: one to stand behind the mother so that she can slip her arms around her, below the armpits, and lift her; two others to kneel on either side so that they can take the weight of her thighs. The three form a natural chair of womanly support, with Salome in front, the fourth point of the compass.

Meanwhile Maryam mixes the herbs that will make labor go faster. Her grandmother favors giant fennel, and Maryam measures the crushed leaves carefully, for the correct dosage is vital. Then she mixes them in oil and a little wine, lifts the pregnant woman's head, and encourages her to drink. Salome watches; she likes the way her granddaughter handles the matter. Many women in labor pains will writhe and twist away, spit out the potions and frustrate a midwife's work. But Maryam's voice and touch seem to soothe them. They swallow the liquid she offers, breathe deep when she tells them, push when she says to.

More often than not, all goes well. The baby appears as it should, head first. Salome reaches up with both hands and with a deft twist brings the child out into the light of day, a bundle of wrinkled newborn flesh cradled in her dark, age-wrinkled hands. Then she calls on the afterbirth to follow without delay.

"Come sister," she chants, claiming it as family lest its spirit come back to haunt the child. "Come into the world."

"Come sister," echo the kinswomen, knowing that the placenta must emerge, or the mother will die.

If the afterbirth delays, some midwives use pepper to make the mother sneeze. Others burn hyssop or thyme and make the mother inhale the fumes to bring on extra contractions. But Salome prefers a simpler, more effective method: she presses her head hard into the mother's stomach, ignoring her cries of pain, and pushes the afterbirth down and out.

Now the kinswomen stand and ululate to greet the new baby into the world and frighten away any evil spirits that might be hovering nearby, ready to enter the vulnerable newborn. The high, sharp trilling wafts out over the village, carrying the good news as Maryam oils and salts the baby—every newborn anointed in its new world—to protect it from evil spirits and illness. Then she puts it into a basket along with the afterbirth so that the child can draw on its power for its first day of life. Salome chants the spells that are expected of her. "El, great god who keeps every living thing alive," she cries. "Give afflictions and enemies no power over this woman and over the child that has emerged from her. I hereby call on the mighty one." And now, shortening the forbidden full name of Yahweh to Yah, she closes her eyes, lifts her head, and offers the abbreviated name again and again into the night, high and piercing: "Yah, Yah, Yah, Yah, Yah . . ."

She knows the infant's life was in her hands and her herbs, and that her spells, like the oil and the salt, are more ritual than practical. But she also recognizes the power of belief. A mother must have faith in her infant's ability to survive, and the very act of chanting a spell is reassuring, even to Salome herself. It is an act of closure, as it were, signifying that her work has been well done and she can return home to sleep in good faith.

She comes back the next day to cut the navel cord. If the newborn is a boy, she circumcises it. A swift skillful nick of the knife, a single cry, and it's done. Then she and Maryam wrap the afterbirth in oil and straw, tie it up in a cloth embroidered by the mother for just this purpose, and bury it along with the blood-soaked soil from in front of the birthing stone. This way, the earth will wait patiently to reclaim the new life, for as everyone knows, we are born of the earth and to the earth we shall return. Ashes to ashes, dust to dust.

The baby won't be named for forty days yet. If it survives, there'll be a feast; the village will celebrate, and the mother will be ritually bathed by her kinswomen. But not until those forty days have passed. You never want to provoke the wrath of the gods by taking life for granted.

Yet sometimes even Salome's best efforts fail. For all her skill and knowledge and experience, the gods will have their way. The mother may keep bleeding no matter how strong the herbs she's been given, growing weaker and weaker until she loses the strength to live. Or the infant is born dead: purple from lack of air, with the cord wrapped around its neck, or so malformed that you can't help but be grateful that there is no breath in its lungs.

Sometimes, and these are the worst, both mother and child die, and then the gathered women keen—a long, deep moaning like an animal in mortal pain—as Salome seamlessly switches from life to death, accepting the one as calmly and as naturally as the other. Maryam washes the bodies as her grandmother mixes myrrh and other aromatic herbs with oil, and then the two women, the old and the young, perform the last act of honor to the dead woman and her child. They rub and anoint the corpses and wrap them in their shrouds.

When I lived in Jerusalem, I used to go walking with friends in the surrounding hills in search of herbs, especially in the springtime. My favorite was wild sage, called *maryamiya* in Aramaic: literally, Maryam's herb. Not the wide-leaved garden sage, but a spindlier mountain species with long grayish-green leaves. We'd take it home and pack it into a glass, then fill the glass with honey and hot water, sip, and feel extraordinarily clear-headed and . . . well, sage.

Whether Maryam's name came from the herb or the herb's name from Maryam, the link remains firm. The sage I collected and drank is certainly the same one she collected and drank. But I was merely dabbling; Maryam was far more professional.

Few people today have any serious difficulty accepting the image of her as a shepherd girl, out in the hills with the sheep and the goats. After all, that fits our picture of peasant life two thousand years ago. Or, indeed, of peasant life today. But there's a certain condescension in this, very similar to the one we adopt when we imagine that people who could neither read nor write were by definition ignorant.

Maryam has to have been far more than just another peasant girl out with the flocks. She would raise a child who would become a revered healer in his time, let alone a divine being after his death. How then did he come by such knowledge?

There have been innumerable theories as to where Jesus learned the art of healing, sending him everywhere from Egypt to China to become a kind of sorcerer's apprentice. Such theories feed off and into the ongoing western fascination with the occult, and the essentially racist idea of the inscrutably mysterious Orient. But not only are none of them helpful; they actually obscure the issue. A quick pass with Ockham's razor—the famous principle devised by medieval scholar William of Ockham which states, in essence, that ornate explanations are both unnecessary and illogical—and we can see a more convincing answer far closer to home.

Let us let go of Orientalist exotica, then, and see Maryam as a healer. An assumption, true, but by no means an unreasonable one, for there is strong circumstantial evidence. Every village of the time included a line of women who passed on the knowledge of herbal and manual medicine to their daughters and granddaughters. They were called "wise women," or perhaps more appropriately in Maryam's case, "sage women." Of course we don't know if Maryam's grandmother was called Salome; there is no record, neither historical nor legendary, of her grandparents. But women such as she were the midwives and pharmacists, the bone-setters and bandagers, the family practitioners and emergency-room physicians of the time.

In the peasant societies of the Middle East two millennia ago, as in many peasant societies still today, it was rare to see anyone without some kind of scar or deformity or suppurating sore. Even the relatively healthy showed the signs of hard labor. Faces we now take for forty-year-olds belonged to twenty-year-olds. Malnutrition led to stunted growth and skin disorders. Rotting teeth, open sores, crippled limbs were all par for the course. The surprise is not that up to three out of five people born would die before adulthood, but that two out of five made it through this minefield of physical threat. And much of that was due to the work of the wise women.

They understood bones and muscles, herbs and drugs. They manipulated limbs and bones in what we now call osteopathy, often with seemingly miraculous results—a fact that should come as no surprise to anyone who has made it to a chiropractor's office doubled over in agony, then risen from the table feeling almost Lazarus-like, able to walk without pain or crutches. They knew how to bind a sprain, how to set a broken bone, how to clean and disinfect and protect an open wound. How to treat eye infections, skin diseases, snakebite, worms, dysentery. And of course how to help in childbirth. These women, without formal training, without literacy, without FDA-approved drugs, saved lives.

The herbs Maryam and her grandmother used were not as reliable as modern drugs, to be sure, but they were the accepted medical treatments of the time. What worked for peasants also worked for the elite of Athens and Rome and Alexandria. There, the Hippocratic tradition was carried on and developed in the work of honored medical men such as Soranus, who authored the textbook *Gynecology*, Pliny with his *Natural History*, and the famed first-century pharmacologist Dioscorides. But not only men. Aristotle's wife, Pythias—named after the Pythia, the woman who acted as the Delphic oracle—specialized in obstetrics. Seneca wrote in praise of the skill of his physician, a woman. And a certain Cleopatra—not the Egyptian queen, but another Cleo—was so expert in gynecology that her book on the subject would remain a standard reference into the sixteenth century.

Women physicians had a major advantage over their male colleagues: though they too were members of the ruling class, they had easier access to the vast knowledge of traditional wise women. They simply had to ask their own slaves and servants. And this was essential. By Pliny's own admission, most of his expertise was based on traditional folk medicine. "The reason why herbs are not familiar," he wrote, "is because experience of them is confined to illiterate countryfolk."

The art and science of herbal healing was in knowing not just which herbs to use, but also how to prepare them, and above all, in what dosage. As with the sage tea I drank in the Judean hills, almost any herb prepared in sufficient quantity or strength will have some effect on the human body. Small amounts of saffron are an exotic spice; large amounts will induce abortion. Small amounts of sage give a subtle flavor to a stew; large amounts act like psychotropic drugs.

The seed, the fruit, the oil of a plant could all have differing effects, as could the bark or the flower. Some were best applied as a suppository, others as an infusion to be drunk or as a paste to be smeared over the affected part of the body. They could be blended into soothing unguents or used in a poultice—a mass of tight-packed leaves, reassuringly heavy on the skin like a cooling hand pressing down.

Maryam would have been expert at spotting fennel; she'd have climbed halfway down a ravine to find it, the spores tickling her nostrils with their bitter, pungent scent. She'd have recognized the small fleshy three-lobed leaves of rue with its mustard-like flowers, or the tiny yellow flowers and feathery silver-gray leaves of artemisia, even then called "the virgin's plant." With her shepherd girl's knowledge of the terrain, she'd have known which plants colonized which slopes and hilltops. The squill that covered the hillside across from Cana could be used to treat vomiting and food poisoning. Wild mint grew lavishly in low places, as it still does in what remains of Magdala, and helped prevent infection of cuts and gashes. Fever-reducing anemones grew thick on the hills in springtime, as did galangal, a sharper, sweeter form of ginger, which stopped vomiting and nausea.

She'd harvest roots and stalks, tie them into bundles, and carry them home in a sling across her back. There, she'd spread the herbs out on the reed roof canopy to dry in the sun. Within a few days, the leaves would shrink and curl, crumbling beneath her fingers and ready to be pounded into powder.

Resins were even more valuable. Salome taught her how to prepare myrrh—from *murra*, Aramaic for "bitter"—an antiseptic and painkiller whose strong scent also made it an effective perfume when preparing bodies for burial. Tap the bark of the myrrh tree in the fall and its resin appeared as a clear liquid, then quickly set into pale yellow tears clinging to the trunk. Scoop off the tears and you could then pound them into powder to mix with oil for salves and poultices.

Maryam never saw the most prized resin of her time. That was a cultivated rarity worth its weight in silver: opobalsam, from the balsam trees in Herod's heavily guarded groves near the Asphalt Sea—the salt lake we now call the Dead Sea. Instead, Salome showed her how to milk the purplish bark of the storax, a kind of gum tree also known as liquidambar. The poor man's opobalsam, it had almost as many uses as myrrh, but was especially valued for bronchial and lung infections and as a healing agent for wounds and skin diseases.

Two thousand years later, peasants in some parts of the Middle East still revere the storax tree. It is considered so sacred that it should never be cut; to use even its dead branches for firewood brings bad luck. Stories circulate that this is the tree from which Moses' rod came, the one that sprouted when he thrust it into the ground. Rosaries are still made from its seeds.

Where did herbs end and faith begin? The very question reveals its modern bias.

In Nain, the village across the Jezreel Valley from Nazareth, where the gospel of Luke has Jesus raising the widow's son from the dead, there is one tiny church. Most of the time, it is locked. You have to go across the road and ask the family who hold the key to open the door for you. The key seems absurdly large for such a small building, and it is also peculiarly ornate, since once the door is open, what strikes you most of all is the utter plainness of the place. No lush adornment, no massive accumulation of gold-encrusted icons, no well-funded renovation. Almost shabby, in fact. A place where faith must do its work unaided by pomp and circumstance. And it does.

Walk to the far end and you find a table pushed up against the back of the altar, seemingly littered with pieces of paper. Look closer, and you see that these are letters written in thanks for miracles, or asking for them. Most are in English, though clearly not from native English-speakers; it seems that pilgrims here believe that Jesus responds better to English. Nearly all the letters concern illness, usually that of someone near: "for my daughter," "for my grandson." The profusion of them behind the altar is testament to the healing powers of prayer, for each one is written in thanks or in anticipation of thanks.

They lie there, open, in no particular order, for everyone to read and renew their faith. Yet when you start to read them, you can't help feeling as though you are prying into other people's private affairs—of both health and faith. When you come to one that starts "Dear Jesus" and ends "Love, Adrienne," you have to stop reading. These are indeed love letters.

Sixty miles to the south, the thick stone walls and carefully tended gardens of the isolated monastery of Saint Gerasimos create an oasis of shade in the heavy heat of the Jordan Valley. One of the three Greek Orthodox monks who lives there tells how Gerasimos tamed and lived with a lion, and how he also tamed "Maria of Egypt," a former prostitute whose story makes Mary Magdalene seem a model of chastity. But Gerasimos is celebrated more for his healing powers than for his taming ones. Behind the altar in the monastery church—as richly decorated as the one in Nain is simple—the wall is covered with flesh-colored effigies of legs, feet, arms, hearts, eyes, babies, even what appears to be a kidney. The larger effigies, some almost lifesize, are made out of wax; the smaller ones out of pressed tin. Heal my hand, my foot, my eye, my heart . . . Each effigy bears witness to personal tragedy, to distress and hoped-for relief.

These are votives, offered to the saint either in thanks for healing the body part represented, or in the hope of it. They're a tradition that goes back two thousand years and more, to the temples of the great goddess Isis, famed throughout the eastern Mediterranean for her healing powers. And they work now as well as they did then, when there was no dividing line between faith and healing, just as there was none between astrology and astronomy, or between mind and body, or even—witness the human disguises of many of the Greek gods—between the divine and the human.

Herbal medicine, folk religion, osteopathy, magic, and formal religion all blended together in people's minds. Just a few years ago, this would have been sneered at as "primitive" or "superstitious," but modern research on placebos and on the mind-body connection clearly shows that the mind does affect the body. Every good healer, whether village wise woman or Harvard Medical School graduate, knows the limits of science, and the importance of faith.

Inevitably, health fused with salvation. The very word began, after all, as a medical term, as in *salve*, or healing ointment. It meant physical healing, and beyond specific healing, deliverance from disease and by extension, from death. A divine function.

By Maryam's time, the Middle East had seen a long line of healing goddesses. As far back as 4000 B.C. the Sumerians worshipped Inanna, the queen of heaven and earth, who embodied the trinity of love, healing, and birth. Later, the Assyrian goddess Ishtar fulfilled the same role, with an emphasis on easing pain. But the greatest of all the healing goddesses, and the longest-lived—she was worshipped from 2500 B.C. well into the sixth century A.D.—was Isis, whose cult spread out of Egypt to encompass the whole of the eastern Mediterranean.

Belief in Isis was not a cult as we now think of the term, but a highly developed culture. She was worshipped by serious scientists who had, perhaps, a greater sense of humility in the face of knowledge than we are used to today. In the fourth century B.C., for instance, the famed university of Alexandria included a medical school established under the pharaoh Ptolemy I, a student of Aristotle. Physiology and pathology were taught at this school, and post-mortem dissections led to the discovery of the system of blood circulation as well as the nervous system. But magical texts and folk cures were also taught, and given equal weight. Moreover, the medical school was attached to the temple of Isis Medica, which was in essence a sanitarium. Faith healing took place there, alongside a range of services that some today would still consider the perfect spa experience: drug-induced sleep and dreams, massage, herbal remedies, purges, bleeding, mineral baths, and a plentiful supply of sacred spring water to be drunk fresh from the source.

The priests who officiated as healers at Isis Medica were known as *therapeutae*—therapeutics—the same name that would later be adopted by an Egyptian Jewish monastic movement in which women participated equally with men. An early gnostic Christian group, the Peretae, worshipped Isis as "the right-hand power of god," using medical analogies that displayed a sophisticated understanding of human anatomy. And even when Christianity began to displace older forms of worship, Isis lived on within it. The gnostics morphed her into Sophia, the personification of divine wisdom, and in the visionary Wisdom of Solomon, Sophia instructs the writer in "the nature of all living things," including the healing uses of plants and roots.

In Maryam's time, Isis was still worshipped as the great healer in major cities like Corinth, Alexandria, and Rome. In Athens, however, she had long had competition from a whole family of divine healers: Asculepius and his daughters, Hygeia and Panacea. A fourth-century B.C. bas-relief shows Hygeia standing in a sexy slouch, one hand on her hip, the other propped against a wall behind the seated figure of her father. The posture, the face, even the dress are stunningly modern, like a fashion model's louche pose. The long, flimsy robe follows the contours of her stance, while a shawl slung over her shoulders flows casually to the ground behind her. Head tilted to one side, she stares out at the viewer almost defiantly, as though to say "You got a problem with this?"

The gospels also blend physical and metaphysical healing. Written in the late first century A.D., they are documents of their time. As a preacher, Jesus would favor faith-healing over herbs, but he had clearly also been well trained in both folk medicine and what we now see as good medical practice. In Mark, when he raises the daughter of Jairus from the dead, saying that she's just sleeping ("talitha kumi"), he then tells her parents to give her something to eat. In this he sounds for all the world like my father, a family doctor in England, who'd tell a worried mother reassuringly, "It's just a bug," and as he was going out the door, "Make sure she eats something and call me in the morning." And when Jesus mixes spittle with clay to anoint a blind man's eyes in the gospel of John, giving him instructions to wash it out afterward, he is carrying out a familiar folk-healing rite. The same powdery yellow kaolin clay is still used by older rural Palestinians to stop fermentation in recipes containing grapes—and to mix into fever-reducing pessaries and compresses.

But of course there was more to clay and spittle than physical healing. The symbolism was clear. It was dust and water, inanimate and animate, heaven and earth: opposites achieving magical effect when brought together. The pattern is there in ancient Egyptian legend, when Isis kneads the spittle of the great god Ra with clay to create a sacred serpent which then bites him; delerious from the venom, Ra reveals his sacred name, and so transfers his power to Isis.

Knowing the name was the key to achieving magical power. Knowledge is power, a piece of knowledge itself as ancient as one of the oldest creation legends, that of Adam and Eve. When Eve picked the apple from the Tree of Knowledge, she was reaching not for food, but for wisdom. Food for the mind, if you like. But since wisdom was power, her reaching for it was a threat to the greatest power of all. She was cursed and, along with Adam, banished from Eden, which was suddenly revealed as a rather unattractive place of deliberate ignorance.

No wonder the names of gods were so often taboo. To know the name and speak it out loud was to steal divine power. In Palestine, in Egypt, in Rome too, a divine name spoken aloud compelled the god to obey the speaker. Roman priests would call on the guardian deity of a city under siege to abandon the city and come over to them. Towns and whole provinces were re-named with each new conquerer or occupier, a practice that would continue through the centuries (Jerusalem alone has been known by at least eight different names over the past two millennia). To name something, whether a city or a god, was to control it.

The same worked for demons. We still talk of wrestling with personal demons, and an essential part of the process of modern psychotherapy is naming and facing them. Two thousand years ago, the process was quicker, and often as effective. Both physical and mental illness were embodied in physical demons, which were then cast out.

Each demon had its own realm of mastery over certain parts of the mind and body. The Dead Sea scrolls—the sacred texts of the Essene desert monastics—included not just apocalyptic and wisdom literature, but also lists of devils' names along with the specific parts of the body and illnesses over which they had dominion. Healers who knew these names would call out the right one, commanding the demon to leave the sick person and doubling the power of the command by proclaiming it in the name of an all-powerful god—as, for example, "in the name of the Father."

Amulets of the time, made for the elite who could afford them, followed established oral formulas for exorcising demons. One surviving Palestinian amulet reads: "Adjured are you, spirit, in the name of I-am-who-I-am and in the name of his holy angels, to move away and be expelled and keep far from Klara daughter of Kyrana. You no longer have power over her. Be bound and kept away from her."

Another amulet addresses the fever itself: "I abjure you, fever and sickness, in the name of Abrasax, who is appointed over you, that he may uproot you from the body of Simon, son of Kattia. I do this in the name of the engraved letters of The Name."

Whoever chanted such incantations—whoever knew the names— would have, at least for that moment, the power of good over evil. Healing, when done in the divine name, was seen as a sign of the grace of god. But there was an inevitable flip side to this: sickness could then be seen as the lack of divine grace. If good faith heals, then bad faith can make you ill.

"Master, who sinned, this man or his parents, that he was born blind?" the disciples ask Jesus in the gospel of John. They are not being deliberately cruel, but merely reflecting a problem explored two millennia later by Susan Sontag in *Illness as Metaphor*, a book that begins in almost biblical language: "It is hardly possible to take up residence in the kingdom of the ill unprejudiced by the lurid metaphors with which it has been landscaped."

Tracing the metaphors of sickness, Sontag went back to the *Iliad* and the *Odyssey*, where disease could be the result of supernatural punishment for a personal fault, a collective transgression, or a crime of one's ancestors. But it could also be the result of demonic possession or of natural causes. The attribution of cause depended to a large extent on the state of available treatment. "Theories that diseases are caused by mental states . . . are always an index of how much is not understood about the physical terrain of a disease," wrote Sontag acerbically. And talking specifically about modern attitudes toward cancer: "Any disease that is treated as a mystery and acutely enough feared will be felt to be morally, if not literally, contagious . . . Contact with someone afflicted with a disease regarded as a mysterious malevolency inevitably feels like a trespass; worse, like the violation of a taboo."

What is striking in the gospel accounts is that Jesus does not have this fear. His followers fear the hemorrhaging woman and the leper as unclean; he does not. When he tells his disciples that neither the blind man nor his parents have sinned, he reveals a down-to-earth awareness of natural cause and effect—an awareness that he must have learned from the experts who raised him. That is, the village wise women.

But though Jesus did not see individual illness as just punishment for some past sin, he did see the sorry state of the body politic that way. The power of casting out demons had a wider metaphorical meaning. As he and other healers and preachers used it, it also meant casting out corruption and foreign rule. It meant purifying the temple, and freeing Judea and Galilee from the influence of Hellenism, Rome, and Herod. Expelling the human demons, that is.

In this, Jesus was very much in the classical prophetic tradition. The metaphor of physical sickness and health was national as well as personal, and was used this way throughout the great prophetic writings. "The eyes of the blind shall be opened and the ears of the deaf unstopped," said Isaiah. "Then the lame man shall leap like a hart and the tongue of the dumb sing with joy."

Illness and cure were used repeatedly as metaphors in the apocalyptic writings of the Essenes, whose very name probably came from the Aramaic *asa*—to heal—meaning not only physical healing, but also, in a forerunner of the latter kabbalistic idea of *tikkun olam*, healing the ills of the world. God will "release the captives, make the blind see, raise up the downtrodden," says the first-century B.C. Messianic Apocalypse, as well as "heal the sick, resurrect the dead, and announce glad tidings to the poor."

Healing was thus heavily politicized. There was no escaping that fact. The fusion of medicine, religion, and national aspiration was built into the culture.

In such a world, the hardest won knowledge was Maryam's: that both health and sickness were natural and that there was no divine reward or punishment involved. No magic tricks, either, such as she'd seen in the marketplace of Magdala, where self-proclaimed miracle workers chanted nonsense while slitting a chicken's throat, then twirled the bird over a sick woman's body, spattering her with blood. Maryam pitied those who lined up to spend what little they had on ornate amulets with prayers and seeds inside them, or on potions made out of powdered lizard tails or frogs' eyes or bats' wings. And she'd turn away, sick to her stomach, from apothecaries who put hair cut from the head of a crucified man inside a bag to be sold as a necklace against fever, or nails from the cross as a charm against attack.

"Charlatans," her grandmother would say, spitting on the ground in disgust. "Crooks. Profiteering scum. Listen to me, child: there is no need to kill in order to heal. No need for sacrifice, not even of a lizard or a chicken, let alone a good man crucified for his courage in speaking out and resisting injustice. No magic here," she'd say, tapping her head with her forefinger. "Just knowledge. The will of God? Knowledge *is* the will of God."

That is why Eve ate the apple of the Tree of Knowledge, of course. Not in rebellion against God, but as part of the divine plan to bring human beings to life—to real, conscious, knowing life instead of the temporary artifice of Eden. Thus her name, Hava in Hebrew, meaning "life."

To play the role of Eve, however, could be as difficult in Maryam's time as it had been for Eve herself. Though the wise women made no claims to divine inspiration, their ability threatened those who claimed a sacred monopoly on healing. The apocryphal first-century Book of Enoch attacked them head on, saying that fallen angels—devils—had taught "the daughters of men" poisons, medicines, spells, invocations, and sorcery.

Such attacks exemplified the nervousness of the temple priesthood. Bad enough that healing power was being practiced by anyone other than they, with their scrolls of spells and medicinal recipes closely guarded in the temple archives. Worse still that it was being done by illiterate peasant women. But most seriously, village healers constituted a political challenge to the authority of the temple priesthood.

The very phrase "healing power" contains the issue: to be able to heal was to exercise power. It meant that the dictates of fate, whether divinely or humanly determined, did not have to be passively accepted.

The phrases you can still hear in peasant villages throughout the Middle East—"That's the way it is," "What can you do?" "It's the will of God"—were put in question by the skill of wise women. There were indeed things that could be done. The will of God could be guided in a different direction by human intervention. Humans, that is, could affect fate. They could assert independence.

To a temple establishment clinging to power and privilege, that was a dangerous message. Two thousand years ago as now, religion was threatened by science. The difference is that then, the scientists were those who practiced alternative medicine: the folk healers. It was establishment medicine, under the temple authorities, that sought to keep healing firmly within the bounds of religion.

Galilee wise women like Salome and Maryam were fortunate in living so far from Jerusalem; they could continue their work without harassment. Others farther south, in Judea, had less freedom to practice. With healing claimed as a divine function by the powers-that-be, their work risked being seen as magic—and if it failed, as it inevitably sometimes did, as black magic, or the work of demons. The most infamous instance of this happening would be sixteen centuries later in colonial America, when many of the women persecuted in the Salem witch trials were midwives and healers. Caught in the seemingly never-ending politicization of healing, their skill was attributed to fallen angels instead of good ones.

There is a terrible irony in this. If Maryam was indeed a midwife and a healer—and her son's powers and style of healing strongly indicate that she was, and that it was she who taught him his skills, breaking the line of female transmission in order to empower her son—then she was fortunate to have lived in first-century Galilee and not later and elsewhere. In seventeenth-century Massachusetts, she would have risked being burned at the stake, in full religious fervor and in the name of her own son, as a witch. Still more disturbing, she might well be the target of similar zealots in American society today: those who kill and yet call themselves pro-life.

Maryam certainly knew as much about how to prevent childbirth as how to assist it. Contraception was widely used throughout the Mediterranean of her time. The most popular methods were coitus interruptus (advocated by Hippocrates, and later approved by Palestinian rabbis as "threshing within and winnowing without"), anal sex ("he plowed in the garden and poured out on manure piles," in a later Talmudic reference), extended breast-feeding, estrogenic herbs taken orally, and spermicidal resins used vaginally in pessaries and sponges. And, if all else failed, abortion.

Aristotle and Plato both advocated early termination of pregnancy. "The proper thing to do," wrote the former in his *Politics*, "is to limit the size of each family, and if children are then conceived in excess of the limit so fixed, have miscarriage induced before sense and life have begun in the embryo." This idea was so enthusiastically adopted by the well-to-do that by the first century, the Roman aristocracy was suffering a major problem of infertility, which is why so many emperors adopted male heirs; they didn't have any surviving ones of their own.

Plautus, Cicero, and Ovid all refer to douching after sex. Saint Jerome in his twenty-second epistle would later speak of young girls who "savor their sterility in advance and kill the human being even before its seed has been sown." Polybius wrote in the second century B.C. that Greek families limited themselves to one or two children— clearly using contraception backed up by abortion.

The famed second-century gynecologist Soranus of Ephesus listed numerous contraceptive and abortive methods using plants we now know to have active properties. His favorite was giant fennel root— *Ferula silphium*—which turned out to be unfortunate for that particular plant. Discovered by the Greeks on the north African coast in the seventh century B.C., it became so sought after as a contraceptive and an abortion drug (the effect depending on the dosage, much as most modern "morning-after" drugs are simply intensive doses of contraceptive estrogen) that it became extinct by the fourth century A.D. Different species of fennel are still used to induce abortion by village folk practitioners throughout Asia.

Other contraceptive herbs included artemisia—wormwood— named after the virgin goddess Artemis for its ability to keep women without the most visible sign of non-virginity: pregnancy. Similarly, the berries of the chasteberry bush did not keep you chaste; they kept the appearance of chastity thanks to their contraceptive action. The seeds of wild rue—the same rue Ophelia hands out in Shakespeare's *Hamlet*, and certainly with the same associations—were crushed and brewed to promote labor, and in a stronger dose, to induce abortion. Rue is still used this way by Beduin, Mexican, and Indian village women.

In addition to herbs, animal secretions were sometimes used, like foam from a pregnant camel's mouth. Absurd? Disgusting? Not when you consider that an extract of pregnant mare's urine is today one of the best-selling pharmaceuticals in the western world, marketed as estrogen under the trade name Premarin and used as a contraceptive, a "morning-after" drug, and hormone replacement therapy.

If such widespread use of contraception and abortion two thousand years ago seems surprising, it is worth remembering that the current religious bias against contraception and abortion is relatively recent. In the eleventh century, the famous Islamic physician Ibn Sina, known in the west as Avicenna, prescribed abortion drugs in early pregnancy, and Arab physicians recommended contraceptive barriers of wool soaked in olive oil, linseed, cedar gum, or opobalsam, as well as irritant pessaries using such items as ground pine bark as abortifacients. The third- and fourth-century Talmudic rabbis who wrote of "winnowing within and threshing without" approved early abortion using "root potions" since they considered a fetus viable only after forty days from conception. Besides, in their odd misogyny, they considered the commandment to "be fruitful and multiply" to apply to men but not necessarily to women. Or maybe they simply had the wisdom to accommodate to accepted practice.

In our twenty-first-century hubris, we tend to imagine that the world was ignorant before the advent of modern science, and that knowledge advances in a linear progression. There is plenty of evidence to the contrary. The very fact that "creationism" is being advanced as a science equal to evolution in some American schools should make us realize that knowledge progresses and regresses according to the social mores of the time and place. Thus American arbiters of morality and "good taste" would doubtless be shocked at a particularly beautiful thirteenth-century-B.C. statuette in the Israel Museum in Jerusalem; it is of a woman—a Canaanite fertility goddess—with the front of her torso cut away to reveal twin infants in her womb, each one reaching up toward a breast while she reaches down and with long, elegant fingers, opens her vagina for childbirth.

How life began was no secret. There are no storks carrying infants in their bills in ancient legend. The gods were sexual creatures in the image of their creators—those who believed in them. If the precise physiology of sperm and ova was not yet known, people certainly had a good concept of seed, how it was planted, and how it grew. Any farmer would. Sperm was seed, as in Onan spilling his in the Hebrew bible. The womb was the incubating soil. In a peasant culture, it's easy to see how women's fertility would be equated with that of the earth, with the seed being nourished, growing, bearing fruit. Like healing, fertility itself carried intimations of the miraculous and the divine, intimations you can still see reflected in the face of any woman bearing her first child.

Under such circumstances, abortive drugs were not given lightly. If the mother's life was threatened, her life was chosen over that of her fetus, with the midwife acting in the true sense of her profession, as the one who is, in the word's German origin, *mit* or "with" the wife. If a young girl was pregnant as a result of rape—and at a time when there was no distinction between combatants and non-combatants in warfare, rape was dismayingly frequent—no village healer would be cruel enough to insist that she carry the child to term. And if a family was so impoverished that they simply could not afford to feed another mouth, induced miscarriage was an accepted way out. The same reasons, in short, that women still seek abortions worldwide.

As a healer, Maryam would certainly have been as expert in contraception and abortion as she was in midwifery. And we would do her far greater honor by recognizing this—recognizing her as a woman of real knowledge and power—than by ignoring or denying it, for it is precisely this knowledge that places her in sympathy with women throughout the world. Her herbal expertise not only saved women's lives; it made her a strong advocate for the poor and the downtrodden, for those who looked to her for some measure of control over their own lives, as, in a sense, they still do. She was the one who held the power of choice. And she held it as much for herself as for others.

Feminist Catholic scholars have made much of the idea that she willingly assented to her conception and pregnancy. As one Jesuit scholar in Jerusalem put it, "God needed Mary's 'yes.' Her willingness to bear the child is the prophetic act par excellence." But though this is certainly true for Mary the legend, it vastly underestimates the real Maryam. Her "yes" was far more active than mere assent. She had a real choice. She could choose whether to become pregnant. And if for any reason the choice of pregnancy was not hers, she could still choose not to carry the pregnancy to term. She knew how.

Maryam, in short, embodies the resolution of the so-called abortion controversy. Knowledgeable in both contraception and abortion, she chose pregnancy and birth. She was, in modern terms, both pro-life and pro-choice.

V

Once a month, on the eve of the new moon, Maryam makes offerings. She cherishes this time of day. The light glows gold on the hills, varnishing them into warm, deep color, and then the sky slowly deepens into itself: first an intense blue, then a gentle, dark purple that gathers almost imperceptibly into black. "The hour of the goddess," Maryam calls it.

She uses her own, simple altar: three flat stones placed one on top of the other beneath her favorite oak. Her offerings too are simple. Sometimes she brings libations: a goat's first milk, still warm from the udder, perhaps, or virgin olive oil from the first pressing of the year. She holds the bowl out from her body and tips it slowly so that the liquid pours down in a fine line, spreading over the top stone and then slowly dripping down the sides. Other times she'll bring fruit: three ears of the tender first wheat, bound with straw into a small bouquet, or a sprig of the first vine blossom. She lays them on the top stone, knowing that during the night either the breeze or some small creature, the spirit of the goddess, will whisk them away. And once a year, on the shortest and darkest day of winter, she brings small triangular cakes filled almost to bursting with pomegranate or poppy seeds: the special cakes of the Virgin, ripe with the seeds of fertility.

These are offerings, not sacrifices. You sacrifice out of fear, with the flesh and blood of the animal standing in for your own flesh and blood. You tender offerings out of love. Those who placate the divine with sacrifice do so to avert disaster; those who please the divine with offerings, seek fruitfulness. "Nourish the divine, and the divine will nourish you," as Salome says.

Women throughout the villages of Palestine make their offerings this way, bringing the fruits of their own labor. There are no priests to intervene between them and the divine. This is private, and personal, and it exists in a different realm from that of Yahweh and his temple far away in Jerusalem. "Thou shalt have no other gods before me," says the commandment, not "Thou shalt have no other gods at all."

Maryam still remembers the first time she heard the story of the Great Virgin. She listened wide-eyed, thumb in her mouth, a three-year-old scarcely daring to breathe as Salome chanted the song of Isis, who made the power of women equal to the power of men. It was a song of life and death and life again. A song of the mystery of life.

Long before anything else existed in the land of Egypt, far to the south, Nuth, the great goddess of the sky, and Geb, the father of the earth, brought forth twins, a girl and a boy. They named them Isis and Osiris. The two were so closely intertwined that they became lovers even before they were born, in their mother's womb, and so they remained in life too. In time, they had a younger brother, Seth, but he was consumed with jealousy at their closeness. So he killed Osiris, cut up his body, and scattered his parts over all the earth. The penis fell with the seed of Osiris into the great river they call the Nile, and this is why that river creates fertility wherever it floods over the earth.

Isis went into deep mourning for her lover and brother, keening and wailing as she searched high and low for the parts of his body. She gathered him up, organ by organ, limb by limb, until she had found all of him except that one vital part the great river had claimed as its own. Then she brought him home and put his body back together again. And when she had finished, she made love with him. In so doing, she brought Osiris back to life, for this is how their son, the god Horus, was conceived.

Maryam has heard this story countless times since she was three years old, but she would willingly have Salome repeat it countless times more. She is in thrall to the power of the story, to the grieving sister, the resurrected brother, the two twinned, mated aspects, female and male, of the one divine mystery. It has never occurred to her to ask exactly how Isis made love to the dead Osiris; this is a divine story, and gods can do what humans can not. That is the point of having gods. A missing penis is no obstacle to physical love. And neither is the most essential aspect of Isis' mystery: her virginity. For only the virgin can resurrect the dead, creating and re-creating life. Only the virgin can distill the essence of fertility.

This is why of all the gods, Isis is the one to whom women turn, no matter whether they are Galilean or Judean, Greek or Roman, Syrian or Egyptian. She understands women as only a wise woman can. Two of her greatest titles are the Lady Who Saves and the Great Sorcerer, for she is the mistress of the art of medicine—the one invoked by village healers and by women in childbirth. She has the grief of a wife in mourning, the midwife's concern for life, the healer's compassion, a lover's devotion, the tenderness of a nursing mother. She is everything a woman is, which is why women in all manner of trouble call on her, offering a lock of a child's hair, or an oil lamp lit in her name, or just a simple prayer. They draw comfort and strength from her presence.

Salome has told many stories about Isis over the years, and as is the way with stories of the gods, not all the versions agree with each other. No matter. Each story has its own mystery, and there are further, multiple mysteries contained within the contradictions. In some, Osiris plays a triple role: not only lover and brother to Isis, but also her son—a pattern which will be echoed two centuries later in the gnostic gospel of Philip, which will call Maryam "sister, mother, consort" of Jesus. In others, Horus takes the place of Osiris, and even while she is still pregnant, Isis says of him, "He shall rule over this earth. He will be our master, this god who is but an embryo."

Maryam, just thirteen, places her hands around the bulge of her belly and repeats the words softly, wonderingly. To know the fate of your child, to know that you are carrying greatness . . . She closes her eyes, and dares to imagine herself saying the words of Isis. And for the first time, feels the baby kick.

She offers up a quiet prayer of thanks. *"Myrionymos,"* she murmurs, the Greek name for Isis that always makes her smile, echoing as it does the sound of her name. *Myrionymos*—She of Many Names.

She has no idea that hundreds of years after her own death, she too will become *myrionymos*, with many of the same names as those used for Isis: Queen of Heaven, for instance, or She Who Is Crowned with the Stars, or Star of the Sea. Or that Isis Lactans—the popular image of Isis suckling the infant Horus in paintings and statues—will merge with the classic representation of herself and her as yet unborn son. Or that a version of herself called the Virgin Mary will eventually take the place of the Virgin Isis—literally take her place, with Isis temples being rededicated to Mary.

If you had told Maryam any of this, she would have been shocked, offended, even terrified. One did not take the powers of gods so lightly as to aspire to usurp them.

In the convent school I attended as a child, we were taught to think of pagans as godless creatures living in benighted ignorance of all things holy. Never mind that all the great thinkers of antiquity were pagan, and that they lacked neither soul nor faith nor a sense of the sacred. To the contrary, they possessed all those things to a far larger degree than most of us do today. A sense of the sacred permeated every aspect of everyday life; it was integrated into the everyday, and awe and wonder were part of being.

Not that those great thinkers thought of themselves as pagan. Then as now, the word was used derogatively. It came from the same root as the word for "peasant" (*pagus* in Latin, meaning a country district), so that to the Roman aristocracy, a peasant was by definition a pagan, and vice versa. High-born Athenians or Spartans or Romans would never for the life of them think of themselves as pagans; they were believers, men and women of good faith. And they believed in many gods.

I would be many years out of the convent school when I realized that paganism really means polytheism, and that most polytheists acknowledged one god above all. Whether this god was called El or Uranus, Zeus or Jupiter, Lah or Yahweh, he was so great and so remote that direct address was impossible. Instead, people turned to a vast array of more accessible gods who would be willing to intercede on their behalf.

Even in the west, people still do. If we could let go of our preconceptions—our lubricious association of paganism with nymphs dancing around naked in the sunrise, for instance—we would have to acknowledge that for all our pride in monotheism, we are still far more polytheistic than we might think.

A degree of polytheism is built into Catholicism in the idea of the Holy Trinity, for example, and in the vast panoply of saints to whom believers pray. Saints—indeed, Maryam herself—have become intercessors, called on for a purpose, in the same way people called on Isis for healing two thousand years ago. Whether we call them lesser gods or prophets, saints or holy men and women, they are sacred figures with whom one can have a relationship. They listen to humans and can do some special pleading, and they can be wooed for this purpose with flowers and candles and gifts: offerings. They are the manifestations of the persistent need to humanize the divine—to give it a name that can be spoken, a face that can be seen.

In a similar manner, observant Jews revere the burial sites of biblical ancestors—Abraham's tomb in Hebron, Rachel's tomb in Bethlehem—and of famous rabbis, to whose tombs Sephardi Jews in particular make pilgrimage on their feast days, setting up barbecues and picnic tables for festive celebrations in the graveyards. And despite all strictures against idolatry, ultra-Orthodox Jews revere the stones of the Western Wall. Never mind that it was never, strictly speaking, part of the temple, but merely a section of the retaining wall built by Herod; modern Jews pray before it, kiss its giant ashlar stones, push written prayers and pleas into the crevices between the limestone blocks.

Throughout the Mediterranean, remnants of ancient pantheistic cults survive in pagan beliefs absorbed into monotheistic ones. The fruit of a fig tree in a West Bank monastery, for instance, cures infertility, despite the fact that women are barred from crossing the threshold. A healing spring in southern Galilee is revered by local Moslems who have named it after an early-twentieth-century Jewish settler. The leaves of an acacia tree growing beside a Moroccan rabbi's grave heal crippled limbs.

None of this is so strange when you consider that in the west, pagan traditions are built into the most agnostic everyday lives. Take the names of days, for instance. In English and German, most of them come from those of Norse gods; in French and Spanish, from Roman gods. We honor pagan deities each time we arrange a meeting or make a date.

Perhaps one of the best descriptions of paganism comes from biblical scholar Paula Fredriksen, who calls it "the rich native religious stew of traditional society in the Mediterranean." And a stew it was, a feast of sacred variety. "In the pre-Christian epoch," as religious historian Walter Burkert wrote, "the various forms of worship . . . are never exclusive; they appear as varying forms, trends, or options within the one disparate yet continuous conglomerate of ancient religion."

The gods of old, in short, were remarkably tolerant. Much more so than the cruel exclusive gods invoked by modern fundamentalists, whose thirst for blood—whether in Moslem suicide bombings, in Christian executions of abortion providers, or in Jewish attacks on Palestinian villagers trying to pick olives—seems primitive by comparison.

Yahweh was far more accepting of other gods than were his high priests and his prophets. Maryam was right: "no gods before me," not no other gods at all. Primacy, not exclusivity. In fact one can read the whole of the Hebrew bible as the history not of monotheism but of its failure, with the prophets railing again and again at their people for following other gods.

Canaanite, Egyptian, Babylonian, and smaller, more local traditions persisted in Maryam's time. They still do. A wealth of Middle Eastern superstitions and small rituals have their roots in far older religions: spitting against the evil eye, for instance, or the open hand held up to ward off evil—the familiar *hamsa* amulet. And religions still crossbreed and interconnect in ways we are hardly aware of.

Jews who avoid walking under a ladder or who cross their fingers for luck are acting out Christian rituals, since both the ladder and the fingers refer to the cross of the crucifixion. Christians who consult the daily horoscope in the newspaper are acting out Babylonian beliefs, where the stars and the planets are the gods of fate. Moslems who face east to pray in the direction of Mecca are facing the rising sun, the focal point of ancient Egyptian sun worship.

Islam is clear in its recognition of the Hebrew prophets who went before Mohammed, as well as Jesus and Mary. Christianity not only acknowledges its basis in the Hebrew bible; the gospels go to great length to establish Jesus as the manifestation of Hebrew biblical prophecy. The Judaic practices in Herod's temple were heavily influenced by temple religions throughout the eastern Mediterranean and central Asia.

This crossbreeding seems to me cause for celebration. The religions that we think of as dividing us, in fact bind us together. No religion rises new, out of nothing, entirely unaffected by the existing religions of the culture in which it arose. In the words of Harvard theologian Harvey Cox, "Every religion is like Peer Gynt's famous onion. If you tried to peel away all they have absorbed from other faiths, which are in turn already conglomerates, you would find only more and more layers underneath . . . The genius of a faith is found more in its characteristic ways of combining things than in some induplicable inner essence."

An Israelite daughter of Yahweh making offerings to Isis was not being unfaithful to the one great god. She was speaking with one form of the divine, with the goddess of the most important thing of all in a peasant society: fertility. And what is the essence of Maryam's story as it has come down to us if not miraculous fertility?

"But was Mary really a virgin?" It's a deceptively simple question, asked sincerely by the faithful, and teasingly, even mockingly, by the cynical. The former want to know if it's possible; the latter take it for granted that it's not.

In modern terms, virginity has been reduced to an either/or matter: Either she was or she wasn't. Given that we define virginity by the hymen, this seems reasonable enough. The hymen is either intact or not—a basic physical fact, but one that even in the twenty-first century, comes laden with immense cultural weight.

The very language we use when we talk about virginity is loaded. Though it seems oddly dated, we still talk of "losing one's virginity," a phrase that implies not just loss, but hapless passivity. A man "takes" a girl's virginity, the implication being that she is the deceived or seduced victim. As in Victorian pornography where innocents are "taken" sexually by ruthless roués, there is a certain lasciviousness in such talk, a sense of swooning female helplessness and rapacious male power that does credit to neither gender.

We still think of being virgin as being innocent. Innocent, that is, of sex. But this surely begs the question of why we should be innocent of sex. To be innocent is to be free from moral wrong, to be guiltless, to have done no evil. Do we then think of sex as morally wrong, guilty, and evil? Whatever modern reason says, our language betrays us. This may be the twenty-first century, but some part of us still subscribes to the antiquated dualisms of virgin and whore, good girl and bad girl, innocent and slut—terms that exist in abundance for girls and women, but hardly at all for boys and men, among whom sexual experience is at least tolerated and usually appreciated.

The idea of virginity as a precious commodity that can be lost—not through carelessness, but more in the sense of a "lost soul," doomed and damned—is often rationalized by the idea of wholeness. From this point of view, an intact hymen is the visible evidence of a state of perfection. Once it is gone, the female body is no longer whole, but becomes used or damaged goods.

Leaving aside the very idea of the female body as goods, used or not, the contradictions built into this viewpoint should give pause to those who hold it dearest: the fundamentalist guardians of purity. If you support the politicization of private life currently known as "family values," motherhood should surely be seen as a state of wholeness and completion. So too, in that case, should the sexual activity that leads to motherhood.

The problem is that sexual activity itself has been politicized, which is why a small biological detail—a mere membrane—assumes such giant proportions. This is also why the hymen has become a far more fetishistic object than a similarly slight male membrane, the foreskin. The absence of a foreskin does not indicate sexual experience; the absence of a hymen usually does.

"The hymen and the foreskin are biologically insignificant tissues that represent momentous psychological issues," say psychoanalysts Deanna Holtzman and Nancy Kulish. At least we assume they are biologically insignificant. The truth is, nobody knows. Holtzman and Kulish did a thorough search of gynecological publications for information on the biological significance of the hymen, and found . . . nothing. They concluded that "there is no known anatomical or physiological function for the hymen."

Something that is not understood becomes both intriguing and alluring, a fertile field for myth and superstition; when it has to do with female sexuality, the myths and superstitions are infinitely multiplied. In the lack of a known physical function, especially in a culture such as ours where it is assumed that everything does indeed have a function, the hymen maintains an aura of mystery. Thus the assumption of "momentous psychological issues." In Maryam's time, however, attitudes toward the hymen were far more down-to-earth.

The word itself is ancient Greek for a membrane, and saw double service as the name of a bridal song or hymn. It was personified by Hymen, the god of marriage, a lissome youth shown carrying a flaming torch and a veil, who died on his wedding night. The symbolism of flames/sex and veil/hymen is clear enough. It would be almost laughable to a modern audience were it not that brides still raise their veils to be kissed at the conclusion of the marriage ceremony, that we still talk of women "taking the veil" when they become nuns, and that made-for-television movies still cut away to flames rising in an open hearth when the action begins to get steamy. But what is most fascinating is the gender of the god involved. It is as though the hymen were the one part of a woman's body that made her somehow not-female, and that is why Hymen had to die. Only then was the woman fully female. Only then could she become pregnant. Only then, fertile.

This would surely indicate that virginity was a liability rather than an asset two millennia ago, especially with such high maternal and infant mortality rates. The earlier a girl began sexual activity, the greater her potential fertility. And the more children she gave birth to, the higher the probability that at least two might survive to adulthood.

An intact hymen did have one singular value, however: it guaranteed that the first-born was indeed the child of the father. In a peasant culture such as Maryam's, where family continuity on the land was the prime value, the hymen was the only absolute assurance of paternity (and would remain so until two millennia later, with the advent of DNA testing). Thus the dire punishment in Deuteronomy, ignored in Maryam's time along with most of the other Deuteronomical strictures, of putting a false virgin to death by stoning. The offense was a legal one. If the woman's first child was male, the hymen determined inheritance rights. By misrepresenting herself, a sexually experienced woman put the system of inheritance in doubt. Physical virginity was not a moral issue, but an economic one.

This is the essence of the legendary emphasis on Mary's virginal conception of Jesus. It was essential to her son's future identity: a guarantee of divine paternity.

But though this may help explain why Mary had to be a virgin—had to become one, as it were—it does not help with the question of whether the real Maryam could possibly have been one. What does seem clear is that our modern emphasis on physiology may be misleading; we may be asking the wrong question. But those who claim to have found the answer elsewhere, in linguistics, appear to be asking merely another version of the wrong question.

The most mundane way of dealing with the virginity question is to focus not on the hymen, but on a detail much noted by biblical scholars: that the author of Matthew's gospel made an error in translation. He used numerous references to the Hebrew bible in order to prove that Jesus was indeed the messiah foretold by the great prophets. But since he wrote in Greek, not in biblical Hebrew, he ran into trouble when he quoted the famed verse from Isaiah rendered in the King James bible as "Behold, a virgin shall conceive and bear a son, and shall call his name Immanuel."

The original Hebrew uses the word *alma*, which referred to any unmarried woman, albeit usually a girl at the age of puberty. Matthew uses the Greek word *parthenos*, which generally meant physical virginity. The difference in meaning was not exactly Matthew's fault. The Hebrew bible had been translated into Greek three hundred years earlier, in Alexandria. That edition, known as the Septuagint after the seventy scholars who reputedly spent their respective lifetimes working on it, was the one the Matthew author would have used, since it's highly unlikely that he knew Hebrew. And the error, insofar as there was one, was one that all translators still know and tussle with: cultural differences give subtly different meanings to specific words, so that there are often no direct equivalents in another language.

This seems a convincing argument at first, though it's hard to think of a more disappointing one. If the whole question of Maryam's virginity can be boiled down to something as elementary as a mistranslation, we are left feeling oddly foolish, if not downright bereft.

Reason has been satisfied, true, but something in us suspects that reason alone can be utterly unreasonable. And in this case, that something is right.

It may be convenient to argue that *parthenos* meant a physical virgin, but that was not always the case. The word was also used for a girl who had been raped or was an unmarried mother. In that sense, it was used much as we use the word "parthenogenesis" today when talking about basic plant forms: reproduction without fertilization. Faced with an evident pregnancy and no known father, the language allowed for there having been no father at all, despite the physical evidence. In short, *parthenos* was an ancient euphemism.

The Romans would later adopt the same attitude, as they adopted so much else in Greek culture. The Latin word *virgo* was used for any woman who was not married, no matter her age and no matter if she was pregnant. A widow could be as virgin as a young girl.

The word "virgin" has been used this way both throughout history and throughout the world. In Babylon, infants born to single mothers were called "virgin births." In ancient Greece, a woman remained a maiden—*kore* or *parthenos*—until marriage, when she became a *gyne*, a woman. Pregnancy and childbirth made no difference. And in the twentieth century, anthropologist Edmund Leach found that in the Trobriand Islands just off what is now East Timor, a widow became a "marriageable maiden" when she finished her mourning period. As two thousand years ago, virginity was a social role, not a physical fact.

The linguistic argument doesn't hold up. Worse, the very fact of its being made leaves something of a bad taste in the mouth. To reduce the whole issue of virginity to a mere translating error—let alone one that may or may not have occurred—is to lose all sense of the grandeur of paradox. And the virgin mother is the supreme paradox. Its fascination lies in the fact, known as widely two thousand years ago as it is now, that a pregnant woman is not a physical virgin. We are talking a human impossibility, and that is precisely the power of the notion. It occurs at the interface between the human and the divine, the place where the mind reels, drunk with impossible possibility.

Claude Lévi-Strauss maintained that the human imagination is trapped in a web of dualisms: the raw and the cooked, to quote his best-known example, or virgin and whore, good and evil, love and hate, sacred and profane. Every myth, Lévi-Strauss argued, is driven by the obsessive need to solve a paradox—a contradiction in terms that cannot, by definition, be solved. If a solution were possible, it would no longer be a paradox, and so would lose its power to haunt and hold the imagination.

But for Maryam, as for everyone in her time, there was no such obsessive need. They had no expectation that everything could be explained. And they maintained a far greater sense of humility in the face of the unknown. Instead of being a challenge to reason and science, the paradoxical was cherished as the source of awe and mystery.

Today, if we talk at all about mysteries, it's usually about mystery novels—an elementary but safe form of mystery, where we know before we even open the book that it will have a resolution. Yet even on this everyday level, there is an inkling of a sense of religious mystery. Beyond the simple page-turner aspect, beyond escape from the humdrum facts and pressures of everyday life, each mystery offers the excitement of coming face to face with the incomprehensible, even the impossible, like the murdered man found inside a room locked from the inside. In fact it is almost a disappointment when the resolution comes. The detailed explanation of whodunnit and how it was done is supposed to be the climax of the story, but it generally feels distinctly anticlimactic. The reader's delight is in the exploration, not in the explanation.

But where mystery novels are essentially spoiled by the convention that they must have a resolution, religious mystery thrives on its defiance of such resolution. That is precisely why it lasts, and why it continues to exert its hold on us. It offers a glimpse, or perhaps just a glimmer, of something far beyond our ken. Something that is by definition not just unknown, but unknowable, and that we therefore call sacred.

As with a Zen koan, one cannot understand a paradox, but one can apprehend it. Throughout the centuries, mystics of all faiths, including Christian gnostics, Islamic Sufis, and Jewish kabbalists, have delved into the paradoxical to reach beyond literal meaning to its underlying mystery, in the hope of at least a brief moment of epiphany. Using techniques such as allegorical interpretation, deep meditation, and even ecstatic dance, they aim at breaking down the dualistic intellect—or rather, leaping beyond it—to approach the ineffable. The paradoxical becomes not just a conundrum, but an essential tool to revelation.

In fact you could argue that a real religious sense cannot exist without paradox. Divinity must be paradoxical, or it loses its power to hold the imagination. Pascal maintained that the only lasting religion is one that goes "against nature, and against proofs." For what is the grandeur of the divine if it does not supersede the known and the human?

Dogma and forms of worship are merely the exterior characteristics of particular religions. They do not even begin to touch the interior, which is the religious sense or spirit: the sense of the sacred, the apprehension of the divine. And since the divine is by definition beyond the physical—metaphysical—the only way we can come close to it is indirectly, through paradox, metaphor, and allegory. That is, through poetry.

All the great religious writings came into being not as "texts," but as oral poetry. And the power and endurance of the prophetic and wisdom writings in the Bible lie in the spirit of poetry. For poetry thrives on the enigmatic. It creates room for the imagination to soar, for the senses to expand, for the mind to marvel. The essence of the religious spirit is poetic; the rest—the legalistic side of what we now call organized religion—is prosaic.

This is why modern fundamentalism is so tragic a distortion of religion. By restricting itself to the most literal interpretations of poetic texts, it becomes blind to the religious spirit. It becomes, in fact, anti-religious. The sacred is reduced to a set of legal strictures; awe and mystery to obedience and punishment. Lacking all sense of the poetic, fundamentalism hates paradox, and denies mystery. Enigma is anathema. It is religion made harsh, and at the same time—why not be paradoxical about it?—made bland.

Perhaps this loss of metaphor was inevitable. The further a religion travels from its roots in place and time, the more it depends solely on the written word. The word becomes sacrosanct in exile, like love letters pored over for every minutia of meaning when a couple are separated by distance. The greater the distance and the longer the separation, the more meaning is read into every word. And each word then becomes over-burdened. It goes stiff under the burden of so much emotional weight, fossilizes under the pressure of need and desire, loses all its seductive ambiguity, all flexibility, all sense of the enigmatic. It gets pinned down to one mundane, literal meaning.

In his *Poetics*, written nearly four centuries before Maryam was born, Aristotle wrote that "the poet should prefer probable impossibilities to improbable possibilities." So too should anyone seeking a glimpse of the divine. It is precisely the knowledge that a virgin birth is not possible that makes the idea so powerful. Indeed, as the question "But was she really a virgin?" makes clear, most Catholics of faith do not literally believe that Mary was a virgin; rather, they nurture the *idea* of it. Otherwise they would not have to even ask the question. They know one thing rationally, and believe another with the deeper kind of knowledge we call faith: the power of trust over proof, of imagination over physical reality. Or, as Aristotle called it, the willing suspension of disbelief.

To seek proof that virginal conception is either possible or impossible, then, is to miss the point. It could be said that those who argue that Maryam was definitely not a virgin have no imagination, while those who maintain that she definitely was, have no sense of reason. And since to be human is to be possessed of both imagination and reason, the one without the other leaves us impoverished, deprived of an essential part of our own humanity.

Surely we need to recognize that the virgin mother represents a metaphysical truth, one that thrives in the realm of poetry, not of physics. It seems a sad comment on our own times that this was appreciated far more two thousand years ago than it is today.

Maryam was born into "a world full of gods," to quote the title of British historian Keith Hopkins' history of belief in the first century—a world full also of goddesses, who had been revered for hundreds and in some cases thousands of years. These were virgin goddesses. And virgin goddesses were fertility goddesses.

Few were remotely virginal in the modern sense of the word. They had, to put it mildly, active sex lives. But their virginity was never defined in terms of the existence of a hymen. Instead, they were manifestations of what Italian classicist Giulia Sissa calls "the enigmatic virgin." They existed in a state of "maidenhood without maidenhead."

Take sex out of the picture, in other words—however shocking that may be to the modern mind—and virginity becomes something infinitely grander and more mysterious than the presence of a membrane.

Isis was the greatest of the great virgins. By Maryam's time, she had been worshipped for some three thousand years, and her renown had spread far beyond Egypt, becoming so powerful in Rome that the emperor Nero would eventually order all her temples destroyed as a threat to the existing order. Not that she needed temples. Throughout the Middle East and the eastern Mediterranean, women in villages like Nazareth worshipped her in small, everyday ways as the wisest of the wise women, the one who understood their most intimate lives.

But the goddess whose legend gave birth to all the others was not

Isis; it was her mother, Nuth, who ruled the sky. In Egypt, Nuth was always shown in an extraordinarily sensuous pose: arched over the earth, long-limbed and long-bellied, with a series of bright yellow disks running the length of her torso. These disks represented the round orb of the sun entering her mouth, traveling through her body, and emerging between her thighs, for as the goddess of all birth and rebirth, she swallowed the sun each evening at sundown, and each dawn, gave birth to it again.

She was the ultimate mother not only of the sun, but of all creation. And as one of her priests recorded, she doubled—perhaps even tripled—the ante of virgin motherhood by giving birth even to herself: "It was Nuth, the mighty mother, who was the first to give birth to anything, and she did so when nothing else had been born, and when she herself had never been born."

Nuth would metamorphose into innumerable other goddesses, taking on different names as her legend traveled through central Asia and the Mediterranean. In one manifestation or another, the virgin goddess held sway throughout the virtual Babel of ancient cultures and beliefs, all borrowing from each other, influencing each other, fusing and separating in constant flux. In Sumer, she was known as the Virgin Inanna, goddess of sex and procreation, whose many lovers included legendary kings. In Babylon, the Virgin Ishtar was not just the firstborn of the gods, but the mother of all gods and all men, proudly insistent on her independence from any male. "It is I alone who gave birth to the people," she proclaimed. She alone, too, who would bring her dead lover, Tammuz, back to life. And in the land of Canaan, Asherah, also called "The Maid" and "She Who Gives Birth to the Gods," was yet another manifestation, as was her daughter Anath, who further defied all human conventions by being the goddess of the exclusively male realms of war and the hunt, as well as the exclusively female one of childbirth.

Anath's legend follows that of Isis as it relates how her lover and brother, the storm god Baal, died and descended to the world of Mot, the god of death and sterility. In deep mourning, she descended to the underworld herself in search of him, as the Greek goddess Demeter would later do in search of her daughter, Persephone. When Anath found Baal's body, she brought it back up to the surface of the earth, ground it up, sowed his seed far and wide, and thus resurrected him.

Meanwhile, in what is now Turkey, a particularly gruesome detail developed in the legend of the Virgin Cybele, who became known in Rome as Magna Deum Mater, the great mother of the gods. She had taken a young human lover, Attis, but youth being as callow and hormones as irresistible then as now, he had been unfaithful to her with a nymph. The wrath of the goddess exacted a high price: in repentance, Attis castrated himself. As he died from the ensuing loss of blood, his seed fell all over the earth, and seeing this, Cybele forgave him, and resurrected him as the god of vegetation.

Again and again, the great virgin and the great mother are one and the same. Defying human preconceptions, she is chaste and promiscuous, tender and bloodthirsty—as contradictory, in short, as only a goddess can be.

Even as she gradually lost supreme power, becoming just one of several deities in the Greek and Roman pantheons, the great virgin still retained her paradoxical nature. Artemis was the goddess of childbirth, yet she was also worshipped as the goddess of the hunt, and so of death. The paradox lived on in the herb named after her, artemisia, which depending on the dosage could be either a fertility drug, or one to prevent or terminate pregnancy. When the Romans appropriated Greek theology, she would become Diana, the virgin goddess whose most famed statue, Diana of Ephesus, shows her positively bursting with fertility, multiple rows of breasts spilling across her chest like a huge bunch of grapes swollen with juice. And later, as Christianity gained ascendance, the great temple of Diana at Ephesus would be rededicated, like many of the Isis temples, to the Virgin Mary.

But no matter what name the great goddess bore, where she was worshipped, or what unique details her legend contained, her virginity was essential. It signified her power. The virgin was her own person, unpossessed and unpossessable by any man, whether god or human. She took lovers, but was never taken herself; she never married. Far from being barren or unfruitful, she was virgin in the same way we still talk of virgin forest or virgin territory. She teemed with life. Untamed, untouchable, uncontrollable, she was the wild, fecund source of creation. Soil, rain, sun; seed, harvest, sustenance; man, woman, child—every form of life began with her.

She was the essence of fertility, and her power was life itself. Throughout the peasant agricultural societies of the Middle East, her legend was the enduring metaphor for the revolution of the seasons. During her grief at the loss of her dead lover or brother or child, the soil lay barren; her resuscitation of the loved one brought the soil back to life again. Male gods or humans provided the seed, but only she could make it fertile.

Anyone who has experienced the first rain in the arid Middle East will understand how powerful an impression is made by this annual return to fertility. Even in the twenty-first century, it induces an almost primordial sense of awe.

In the Galilee, the first rain comes in early autumn, around the time of Rosh Hashanah, the Jewish New Year—literally, the head or start of the year. Sometimes, it even occurs on the day itself, and then it seems like all the ancient traditions have magically come together to create new life.

You sense it first in the air. The earth is baked and cracked from the long summer drought; the dust in your nose and ears and mouth is so constant that you barely notice it. But something is different, and you lift your head to what you slowly realize is the first hint of moisture after months of dryness. An hour passes, perhaps two, and then you hear the sound: like someone dropping marbles onto flagstones outside the window. You don't know what it is at first, it's been so long since there was rain. And then you look outside and you see it: huge, heavy drops coming down one by one, hitting the bone-dry ground and bouncing off it as though each drop were solid. Then more come down, and more, until within a few minutes they're beating on the ground with the rhythm of a tabla player, the rapid heavy beat of the Middle East. Only the first rain is ever so loud.

Birds wake out of their torpor and join in like flutes to the drumbeat. Thunder rolls over the hills, adding in bass. Giant black clouds move over the landscape, sweeping in as the wind picks up. And then suddenly the rain is slashing across the valleys in huge white curtains, water is running down the rocky hillsides, spilling over stone terraces, cascading through dry wadi beds in flash floods that seem to have come from nowhere. Hillside alleys become streams, waterfalls splash down off roofs. Children run outside and turn in slow circles with arms spread, mouths wide open and faces turned up to the sky to drink the rain as it falls.

An hour later, it's over. Only the smell remains—the smell of damp earth, of bushes and trees coming back to life, of seeds long dormant pushing up through the stony soil. It's the scent of renewal, the primal knowledge in the air that new life, a new year, has begun.

This is the ancient gift of the virgin—the powerful pulse of life in the making. Hers is the mystery of fertility, the wild unpredictability of it, which we acknowledge even today when we call droughts or floods or other natural disasters "acts of god." As any villager in Nazareth could have told you, when you live on the land, you can never take it for granted. One way or another, fertility is always miraculous.

VI

If she could—if there were such things as time and luxury in her life—Maryam would sit for hours at a time with her hands folded across her belly, feeling the child growing inside her. She is surprised at this. After all, she is used to birth. She has pulled lambs and kids out of their mothers' wombs—released them from their placentas, wiped off the blood and tissue, massaged the mothers' teats until the milk began to flow. She's done the same for women and their newborns, countless times. But she's always been so focused on birth that she never really thought about the months that went before.

She thinks of how pregnant women look as they straighten up to rest their backs in the fields, or pause on the way back from the well—of the way they stare down at their swollen bellies, eyes wide in a kind of tender amazement. "Look what I have done," they seem to be saying. And when she searches for the word to describe that look on their faces, what she finds is "awe."

But now Maryam realizes that there's no understanding the depth of that feeling until it happens to you, until it's your own belly you look down on, your own skin stretching, your own knowledge that there is another being growing inside you. Now she knows it *be-basara*, as the saying goes—on her own flesh. A different kind of knowledge. And with this new knowledge comes an immense sense of both pride and humility.

She didn't have to tell Salome. All the old woman needed was one glimpse of her granddaughter sitting with her hands across her belly, and she knew. "Blessed be the Name," she said, and the ritual phrase rang fresh in Maryam's ears as the old woman hugged her close. "Blessed be the woman."

And Maryam truly feels blessed. A new life is growing inside her, a small miracle growing larger by the day. As her belly swells and the village sees she is pregnant, the child is welcomed even before it is born into the world. The ritual yet heartfelt words are repeated—she is blessed and blessed again—because every pregnancy offers the hope of new life, and each new life is hope.

She feels like climbing high above the village to the top of the ridge and ululating so that the whole world can hear. Imagines the piercing trill echoing through the hills, proclaiming her pregnancy. But she knows it would be bad luck to do that; she needs to be patient. First, the child must be born, alive and healthy, and then it must survive the first dangerous weeks of life. Forty days must pass before a celebration can be held. Yet Maryam has no doubt. In her heart, she is already celebrating.

"You are carrying a boy," Salome says firmly. "Hands across the belly mean a boy."

Maryam is surprised; she'd assumed it would be a girl, and that she would do for this child what Salome had done for her—bring into being another in the long line of wise women. Salome laughs. "This is how wise men are born," she says. "The sons of wise women can take the knowledge of women into the world of men, and change it. You will teach him as I have taught you. Teach him well, and he will teach others."

Soon Maryam is too heavy to go out on the hillsides with the flocks. Salome takes charge of her, setting her to work in the courtyard pounding wheat and beans and herbs, cooking, weaving. When the old woman sits back on her heels to rest, it seems to her that she can see her granddaughter change by the day from girl to woman, heavy-breasted and large with life. Once a week, she spreads virgin olive oil on the girl's belly to ease the expanding skin. She strokes the cloudy green lotion in small circles, each leading on to the next in spirals all around the belly, encircling the child within. Salome talks silently to the child through her touch, sure that her words reach through his mother's flesh, into the womb. She can feel him move beneath her hands, already eager for the knowledge in them. Maryam feels it too. And she knows that when his time comes, he will slip quietly and quickly into the world with ten fingers and ten toes, perfectly formed, protected by the great goddess of childbirth.

Their kinfolk have already set about finding a husband for Maryam, a father to adopt her child and give him his name. Meanwhile, as Salome says, "A father there has been, and another father there will be. Between the two is God the father."

The absence of the first father is no cause for concern. His work is done. They say there are three partners in the creation of life: the father, the mother, and God, whom they call "the Name" to avoid the forbidden act of saying "Yahweh" out loud. The father provides the white stuff, the sperm, and out of this are built the bones and the sinews, the nails, the white matter of the brain, and the white of the eye. The mother provides the red, the menstrual blood and the blood of birth, and this builds the skin and the flesh and the hair and the black of the eye. But it is Yahweh who makes the infant truly live, who gives the spirit and the soul and the use of all five senses: the sight of the eyes, the hearing of the ears, the scent in the nostrils, the taste in the mouth, the touch of skin on skin, hand on hand, mouth on breast. It is Yahweh who knits all these together and gives understanding and thought. And when the time comes for a person to die, it is Yahweh who takes his portion back.

"The man lies with the woman, and the Name creates," says Salome, smiling, for who knows when a child will be conceived? A man and a woman can lie together for years and nothing will happen; others can lie together just once, and the woman is pregnant. Sometimes Yahweh plays his part, sometimes not, and there is no knowing why one time he does, and another he doesn't.

They say too that a woman conceives when the angel Gabriel kneads soil into a small ball and plants it in her when her husband comes to her at night; but when the soil is infertile, so dry it's mere dust, then there is nothing into which Yahweh can breathe spirit. Salome just smiles. Let them believe what they will; one explanation is as good as another. She knows that the peasant life is hard on a woman's body, and that malnutrition and disease work against fertility as surely as the whims of the divine. Her herbs can help make a woman's body more receptive to conception, but even the wisest of midwives must acknowledge how much remains unknown. For what is wisdom without humility? No longer wisdom, but delusion, a closing of the mind to the unknown.

A father there will indeed be. So many women die in childbirth that there are always widowers needing young able-bodied girls for wives, whether from Nazareth itself or from a larger village like the Galilee Bethlehem to the west. This is how marriage is done—the wife just out of adolescence, with many years of childbearing ahead of her, and the man older, twice her age, able to set up his own household within the *hamula*, the family clan. It is a good arrangement for children, and a bad one for the women who survive childbirth and live on to become widows, their husbands and children dead long before them, like Salome.

It will be arranged, as all marriages are arranged. Kinsmen from either side will meet, drink wine mixed with water, talk amiably until they come to an agreement. Of course the father they find will not be the one who lay with Maryam when she became pregnant. Her child will inherit nothing, even if he is a boy, and even though her firstborn. That is understood. But there will be a pallet to sleep on, a reed canopy to sleep under, food to eat, other children to call brother and sister.

This is how Maryam will be looked after, because she is not only a daughter of Israel and a daughter of Yahweh, but also a daughter of Nazareth, and the villagers look after their own. And like every child born here, her son will be *bar-Natzrat*, a son of Nazareth. And *bar-*

enash, son of man, a human being. And *bar-elohin*, a son of god, as they all are children of god.

Maryam is pregnant, this we know. But how exactly she became pregnant is another story—or more accurately, several possible stories.

"A biography may be considered complete if it merely accounts for six or seven selves, whereas a person may well have as many as one thousand," Virginia Woolf once wrote. She exaggerated, of course, but we get the point: to limit any person to a single neatly explainable package is to create a fiction. We are all far too complex for that, and it is precisely that complexity—the unexplainable contradictions in our lives—that makes us interesting. And human.

The same applies to events. In what has become the paradigm of multiple points of view, the great Japanese film director Akira Kurosawa contented himself with "merely" four conflicting accounts in his classic *Rashomon*, which can be seen as the biography of an event.

The first line of the film, repeated three times, is "I don't understand." Under the huge Rashomon gate, during a violent rainstorm, those taking shelter hear four radically different accounts of a rape and murder: a bandit's confession to the crime, the raped woman's testimony, the story of the murdered man (via a medium), and the account of a woodsman who, by chance, has witnessed it all. Each successive version is utterly convincing. Each seems that it can only be the truth. And so each raises ever increasing doubts as to the reliability of human testimony. What is true and what do we merely convince ourselves is true, or represent as true because it's how we want it to have been?

Crime investigators know just how fallible memory can be, whether due to eagerness to produce facts, to mistaken impressions, to self-aggrandizement, or to self-interest. This, Kurosawa implies, is the nature of humanity. It is what makes our stories so complex, so compelling, and so inherently unreliable. Yet if this seems a dark take on human nature, he provides redemption at the end of his film. As the storm eases off, the sheltering men hear the cry of an abandoned newborn. The woodsman decides to adopt the infant—what's one more mouth to feed, he says—and walks off into the faint post-storm sunshine, the child cradled in his arms.

The ambiguity of the *Rashomon* story is precisely what makes it so powerful. It resonates in the same way that classic myths do. "No sooner have you grabbed hold of it than myth opens out into a fan of a thousand segments," says classicist Roberto Calasso. "Everything that happens, happens this way, or that way, or this other way. And in each of these diverging stories all the others are reflected, all brush by us like folds of the same cloth."

And if only one version of a mythical event survives? Then, says Calasso, "it is like a body without a shadow, and we must do our best to trace out that invisible shadow in our minds."

Over the centuries, Maryam's conception of Jesus has been made into such a single-version event. Though it is often called a mystery, it is in fact quite the opposite, for to advocate a definitive "this is how it happened, this way and no other" is to deny mystery altogether—not only Maryam's, but the mystery of any life, the imponderables that make us human.

Mystery is not in what we know, or even in what we believe, but in what we think may be so. Mystery is wonder, literally, in the sense that we can say, "I wonder . . ." If we can keep our minds open, rejecting the security of conviction and forgoing certainty for possibility, we may then—perhaps—approach what could be called truth.

Truth is always an evolving idea, wrote William James in his essay on pragmatism. It is always temporary, and always constructed from our own experience. "The 'absolutely' true, meaning what no further experience will ever alter, is that ideal vanishing point towards which we imagine all our temporary truths will some day converge. It runs on all fours with the completely wise man, and with absolutely complete experience. Meanwhile we have to live by what truth we can get today, and be ready tomorrow to call it falsehood."

And yet there does exist another way of approaching the matter of the conception of Jesus, one far closer to that of Maryam's time. As in Calasso's description of the Greek myths, there may be more than one truth, even several truths, each equally valid in a very different way and on a very different level of reality. And each one may perhaps point us toward a greater, perfect, impossible truth such as James talked about.

True believers and true skeptics alike will have a hard time with such an approach. But to quote James again, "so far as man stands for anything, and is productive and originative at all, his entire vital function may be said to have to deal with maybes. Not a victory is gained, not a deed of faithfulness or courage is done, except upon a maybe."

Who was the father of Maryam's child? The largest "maybe" of all is both the most widely held theory and, at least on the face of it, the most impossible: that the father was God.

To believe this would seem to be a matter of faith, way beyond the bounds of historical inquiry. But the need to retain an open mind works both ways—not just on the part of the faithful toward the evidence of reason, but also on the part of the rational toward the evidence of faith. Unless a reader is so deeply committed to atheism that it has itself become an article of religious belief, there may be more in the idea of divine paternity than many of us suspect.

Conception, despite all our scientific knowledge, still has a certain element of divine mystery. Television nature programs refer to "the miracle of birth," and even in the age of genetic engineering, every woman pregnant for the first time feels the same tender amazement Maryam felt as she stared down at her swollen belly. When the baby kicks inside the womb, the first-time father-to-be smiles in bashful pride, as though he can't quite believe what he has done. The word for what the parents feel at that moment is still awe. In this most physical of moments, they touch the metaphysical.

"Blessed be the Name," said Salome, and this is the ritual phrase still used in modern Hebrew: *baruch ha-shem*, God be blessed. Among religious and Sephardic Jews in particular, it is almost a verbal tic, like saying "Bless you" when someone sneezes. In Arabic it is used the same way, to indicate that everything's fine, or to express relief or joy at good news. "Allah be blessed, she is pregnant," they still say in Palestinian Arab villages, echoing the gospel "Blessed art thou among women."

Now as two thousand years ago, the divine haunts both language and thought in the Middle East. The Hebrew *be-ezrat ha-shem*, "with the help of God," gets tacked onto any hope for the future, large or small, as does the Arabic *insh-Allah*, "by the will of Allah." Both are gestures of humility, acknowledgements of the limits of human purpose.

But God's help is one thing; God's sperm another. An act of intercourse between the human and the divine, resulting in the birth of a child both human and divine? To take the idea literally borders on obscenity. The question is, who does indeed take it literally?

Anthropologist Edmund Leach tackled exactly this question when he discussed the belief in virginal conception among the Trobriand islanders. Earlier anthropologists had interpreted this belief as simple ignorance of physiology. Leach had a sharp reply. "What seems to me interesting," he said, "is not so much the ignorance of the aborigines as the naiveté of the anthropologists." The only way an anthropologist could take such stories at face value was if they matched "his own private fantasy of the natural ignorance of childish savages."

Indeed, when asked, the islanders freely acknowledged the role of sexual intercourse in conception. The women, who were less involved in religious ritual, said that conception was the result of sex with a man; the men said it was both sex and the intervention of the divine. So far as they were concerned, said Leach, "a child is of the same legal lineage as the holy spirit which magically enters the mother's body by an un-natural route at the moment of conception, while the child's human substance and appearance derives from the mother's husband."

Doctrines about conception without male insemination do not stem from innocence and ignorance, Leach pointed out. "On the contrary, they are consistent with theological argument of the greatest subtlety. If we put so-called primitive beliefs alongside sophisticated ones and treat the whole lot with equal philosophical respect, we shall see that they constitute a set of variations around a common structural theme: the metaphysical topography of the relationship between gods and men."

As in the twentieth-century Trobriand Islands, so too in first-century Palestine. Maryam lived in a place and time when the metaphysical element in human conception was publicly acknowledged. All human birth was divinely empowered, and every child was thus a son or daughter of God.

The idea of God the father was so intrinsic a part of the culture that it was fused into the names of the Hebrew bible: Yoav ("Yo/Yahweh is my father"), Eliav ("my god is my father"), Aviel ("my father is god"), Abram ("exalted father"), Abraham ("merciful father"), Aviram ("my father is exalted").

The paternal metaphor continues in well-known Jewish prayers such as the Kaddish, the prayer for the dead: "May the prayers and supplications of all Israel be acceptable before their father who is in heaven." The Lord's Prayer, beginning with "Our father who art in heaven," is thus solidly in the Jewish tradition, as is Jesus himself, who consistently refers to God not as his own personal father but as the father of all: "your father" and "our father."

Nobody who heard Jesus use these phrases would have been so naive as to imagine that he meant that everyone was conceived through divine insemination. Paternity was understood as a matter of identity. And it came in many different forms, not just biology. In Rome, for instance, adoption was as accepted a method of creating an heir as procreation. The voluntary father-son bond was as strong as the biological one, if not even stronger because actively chosen on the part of the father. Throughout the peasant cultures of the Mediterranean meanwhile, the patriarch of an extended family was considered the father of everyone in it.

In both Hebrew and Aramaic, "son of" was regularly used in the same way as "citizen of" or "member of," much as it is used today in such disparate American organizations as Bnei Brith—"sons of the covenant"—and the Daughters of the American Revolution. Similarly, when the prophet Malachi called a heathen woman "the daughter of a strange god," he meant that she was from a people who worshipped another god. And when the Essenes talked of an apocalyptic battle between the sons of light and the sons of darkness, they weren't envisioning a sci-fi/fantasy battle, but a war between the enlightened and the benighted.

All this would have been clear to anyone living in the Middle East, where family relationships—not only father, but also mother, brother, sister, and cousin—were and still are used to refer to close ties other than blood ones. Ties as close as blood, that is. And it would have been equally clear to anyone living in the Hellenistic world, where dual paternity—divine and human—had long been established as part of the legend of great men and heroes.

Perhaps the most famous instance of divine paternity in Greek myth is Helen of Troy, apparently conceived when Leda was raped by Zeus in the guise of a swan. That is the premise of the W. B. Yeats poem "Leda and the Swan," known above all for its voyeuristic quality:

> A sudden blow: the great wings beating still
> Above the staggering girl, her thighs caressed
> By the dark webs, her nape caught in his bill
> He holds her helpless breast upon his breast.

And that's just the beginning. Yeats goes on to describe "her loosening thighs" and "a shudder in the loins" before the swan finally lets go. It is as explicit a sexual act between human and divine as there could be, more so even than the renowned ecstasies of Teresa of Avila. But in fact it's doubtful if Homer or any other Greek ever intended such a lascivious vision, for the full version of the legend makes it clear that

Leda had sex with her husband the same night she was raped by Zeus. Helen of Troy was the result of dual paternity: her physical father, and the spirit of Zeus.

In nearly every instance of gods siring legendary humans, they worked *with* men, not instead of them. Theseus was indeed the son of Poseidon, but he was conceived when both Poseidon and a human lover lay with his mother on the same night. Asculepius, the human who would become the god of healing, was the son of Apollo, but he was conceived when his mother lay with both her husband and the god at the same time. And many human offspring of Zeus, the master of disguise, were conceived when he took on the simplest and most deceptive guise of all: that of a man. Hercules was born after Zeus lay with his mother in the form of her husband, for instance, and Dionysus was conceived when Zeus took the form of a man to rape the maiden Semele.

Miraculous conception accrued to real people too, if they were famous enough. Alexander the Great was said to be conceived when Zeus took the form of a snake to couple with Olympias. The emperor Augustus was born after his mother fell asleep in the temple of Apollo and was impregnated by the god. Pythagoras and Plato too were sons of Apollo. And as with "the daughters of strange gods," the "great man" legend also applied to great women. In the Egyptian temple of Deir el-Bahri at Karnak, a relief in praise of Queen Hatshepsut shows her mother seated on a couch alongside the god Amon, who proclaims: "Hatshepsut shall be the name of this my daughter whom I have placed in thy body."

Divine paternity was, in a way, an act of conceptual art: a creative act that took place on the level of mind, not body. This is how sorcerers and seers could believably declare, "I am the son of the living god," a formulation that appeared frequently in Greek magical papyruses. As historian Morton Smith has pointed out, it was not to be taken literally. It was a way of calling down the power of the divine, of saying, "At this moment, I am inspired by, and act and speak for, the god."

But there was one vital difference between the concept of dual paternity in Middle Eastern cultures and in Hellenistic culture. As the idea spread north and west to Athens and then to Rome, it lost its democratic quality. In Israelite culture, as in the Trobriand Islands, everyone was a child of God; in Hellenistic culture, only the great, the powerful, and the high-born. This meant that early Christians outside Palestine had no difficulty with the idea of Jesus being both the son of Joseph and the son of God. Since they lived within the Hellenistic cultural tradition of divinely born great men, they expected it. It was a confirmation of his greatness, a rationalization of their faith.

Which was the biological father was not a question. Nobody imagined, like Yeats, literal sexual intercourse between human and divine. Just as we still use the words "ghost" and "spirit" interchangeably, so the Holy Ghost "coming upon" Maryam in Luke was the spirit of God, not God personified. It was a union of the spirit, not of the flesh.

If she had heard the story, Maryam would certainly have understood it this way. She never did hear it, of course: the gospel account wasn't written until decades after her death. But then, she didn't need to hear it. She already knew.

No midwife or healer could possibly work without an understanding of the biology of reproduction. Nor, if she was good at her work, could she ignore the mystery of it. Maryam knew there was no explaining why conception occurred at one time and not another, or why one delivery might be easy and another difficult. And she knew that beyond these was a greater mystery: the sense of awe and wonder she felt anew each time a child emerged into the light of day with all ten of its fingers and all ten of its toes, and the surge of joy inside her each time she heard that first intake of air into newborn lungs and then, on the exhalation, the first loud cry of life.

For all her skill—indeed, because of her skill—she had a strong sense of the mystery inherent in every conception and every birth, of the influence of something more than the rough, urgent couplings of men and women under cover of night. Was the spirit literally there? Did swan's or eagle's or dove's wings beat in frantic accompaniment? Of course not. The spirit was in the idea, in the acknowledgement that every act of conception was an act of both human sexuality and what could be called chance or fate, though as people have throughout the centuries, Maryam preferred to think of it as divine intervention. Conception, birth, survival—all took place *be-ezrat ha-shem*, with the help of God.

God was the father as God was always the father. But the sole father? Maryam would have laughed at the idea, hiding her laughter in her sleeve, perhaps, so as not to offend, but unable to keep it out of her eyes. No, there was a human father too, and anyone looking for him two thousand years later has to start with the one we are given in the gospels: Joseph.

Joseph is a comforting presence in our imaginations. He is there for Maryam when she needs him—someone to look after her, like a good shepherd. A father to her, it seems, more than to Jesus.

In classic patriarchal fashion, he is always shown bearded. True, all but the most Hellenized men had beards in the Palestine of the time. To be clean-shaven was a Hellenistic affectation, a sign of the urban elite. But beards are comforting; they soften a face, make it seem kinder and wiser. Or perhaps we are biased in this by the fact that God is always personified as bearded, as is Jesus, or that orthodox rabbis and imams are usually bearded, and luxuriantly so—no spiffy little goatees or carefully trimmed three-day fuzz, but luxuriant manes that make a young man seem older and experienced, and an old man seem venerable and infinitely wise.

But above all, a beard hides a face. It is harder to tell who the person is, to read the cues we normally read from facial features such as the set of the lips, the jut of the chin, the angle of the jaw. A beard confers mystery. It is the male equivalent of a veil.

And Joseph is a veiled presence in the New Testament gospels. He never even speaks. He appears hardly at all, though his first appearance, in Matthew, is surely significant: the Annunciation is to him, not to Mary. Yet the only thing we hear of him throughout Jesus' childhood is as one of "his parents" fetching him from the temple at age twelve. And after that—nothing. He fades into the background, and without us even noticing it, disappears. He is almost the archetype of the absentee father.

Yet knowing practically nothing about him, we like him nonetheless. He's what we want for Maryam. He has the reassuring solidity and stability of the caretaking husband, one who doesn't judge but—with a little prodding from an annunciating angel—accepts her as she is, pregnant.

Yes, definitely a father figure. A perfect human stand-in for the divine father. You would think he would get more appreciation for this, but even in the convent school I went to, the one named after him, he made barely any impression. While Mary was a bright, colorful presence in the school corridors, a flash of radiant blue at practically every turn, there were just a couple of Joseph statues, and they were dull by comparison. He was clothed in monklike brown, the antithesis of his namesake in the coat of many colors.

There was only one hymn devoted to him among the dozens we sang in morning prayers. "Hail, holy Joseph, hail," it went, "husband of Mary, hail. / Chaste as the lily flower in Eden's peaceful vale. / Hail, holy Joseph, hail! Father of Christ esteemed, / Father be thou to those thy foster Son redeemed."

The hymn writer clearly suffered some confusion as to Joseph's precise role, settling in the end on "foster father." This odd phrase makes it sound as though Joseph had never even met his son's mother, but was a stranger brought in to raise the child. Yet it does provide an extra level of remove, forestalling any possibility of broaching the taboo subject of sex. In the convent setting, Joseph had to be as de-sexed as Mary.

Who was he? A carpenter, everybody knows that. Except there would have been little work for a carpenter in a place like Nazareth.

In the west, whole houses are still made of wood, but not around the Mediterranean, and certainly not in the Palestine of two thousand years ago. Peasant houses are always built of what's readily available, and as anyone knows who reads or watches current news reports from the Middle East, what is readily available in Palestine, now as then, is stone. Stones are the one thing besides thorns that Palestine has in abundance. No matter how hard you work at clearing the soil, at moving stones into terraces, walls, and houses, more always get forced up to the surface by the next winter's cold. A field you thought you'd cleared one year is stony again the next.

There were trees, to be sure, but not in the quantity and quality that would support a carpenter, and besides, there was no demand. Few peasants had tables or chairs in their houses. A bed was a reed pallet on the dirt floor; containers were made of clay, storage boxes of stone. And families built their own houses, as they still do in the villages of the West Bank.

Could Joseph have been a wheelwright or cartwright, then, as some scholars have speculated? If he had lived more than a hundred years later, perhaps. But there were no carts in Palestine in his time; the Romans would only begin building roads there in the second century, under the emperor Hadrian. Until then, wheels were not feasible; they would have broken on the stony dirt tracks. Donkeys and mules still held sway, and the camels of the long-distance caravans.

Maybe he made plows? They were wooden, certainly, but again, each family made their own. As in most rural communities still today, farmers were multiply skilled; no farmer who was not could survive. Only when you left the village—when you were forced off the land and had to hire yourself out in the city—did you begin to be determined not by your family and kin, but by a particular skill.

The whole image of Joseph as a carpenter is based on no more than a passing reference in Matthew, when the villagers of Nazareth refer to Jesus as "the carpenter's son." The Aramaic word used for carpenter, *nagar*, actually meant a craftsman, anything from a mason to a blacksmith, while its Greek equivalent, *tekton*, meant a builder, as in the word *architect*, or arch builder. All these professions would have been in demand not in a small peasant village in the Galilee, but in a city with large building projects such as Jerusalem or Antioch or Athens. A city, that is, such as those where the gospel writers lived.

We do not know the names of the individual men who wrote the New Testament gospels; like most such writing of the time, these books were pseudo-epigraphical—written under the name of a well-known figure from the recent or even the distant past, like the apocryphal Wisdom of Solomon, or the Book of Enoch. But we do know that their authors were part of the Hellenic world of Antioch, Ephesus, and Athens, as was their audience. They wrote in Greek for Greek speakers, which is how Matthew could create an arch builder in a small Middle Eastern village where no buildings were so grand as to have arches. His Joseph is essentially a city man transplanted by authorial fiat to a Galilee village. And, as it were, abandoned there.

Joseph's main function, in Luke as well as in Matthew, seems to be to establish Jesus' lineage not merely as "the carpenter's son," but as a descendant of King David—a descent that would make Jesus' birth accord with Hebrew biblical prophecy. Yet the angelic annunciation in Matthew ensures that Joseph will be a husband in name, but not in biological fact: that he will, in essence, be an escort for Mary, not a real husband. Stranger still, in Mark, now recognized as the earliest gospel, Joseph's existence is not even implied, let alone named. Instead, Jesus is referred to as "the son of Mary." This is a phrase that may seem natural enough today, but in first-century Palestine, where children carried the names of their male ancestors, it would have been highly unnatural.

Then there is the way Jesus refers to himself: not as the "son of Joseph," nor, for that matter, "son of Mary" or even "son of God," but "son of man." This is a direct translation of the Aramaic *bar-enash*, which could be used to indicate simply any man, or an anonymous man—son of all men and no man in particular—or, as with the modern

Hebrew *ben-adam* (literally "son of Adam" or "son of the earth"), a good man or "a mensch." The one thing that is for sure is that it does not refer to Joseph; Jesus never refers to him at all, let alone speaks to him directly.

Joseph begins to sound suspiciously like a fiction. It is probably not surprising, then, that the most intriguing explanation for his near absence in the New Testament is a fictional one. In *The Gospel According to Jesus Christ*, Nobel-winning novelist José Saramago has Mary conventionally married to Joseph, and Jesus conventionally born. The boy is just twelve when a friend of Joseph's goes from Nazareth to Sepphoris to sell a mule, and gets caught up in a riot. Fearing that his friend may be in danger, Joseph gathers up his courage and goes to Sepphoris himself to look for him. His fears are well-founded: the friend is dead. Worse, the authorities are rounding up anyone they find in the streets. Joseph is arrested, and in short order, without benefit of trial or appeal, is crucified along with hundreds of others in the classic Roman method of collective punishment. This becomes not merely an omen of what will happen to his son, but an essential motivating factor. Where the father is crucified by chance, for simply being in the wrong place at the wrong time, the son will choose his crucifixion, thus giving meaning to his father's death.

Yet despite even Saramago's best efforts, Joseph remains a shadow character. He is a mechanical story device more than a person. Surely then we must ask if he ever did really exist. Could this good, bearded man in fact have been a metaphorical beard—an escort who exists to divert public attention from someone who for one reason or another needs to remain secret? Could his presence hide that of another? Or the absence of another?

VII

One moment, she is free—a shepherd girl on the hillside. The next . . .
There is no next. It is as though she has suddenly been taken into
another world, another state of being. One that has nothing to do with
her existence in this world.

It feels like a blow, a hard blow at the nape of her neck. And then
comes the sensation of falling, tumbling and twisting as she goes until
it seems that she will fall forever, down into a deep night of being, a
dark night of the soul. She knows what is happening, but it takes place
so fast that she has no time to react. Not even to protest, let alone
struggle.

The weight is the worst of it. It bears down on her. It pins her to the
ground and smothers her like a huge dark cloud until she can't speak,
can't cry out, has no voice at all. A giant hand seems to cover her face—
her eyes, her nose, her mouth. She is suffocating. No sight, no voice,
no breath in her for so long that she is sure she will never see, speak,
breathe again.

And then, as quickly as it began, it is over. The weight lifts. Light
floods her eyes, so bright she has to close them. If there is the sound of
someone scrambling quickly away over the hillside, she doesn't hear;
she is too busy breathing. Her lungs surge in relief as she gulps air in
deep, painful gasps.

Gradually, her heart stops thumping so hard inside her chest, and
pieces of the world come back into being. The rustle of the breeze in
the scrub oaks. The jagged edges of rough pebbles between her

shoulder blades. A fly buzzing. She lies quietly, thinking that if she can sense these familiar things, all will be well.

Something rustles nearby. She hears a muted murmuring, then a soft bleat. A wet snout nuzzles into her shoulder. A rough tongue licks at her face. She opens her eyes to see the liquid eyes of a lamb staring down into her own, as though willing her back into this world.

She sits up, looks around. Nobody in sight. If it weren't for the pain in her head and between her thighs, she could almost have imagined it all. Just a moment, after all. One long, dark moment in this brilliant sunlit day. And yet she knows that this one moment has irrevocably changed everything. That nothing in her life will ever be the same. Nothing in the world. The seed of something utterly new has taken root deep within her, and it is hers now, hers alone, to care for, to tend, to release into the world.

We don't want to think it happened this way. If Joseph was not the father, then better by far to let the romantic imagination run wild and see the innocence of youthful love, even a kind of Romeo and Juliet scenario: a boy from a family in a feud with Maryam's own, perhaps, or worse, from the garrison town of Sepphoris, just a few miles away yet enemy territory. The Hollywood-soaked imagination conjures up two teenagers under the olive trees, under the stars, under the full moon . . .

But there was almost certainly no romance. The concept did not exist—would not come into being, in fact, until the Middle Ages. People didn't marry for love; they married for advantage and inheritance. Whether high-born Roman elite or low-born Palestinian peasants, marriage was arranged by others, and became an arrangement between husband and wife. If you were fortunate, love might develop, but it would be the love of fondness and respect, not of romance. That was an unimaginable luxury.

Instead, we are forced to consider a far greater likelihood—the complete antithesis of the romantic fantasy, and one far harder for the modern mind to deal with—and that is that Maryam became pregnant as a result of rape.

The initial reaction to the very idea is horror. The mind revolts. To even think in such terms seems an insult. But given the place and the time, we do need to consider the possibility, however unwillingly. And we may find that on closer examination, it is anything but insulting.

The gospel account of the Annunciation to Mary can itself be seen as raising the issue. "The Holy Spirit will come upon you," says the angel Gabriel, "and the power of the Most High will cover you with its shadow." The image of Mary being overshadowed is disturbing enough. But in a Hellenistic setting, a ghostly presence bearing down on her like a dark cloud would immediately bring to mind images of Zeus swooping down on human maidens in the guise of wind or rain, swan or eagle. Or in this case, dove.

Because the Greek myths are "classical," we tend to blur the basic fact that what Zeus was doing was rape. The human virgins were mere objects of his desire with no will of their own, no voice in the matter, no ability to repel his attack. They were essentially terrorized by a god, yet would be honored rather than dishonored for it. And their children, products of rape, would become the semi-divine heroes of legend.

Many biblical scholars have seen Mary's response to the Annunciation as a radical act of affirmation. "Behold the handmaid of the Lord," she says to Gabriel. "Be it done unto me according to thy word." Without Mary's assent, they argue, the very existence of Jesus, let alone of Christianity and the last two thousand years of western culture, would have been impossible. They interpret her words as a queenly "Let it be." But that is indeed an interpretation. What she says can as easily be read as a cowed "Yes, sir."

This is why Catholic feminists like Mary Daly see the conventional image of Mary as setting her up as the model rape victim. Meek and mild, Mary assents to the inevitable. She has no will of her own to exert, and no active role; what will happen will be done *to* her, not *by* her. She lacks even a voice of her own, for the Magnificat, her hymn of praise following the Annunciation, is a direct adaptation of the hymn of Hannah in the first book of Samuel, much of it almost word for word.

That is how it is in the world of the gospels, the books that literally mean "good news." And in the real world? In Maryam's violence-ridden first-century Palestine, rape was so common that it began to put the whole system of patrilinear descent and inheritance in doubt. When the Mishnaic rabbis decided two centuries later to change the patrilinear definition of Jewishness and to make Jewish descent matrilinear, they were probably making a practical accommodation to the realities of the time. In the face of uncertainty as to who the father was, at least the mother was known for sure.

Early anti-Christian diatribes contain persistent rumors that Maryam was raped. The most common candidate for the rapist is a Roman soldier named Panthera—a suitably predatory name. In fact it was not only a fairly common Greek name, but also the name of a Roman legion. This legion was indeed sent south out of Syria into Palestine in both 4 B.C. and 6 A.D., the two years scholars now consider the earliest and latest possibilities for the year in which Maryam gave birth. And where the Roman legions went, they raped.

Seventeen centuries before the Enlightenment and nineteen centuries before the first Geneva Convention, war was a matter of all-out predation. Rape and pillage were as standard procedure as hand-to-hand combat. What could be taken was taken, whether life, food, loot, or sex. Soldiers didn't fight so much as rampage, instituting a reign of terror whose goal was total subjugation of the civilian population. And indeed rape as a means of warfare still continues, most infamously in recent history in the former Yugoslavia, where it was used not just as a sadistic exercise of power, but also as a means of collective punishment and terrorization.

The mind revolts, yes. Most of us can accept that Maryam was not a physical virgin. But raped? "Anyone else, perhaps, but not her," we say to ourselves. Just to consider the idea forces us to abandon the construct of a desexualized figurehead built up over the centuries, and to see her as a real woman. Too real. It breaks through the idealized image to a horribly vivid reality, and however ready we may think we are for that, some remnant of traditional piety reaches out to hold us back.

But to think of Maryam raped is not completely negative; it forces us to re-examine our attitudes toward rape itself. If it offends and violates our traditional image of her, this is exactly what rape is about: the deepest kind of psychological as well as physical violation, not only of a woman's body, but also of the terms of her existence in this world. All sense of safety—gone. All sense of her body as her own—gone. All sense of herself as anything other than the possible object of someone else's violence—gone.

Susan Brownmiller's pioneering *Against Our Will* revealed rape for what it is: not an act of sexual desire, but one of violent aggression. The very fact that there can be deep offense in the idea of Maryam raped reveals how little our attitudes have really changed since Brownmiller wrote that book in 1975. Some part of us still conceives of rape as a shameful kind of sexuality on the woman's part: some part of us still sees it as dirtying, dishonoring, and degrading the woman.

This may be why we find rape so much more offensive for Maryam than for the western woman who makes her way to the nearest rape crisis center, or even for the political prisoner who is tortured by rape. The last way we want to think of her is as dirtied, dishonored, and degraded. Nor should we. For our sense of offense may be the means by which we can finally reach out of our moral numbness about rape. Just as there is no good reason to collude with rapists by thinking of any raped woman as dirtied and degraded, so too with Maryam. To think of her as such is the real dishonor, not only to her but to the millions of women throughout the world who have been, are being, and will be raped.

In fact, Maryam raped could be a far more powerful symbol than the conventional one of her as inviolate, because one thing is clear: if she was indeed raped, she refused to be victimized by it. She refused to feel shame. When she found herself pregnant, she had the power to terminate the pregnancy—as a healer, she knew how—but decided instead to carry the child to term, to give birth to him, and to raise him as her own: "the son of Mary."

She would grace him with the name Yeshua: Iesu in Greek, and thus Jesus in English. In Hebrew, the name uses the abbreviated form of Yahweh—Yah—and means "Yah saves." And it would be an extra-ordinarily appropriate name for the child of a raped woman. In Deuteronomy, if a man rapes a betrothed girl in open country, he is held guilty but she is not, because even though she cried for help, *en moshia la*—"there was nobody to save her." What an amazing gesture, in that case, to defy the victim model of the raped woman by naming the child as a salvation. The act that was intended to shame is transformed into pride, violence into tenderness. Grace is created out of disgrace.

This is surely the essence of Christianity as Jesus preached it. The transmutation of opposites is the basis not only of the Sermon on the Mount—shame into pride, violence into tenderness, disgrace into grace, distrust into trust—but of much of his teaching. The poor shall be rich in spirit, the rich cursed by their wealth. Sinners shall be blessed, and the despised shall be honored. Those who weep shall laugh, while those who laugh now shall weep. It is a new world where everything that seemed immutable about peasant life under occupa-tion—hunger, powerlessness, shame, suffering—is transformed.

Of course there is no way to say for certain if Maryam was indeed raped. The rumors themselves were predictable, not just because rape was common in that time and place, but because by the time the rumors surfaced in the late second century, Maryam's elevation into the Virgin Mary was already under way. As the image of the holy virgin and the insistence on physical virginity became increasingly central to emerging Christianity, its opponents seized on the opportunity for defamation. And their charges still feel depressingly familiar. Sexual rumors surround famous women—especially politicians—even in the twenty-first century. Their opponents resort to the ancient tactic of trying to disparage their sexuality as a cover for the real agenda: attacking their presumption in aspiring to power and attempting to exercise it.

What can be said with surety, however, is that the idea of rape does no dishonor either to Maryam or to her son. On the contrary, it would make her a far greater role model than the Vatican image. Maryam raped is not less deserving of respect in any way, but more. She is a woman who not merely survived adversity, but transformed it into good. Who refused to accede to the image of herself as a victim. And who turned an act of deliberate disgrace into the ultimate grace.

Anonymous soldiers are not the only ones who can rape. In fact a soldier—whether a Herodian one stationed in Sepphoris or a mercenary from one of the Roman legions based in Syria—is almost too convenient, the perfect fictional device for early anti-Christian propagandists. Which is not necessarily to say that there was no rapist at all. It could as well have been anyone else on the hillside tracks leading to Nazareth: a trader, a shepherd boy from another village, even someone from Maryam's own village. This last, in fact, is much likelier. To catch a shepherd girl unawares on an open hillside would be difficult, whereas someone she knew could approach her easily. As we know today, despite the horrifying headline cases of brutal attacks by strangers and the persistent use of rape as a means of subjugation in war, the vast majority of rapes do not occur as random opportunism. Rapists usually know the women they attack. And sometimes, they take advantage of positions of trust. Even priestly ones.

A story of Maryam growing up surrounded by priests appears in several apocryphal "infancy gospels" or "nativity gospels." These were immensely popular from the third century on, and for good reason: they were an early equivalent of supermarket bodice-rippers, their stories filled with graphic detail under the guise of piety. The father of them all, as it were, was the late-second-century Book of James, also known rather more impressively as the Protevangelium of James. An extraordinarily vivid account of Maryam's birth, childhood, and delivery, it was the basis for much of her legend as it developed over the next few centuries.

This gospel has Maryam "presented as a gift" and as a "ministering servant" by her parents when she is three years old. A ward of the temple, in short. On her arrival, the high priest kisses her and places her on the third step of the altar, and there "she danced with her feet, and all the house of Israel loved her." She stays in the temple "like a dove being fed" until she is twelve, when her service there has to come to an end since, under Jewish law, no menstruation is allowed inside the temple precincts. The high priest is instructed by the angel Gabriel to call "all the widowers of the people" to the temple, "each of them bringing his rod." When a dove emerges from the tip of Joseph's rod, it is the sign that he is to be the chosen husband.

At first it seems a charming fable, even down to the Freudian symbolism of the dove emerging from the rod. Never mind for now the disturbing image of a three-year-old dancing for her supper, or the idea of her as a caged dove, being fed and fattened. The story appeals to the desire for Maryam to be special, singled out, and what could be more special than to be the favorite of the temple?

But what did it really mean to be a ward of the temple? The practice was indeed an integral part of organized religious life in Babylon, Greece, and Rome. Young girls were given to a temple by their families either in payment of financial debts or in fulfillment of religious vows. Most such families considered it honorable to offer up a daughter this way, much as many traditional Catholic families used to regard having a daughter enter a convent.

These girls were not "temple virgins" like the Vestals in Rome, however. They were simply menials. They hauled, cleaned, sewed, fetched, cooked, swept—any and all of the host of everyday tasks that we barely notice being done until they are left undone. Their reality was nothing at all like the fairy-tale one of the Book of James. Far from being adored playthings, they were at best ignored, at worst abused.

There is no record of such temple wards in Jerusalem—all records were destroyed when the complex was burned down by the Romans in 70 A.D.—but it seems quite likely that Herod's deeply Hellenized temple adopted this practice from the rest of the Hellenic world. Fathers did sell their daughters in the Palestine of the time; they pledged them away in repayment of debt, much as still happens in many impoverished parts of central Asia. The daughters became bond servants—debt slaves—working out the fathers' debts in services rendered. And since the Jerusalem temple was a major source of debt for peasant Palestinian families, many daughters were undoubtedly given up this way.

If Maryam was one of them, however, she would not have worked inside the temple itself. That was considered an honor, not work for a virtual slave. But the huge mansions of the high-priest enclave on the hillside across from the temple relied heavily on slave labor. There, Maryam would have worked in the women's quarters, for the rich could afford such luxuries as separate quarters for men and women. She'd have bathed and dried and perfumed her mistresses, spoon-fed them when they were ill, laundered their clothes, their underclothes, even their menstrual rags. And as she reached adolescence, as part of the property of the head of the household, she would quite likely have become part of his sexual property too. Sexual abuse of servants and slaves, both girls and boys, was common practice among wealthy families throughout the Hellenistic world, as indeed it always has been when wealth and power give one group of people absolute control over another.

A member of the high priesthood might seduce such a girl in a way we now know as all too familiar. A lecherous guru with an obedient young adept, a philandering televangelist with an adoring congregant, a pedophile priest with a shy and embarrassed altar boy—no matter what religion they profess or represent, they operate the same way, whispering of the sacred while acting out the profane. More likely, however, a first-century priest would dispense with such niceties as seductive whispers; the girl was the property of the temple, after all, and *en moshia la*—there was nobody to save her.

And if, as a result of such abuse, she became pregnant, the temple would cover for him. Someone would be found to marry her. Someone had to be found, for the law stated that anyone who raped a virgin had either to marry her himself or find an alternative in the form of another husband, a man persuaded either by authority or by money, and probably both, to take the place of the father. A Joseph, that is.

Much is temptingly explained, at least in psychoanalytic terms, by such a scenario. Where should Jesus be at age twelve but literally "about my father's business" in the temple? How could he not later bitterly criticize the religious establishment that abused his mother and then cast her out, pregnant? How not become a crusading rebel rocking the uneasy status quo between the Roman occupation and the politico-religious establishment of which his biological father was a part?

But the desire to explain can skew our grasp of probability. As with all successful fictions, there is indeed a seed of the possible in the Book of James. But only a seed. To actually believe that Maryam was a ward of the Jerusalem temple is a stretch, and a very long one at that. The gospel writers were a century closer to Maryam than the Book of James, and they certainly would not have overlooked a temple connection if one had existed. It would have been just too good a story, as it still is— too good to be true.

The question is why so many people were eager to believe it, and why some still are. And the answer seems to lie in the strange kind of snobbery that haunts legend and fantasy. Those who believe they led past lives were never ordinary peasants, but inevitably of high-born blood. Old fairy tales and modern fantasy stories often revolve around a noble birth concealed and then revealed. Even the best writers fall prey to the syndrome. In his novel *King Jesus*, Robert Graves ignored first-century politics altogether for the idea that Jesus was the secret grandson of Herod, and thus the hidden "king of the Jews."

We are not nearly as democratic as we like to think we are—or as Christian, for that matter. Our imaginary heroes tend to be elite figures of high birth, not sons of impoverished peasant girls. Like the Matthew author so eager to establish Jesus' descent from King David that he spent most of his first chapter tracing a line from Joseph all the way back to Abraham, some part of us still believes in lineage, even though the most basic point of Jesus' teaching is that he came from and spoke for peasant people.

The image of Maryam being fed tidbits from the priestly table instead of doing the back-breaking work of coaxing wheat from the stony soil of the Galilee is an insult not just to her own reality, but to Christianity itself—at least insofar as Christianity may be said to represent Jesus' preaching. The transformation of the hard-working Maryam into the cosseted Mary is at best a blind eye to "Blessed are the poor, for yours is the kingdom of heaven." At worst, it is an outright rejection.

And so we come back to Joseph, ever present even as he is ever absent. It is the absent part of him that makes it so much easier to conceive of paternal possibilities bordering on the sensationalist than what should surely be the most obvious one of all: that Joseph was a quiet, constant presence in Maryam's life, and that Jesus was born nine months after he and Maryam married.

This is the simplest answer, and according to the law of William of Ockham's razor, its simplicity should work in its favor. Matthew's tracing of Joseph's descent (and Luke's repeat of it, all the way back to "Adam the son of God") would seem to be stunningly irrelevant unless Jesus were indeed the biological son of Joseph. In fact Luke has him known as such in Nazareth. "Is not this Joseph's son?" say the villagers. Later, in John, they twice call him "Jesus, the son of Joseph."

Still more important is an indirect piece of evidence from Paul, since he wrote a generation earlier than any of the gospel authors, just twenty years after Jesus' crucifixion. Though Paul never mentions either parent by name, he does imply Joseph's paternity with his reference to "God's son Jesus Christ our lord, made of the seed of David according to the flesh." The seed of David, that is, being the sperm of Joseph. Early church writers like Ignatius, the second-century bishop of Antioch, took their lead from Paul. Jesus "was sprung both of the sperm of David and from the Holy Spirit." That makes him a perfect example of dual paternity, with human royalty on one side, divine inheritance on the other.

Everything else—the ambivalence about Joseph in the gospels and the ambiguity of Maryam's marital and physical status—is the result of the gospel writers trying to make the story of Jesus' birth conform to Hebrew biblical prophecy. In fact they were quite open about this. The gospels abound with phrases such as "this is what the prophet wrote" or "to fulfill what the Lord has spoken through the prophet." The writers needed Maryam to be virginally pregnant before marriage in order to create not just a miraculous birth, but a prophesied one. Joseph's real-life role had to be played down in favor of divine paternity. He was handed his brown robe, and made to fade into the background.

That was easy enough to do, since the gospel writers did not really care much about where Jesus came from. His physical reality was not the point, which is why he is never even described. What did such trivial details as appearance or family relationships or village politics mater when the kingdom of heaven was at hand? They were writing theology, not biography. What was important for them was the message. The messenger would die, but the message would live on.

No wonder the gospel portrayal of relations between Jesus, Mary, and Joseph is so oddly uneasy, even antagonistic. Jesus speaks as a divinely inspired preacher of a new social order, not as a son of human parents. On the two occasions he is shown talking directly to Maryam, he calls her "woman," not "Mother." And he never addresses Joseph at all. In fact he seems to disdain the very idea of family. "If anyone does not hate his father and his mother and wife and children and brothers and sisters, and himself too, he cannot be my disciple," he says in

Luke. And in Matthew, "Call no man father on earth, for you have one father who is in heaven." It is as though he considered his biological birth a meaningless accident. Only rebirth could engender meaning: "Unless a man is born again, he cannot see the kingdom of God."

Some scholars have argued that Jesus was speaking as someone who indeed had nobody on earth to call father. That is, as an "illegitimate child." It is an oddly literal reading, especially since the term was as irrelevant in the first century as it has become in the twenty-first. In Maryam's Palestine, a child was only defined as a legal bastard if born to a married woman and fathered by someone other than her husband—if, that is, the mother had jeopardized the system of inheritance. Otherwise, every child was a legitimate member of society, born into a family clan or *hamula* rather than a nuclear family, and addressing the head of the *hamula* as "father" regardless of biological paternity.

Being born again was clearly intended as a metaphor, and just as clearly it was understood that way, especially since it was a factor in many pagan faiths of the time.

Joseph may have been the biological father, or the stand-in. We can see him as a kinsman who took the pregnant Maryam into his home, whether as a duty to the *hamula* or, as Matthew has it, because he was instructed to do so by an angel. Or we can see him as a normal husband of the time, his marriage to Maryam arranged as all marriages were, the bride taken to his home along with her dowry, and his first-born son delivered nine months later. Or he may simply not have existed.

We will never know for sure. And perhaps what we really need to ask is if this even matters.

The search for "the real father" seems an oddly sentimental quest not only for Maryam's time, but also for our own. Nearly a third of all births in the United States are now to single mothers. In Norway, single mothers account for half of all births. In Iceland, 62 percent. In Britain, 38 percent. In France, 41 percent. And in deeply Catholic Ireland, where legal abortion is still not an option, 31 percent.

The phrase "single mother" may or may not mean that there is no father—that is, that the father is absent and takes no responsibility for his child. Many single mothers are still involved with the fathers of their children; they simply do not marry them, whether out of principle or lack of choice. What they do choose is motherhood. Though abortion is generally safe, legal, and relatively inexpensive, they choose to carry their pregnancies to term and raise their children as the sole legal parent. Their children take their mother's name, not their father's.

From everything we know of Maryam—her resilience, her ability, her courage—she may very well have made the same choice. But that does not mean she was a single mother. There was no such thing in the peasant villages of Palestine of two thousand years ago. She and her child would have been absorbed into the *hamula*, and the child raised by the extended family, as was the custom. The absence of a husband would not have been at all unusual. Since women were married at puberty to husbands twice their age, many were widowed, and their youngest children grew up never knowing their biological fathers. Disenfranchised men often went far away to work for months and even years at a time, leaving their wives and children in care of their kinfolk; their wives were "grass widows," but their children were anything but orphans.

Maryam was the mother, and that was enough. For us, it should surely be more than enough. Perhaps she married, perhaps not. Perhaps Jesus knew a human father, perhaps not. But any way you look at it, everything hinges on Maryam. She was the active one. Her decision to carry her pregnancy to term and give birth is what determines the whole of western history of the last two millennia.

Without Joseph, nothing would be different. Without Maryam, everything would. It was Maryam who chose her son, Maryam who gave birth to him, Maryam who nursed him and raised him and taught him all she knew. Maryam, *be-ezrat ha-shem*.

PART THREE

HER WOMEN

VIII

They call it Skull Hill. Golgotha in Aramaic. The place of execution, just outside the northeast gate of the city.

It's really more a rise than a hill, but the name fits nevertheless. There are indeed skulls rolling in the nearby ravine, along with leg bones, rib bones, arm bones—all that remains of crucified men, their bodies tossed there by the soldiers to be picked clean by jackals and hyenas, buzzards and vultures.

If you enter Jerusalem from this direction, you cannot avoid Golgotha. Even when there is nobody hanging here, the place still reeks of death. The uprights of the crosses are permanently embedded in the rock, waiting for the next victims to be nailed to heavy crossbeams and hauled up. All too often, the crossbeams are already in place. Usually just a few victims, but when there's been a disturbance or a riot, dozens. At times, there have been hundreds. Or rather, the remains of hundreds.

Some are still alive, if you can call that life. Each rasping breath is a struggle, a massive effort of failing muscles. They are already dead men in effect, just waiting for the mercy of a last breath. And below the crosses, kept at a distance by the soldiers, those they loved in life keep vigil, enduring a slow death of their own—a death of the soul.

The sun shines, but it does so in some cold, clear reality that is utterly remote from Maryam. For her, the world is darkness. Everything she took for granted, everything that once seemed real and solid, is now crumbling, breaking away. Even the ground beneath her feet.

Her whole body trembles, and the earth seems to tremble with her in horror and protest.

A slight breeze carries the sounds of the city over the walls. But how can birds sing and donkeys bray and people chat and barter and gossip when this is going on? How can there be anything but a terrible silence, a silence so loud it rings in her ears, blocking out all sound, all vision even, all sense of anything but this one vast agony that encompasses everything—her body, her mind, her world.

It is mid-afternoon, and the sun is at its most relentless. The women around her try to persuade her to at least drink some water, if not eat. She ignores them. What mother could eat or drink as her son slowly dies before her eyes?

She has heard it said that as you die, scenes from your life flash before your eyes. Now she knows that if your son is dying, part of you is dying too. She sees herself all those years ago, huge-bellied, riding on the donkey led by Joseph. She almost smiles as she remembers him picking out the smoothest path he could, for even the most minor bumps and stumbles jolted through her. She should have been at home with her women kinfolk gathered in the room and Salome crouched between her legs, waiting for the contractions to come quicker. The women humming birth songs, and the gentle strength of Salome's hands on her stomach, pressing down. Instead, she was riding along the hilltop ridge from Nazareth to the Galilee Bethlehem to register for the census. That evening, in the house of Joseph's kinfolk, women who were strangers would lay her down to give birth in the dank warm straw of the stables beneath the house. And the next day, the Herodian scribe would register a newborn of Bethlehem, resident of Nazareth.

Now she is indeed far from home. She shakes her head, trying to focus on what should surely be the simple task of standing upright, with eyes open. She resists the impulse to collapse to the ground and curl up into a ball, arms over her head to block everything out. If all she can do now is witness, then by God that is what she will do.

She barely remembers screaming when they nailed his hands and feet, though her body still aches from the force with which she shuddered at each blow of the hammer. How long ago was that? Hours, yes—it was just after dawn when it began. But it feels like an eternity, or rather, like one single moment that will not let go, that refuses to move on, as though time itself has stopped dead in its tracks.

She has a vague recollection of hurling herself at the soldiers as they hauled the crossbeam into place. Of ripping at her thin shift, trying to tear it away from her body. Of hearing the pleas pour out of her: "Take me. Take me instead!" The other women reached to hold her back as the soldiers jeered and then taunted her with stinging obscenities. "He's my only son," she cried. "My one and only son. Just let him live, that's all I ask, and you can do anything you like with me. Anything at all!"

And the soldiers laughed and turned their backs on her.

What else could she expect? These soldiers are from the Antonia fortress, the Roman garrison overlooking the temple. Mercenaries from Syria, they're crude men—men who hate being here and so hate the people who are the reason for their being here. What do they care for a desperate mother's pleas? They've seen and heard it all hundreds of times before.

Maybe they never knew their mothers. Never had a mother's voice to tell them stories as they drifted into sleep. She sees her young child's eyes shining as she tells him stories Salome had told her when she herself was young, open-ended parables creating mysteries to sleep on. Remembers him fascinated by the story of the prodigal son who "was lost and now is found." Or begging for her to tell him more even as he sank into sleep with the parable of the wedding feast echoing in his mind: "For many are called, but few are chosen." There was a look of determination on his face then, strangely adult in one so young. And when she told the stories of Hezekiah and his brave resistance fighters, that look would turn fierce, and he'd fall asleep frowning slightly. He dreamed then, she thought, of freedom, of liberty and justice for all. As though he could change the world.

Is this, then, what he was chosen for? The sun still shines over Golgotha as though nothing is happening. The world is not changed. People go in and out of the city gate and look the other way. Some of the soldiers are throwing dice, gambling to pass the time, seemingly deaf to wracked breath rasping out of tortured lungs.

The end must be near, surely. To her horror, she finds herself praying for her son to die—praying to the sky, to the air, to the hills, to whatever power in heaven or on earth can put a stop to this. Death, she knows, is the only way out of the agony. For him, that is. For her, it will continue. That is the curse of the survivor.

Perhaps she should never have taught him what she knew. Never have answered his questions as she and Salome prepared their herbs. Yet he was so quick and apt a student, as though the healing power were in him all the time, just waiting for her to release it. She remembers her pride at the deftness with which he first mixed powdered yellow clay with saliva, as though he had been doing it all his young life. The assurance with which he laid the mixture on the pus-covered eyes of a newborn lamb. The calm nod he gave when the lamb's eyes healed, as though he had never entertained the idea that they would not.

That pride was dangerous, she realizes. What healing can there be now?

One of her son's followers approaches the gambling soldiers. He walks with the air of authority that comes from wealth. Joseph, she remembers his name is, Joseph of Arimathea. They talk briefly. One of the soldiers stands, and something glints in the sun as it changes hands: a gold coin. The soldier goes up to the cross her son is on.

There's a sudden movement. A flash of metal thrusting into her son's side.

She gasps as though the spear had entered her own flesh. As though that were her own blood running free from the jagged wound. Her own head lolling. Her own cry of pain no more than a barely audible sigh.

The soldier wipes his spear on the ground and spits in disgust, and something about that gesture snaps her immobility. She breaks free of the cordon of women around her and runs for the cross. All she knows is that she must get as close as she can, reach out and touch her son one last time. She hurls herself at the foot of the upright, arms around it as though they were already trying to pry her away. Looks up and sees her son's bloodshot eyes staring down at her.

What she sees there terrifies her. They are the eyes of a stranger who has slept at her breast. The eyes of a gentle man subjected to excruciating violence. Of a son so far gone that he no longer even recognizes his mother. Hanging onto this world by a thread, he seems to be looking over the edge of a chasm so deep there is no end to it.

She hears a sound that seems to come from all around her—a long low moan, more primitive, more primeval, than any she has ever heard before. She has heard animals in mortal pain, she has heard women in childbirth, she has heard far too many times the agonized groans of men hanging on crosses. But never has she heard a sound as terrible as this. It is a sound to make the hairs stand up all over your body, to make you shiver uncontrollably in the hottest of heat waves. A sound to penetrate deep into the soul of anyone within earshot, to lodge there and haunt you until the day you die.

And slowly, it dawns on her that her mouth is open, and that this terrible sound is her own. It surges up from the very depths of her being, born out of her into an uncaring world.

Walk around the Israel Museum in Jerusalem, and without warning, you find yourself staring at a human ankle bone, hung on a wall at just about eye level. It seems almost innocuous, if oddly out of place—this is not the Museum of Natural History, after all—until you realize that there is a nail stuck right through the bone. A crude six-inch nail. And then you realize that the nail is there because it is bent, and so couldn't be pulled out to be re-used on the next victim.

The shock that goes through you is visceral. You feel your stomach rising. The hairs stand up on your arms. For the first time, the reality of crucifixion is literally right before your eyes.

It is a ghastly one. Even today, when methods of torture have become "sophisticated" by comparison, the very idea of crucifixion still produces a shudder of horror. Not the crucifix itself, which is an icon. Nor even paintings of Christ on the cross, with their strange mix of the pious and the erotic. But the physical evidence of crucifixion is another thing altogether. It was an excruciating way to die.

They used iron nails. Not always, mind. Sometimes they just tied the victims to the crossbeam with rope. Others, they nailed only the hands. Others again, both hands and feet. The owner of that ankle bone in the Israel Museum had his feet nailed either side of the upright.

Some of the uprights had a footrest, but there was no respite in that. The footrest just prolonged the agony. The tortured man would try to balance on it in a doomed battle to retain muscle control. In a feat of endurance that he had no choice but to perform, his muscles automatically struggled to hold his weight and prevent him from hanging by his arms alone. But they could only do this for so long. Eventually, inevitably, they gave way, and then what killed him—after a few hours if he was fortunate enough to be weak, a few days if he was unfortunate enough to be strong—was asphyxiation. The trapezius, the rhomboids, the deltoids, all the muscles of his shoulders and back and chest failed, and then the weight of his body hanging from the shoulders collapsed his ribcage, blocking his windpipe and his lungs and cutting off his breathing. In effect, he was killed by his own body.

If he was lucky, he would be flogged first. Yes, lucky. The flogging would weaken him, so that he'd die quicker. And this was an essential part of the horror of crucifixion. It made preliminary torture into a mercy. It turned things topsy-turvy, so that what now seems cruel was in fact kind, and vice versa. The footrest made death more drawn-out and more agonizing; flogging made it quicker and easier. Crucifixion attacked not only the body of the victim, but also the most basic concepts of human morality.

Sometimes the soldiers in charge of the crucifixions would thrust a spear into the side of the man on the cross, who would then die quickly from loss of blood. Others, they'd take a club and break his knees or his shin bones, so that he couldn't use his legs to support his weight, and so died quicker. But these were not acts of mercy. The soldiers may have been bribed by relatives to hasten death. Or they simply wanted to entertain themselves, like young psychopaths torturing a helpless animal, which is why they'd sometimes hang people on the crosses upside down, or even in obscene positions. They may have done it out of mere boredom—anything to liven up the slow, drawn-out process. Or perhaps it was simple impatience—they wanted to get back to their beds or to their supper, and they were tired of the sounds and the stench of the dying.

That stench is one detail that is rarely mentioned. Crucifixion was an utterly humiliating way to die, not the least because the victim would lose control of his sphincter muscles, and in plain sight of all who cared to look. Again, religious paintings of Jesus' crucifixion are misleading; out of respect, or perhaps simply wishful thinking, they show him wearing a loincloth, although those being crucified were usually stripped naked before being nailed or tied to the crossbeam. It was a stripping away of whatever remnants of dignity a victim might have managed to retain up to that point. All he could hope for then was the inadvertent kindness of a spear to the side or a blow across the knees, and a quick death—in hours, that is, instead of days.

Nobody knows exactly how many people were crucified in Palestine during the years of Roman control, but it is safe to say that it was in the thousands. Crucifixions were rarely individual affairs, or even, as in the traditional representation of Jesus' crucifixion, a mere three at a time. In 4 B.C., the Roman general Varus dealt with the uprising that followed the death of Herod the Great by having two thousand "troublemakers" crucified in Jerusalem alone—a number that, in a city of perhaps fifty thousand, was literally a decimation of the male population. Add all the crucifixions mentioned by the historian Josephus during the several Judean rebellions against Roman rule, and you find almost ten thousand. And this total does not take account of the unknown thousands of crucifixions carried out in relatively normal times, whether for common crimes of urban poverty, like petty theft, or for real or imagined crimes against the state.

Individual suffering was not the real point of crucifixion, however. The real point was the display of total, ruthless power, along with the corollary of that display: the creation of fear in those who witnessed it—fear not only of the death itself, but of its sudden, merciless application.

There were no trials. No due process. No defense. You could literally be grabbed out of the fields or off the street, be identified, whether rightly or wrongly, as a threat to imperial property, public order, or state security, and be hung by the arms until dead. "Justice" Roman-occupation style was swift and ruthless.

Inevitably, totally innocent people were crucified. Some were simply in the wrong place at the wrong time, as was Joseph in José Saramago's novel *The Gospel According to Jesus Christ*. Many others were guilty of nothing more than voicing an opinion, being related to the wrong person, or having incurred the enmity of someone who then accused them of inciting rebellion against Rome. Guilt was not the issue; power was. The fear this engendered was, and still is, the main weapon of a totalitarian state, where the aim is to keep the population subdued and compliant, forestalling even the possibility of opposition.

As biblical historians Richard Horsley and Neil Asher Silberman put it: "Crucifixion was one of the purest forms of governmental violence. It was as much communal punishment and state-sponsored terrorism as it was judicial vengeance against a particular crime . . . The crosses planted outside the cities warned potential rebels, runaway slaves, and rebellious prophets of what could happen to them." Warned them, that is, and anyone who aided and abetted them.

Crucifixion had been used this way for hundreds of years by

Maryam's time. The Romans probably adopted it from the Carthaginians, though we know it was also used by the Persians, and before them by the Assyrians and the Scythians. It had even been used by Judeans against Judeans.

The Temple Scroll, part of the cache of Essene scrolls found at Qumran on the Dead Sea, lists "hanging from a tree" as punishment for betrayal of the group. And though it is unclear if the Essenes ever carried out the punishment, it is very clear that the Hasmoneans made what could be called liberal use of it during their hundred-year regime. Alexander Janneus, for example, one of the most expansionist and tyrannical Hasmonean rulers, had eight hundred captives crucified as entertainment while he feasted with his concubines.

Throughout the Mediterranean and the Middle East, hundreds of thousands of people—mainly men, but occasionally women too—were put to death this way. The crosses were the inevitable aftermath of slave rebellions in Rome or Carthage, or of popular uprisings in Palestine or Alexandria. But for all its deliberate ghastliness and humiliation, crucifixion was far from a shameful death. On the contrary, it was the punishment for daring to dream of freedom.

"Anyone who was put to death by Pontius Pilate—one of the most notorious thugs in the history of the Roman empire—would have been a hero," as A. N. Wilson noted. He was no longer merely a victim, but part of something much larger. The punishment intended to deter resistance instead inspired more of it. To knowingly risk such a death was the ultimate badge of courage.

By the time Maryam stood vigil at the foot of the cross, crucifixion had become the symbol of resistance. Ever since childhood, when she saw the rebels occupying the garrison town of Sepphoris crucified en masse, she had known that this was the fate of the noblest and the bravest. That sight had created in her what it created in so many others of her time: not the submissive resignation that the Romans intended, but quite the opposite. Like others, she came away full of a fierce despair, committed more strongly than ever to the idea of rising up against oppression, no matter how many lives that might cost.

As in modern Palestine, so two thousand years ago, shame was converted into honor, humiliation into pride. To be killed in the struggle for independence was to achieve a form of immortality. It was to be celebrated in song and story as a death chosen rather than one imposed. Whoever died this way became a model to be emulated by others, his death seen not merely as a physical sacrifice, but as a metaphysical one. His life would be glorified, elaborated, mythologized. He would become greater in death than he ever had been in life. He would become a martyr.

Then as now, the figure of the martyr rose out of the combustible mix of politics and religion. Inevitably, legends were born out of that mix. What actually happened was not nearly as real as what should have happened. As the legends were told again and again, they were embroidered, shaped, honed to the purpose of their telling, until they reflected more about the thoughts and desires of those telling them and listening to them than about the events they related.

When the gospel writers took pen to parchment to record the story of Jesus' life and death some three generations later, they did not set out to write fiction; but neither did they intend to record history. Their concern was theology, and their aim was to do what only theology can do: to create new life out of death. They wrote to inspire their readers by linking what had happened to what had been foretold. Or, as the John and Matthew authors wrote repeatedly, "to fulfill the words of the prophet" and "to fulfill the scripture."

The gospel accounts of the crucifixion refer back again and again to the Hebrew bible. Jesus' last words in Matthew—"My God, my God, why hast thou forsaken me"—are from the start of Psalm 22. His last words in Luke—"Father, into thy hands I commit my spirit"—are from Psalm 31. The "darkness over the land" is from Amos; entering the city on "the foal of an ass" from Zechariah; the vinegar-soaked sponge from Psalm 69; the pierced hands and feet, along with the casting of lots for the garments, from Psalm 22. As always, those seeking signs of scripture revealed, could find them. The gospels provided what biblical scholar John Dominic Crossan has called "prophecy historicized."

Most scholars now agree that there could have been no trial in front of Pontius Pilate. There would be no reason for a peasant preacher like Jesus to be taken high up the chain of command for formal interrogation, let alone for trial. There was no earthquake as Jesus neared death, no eclipse of the sun, no rending of the great temple curtain at the entrance to the holy of holies. These are all things that should have been, and so, in the telling, became. Like the massacre of the innocents, like the flight into Egypt, like the visits of the three magi, they were all part of what Joseph Campbell called "the adventure of the hero."

"Those who told the story to each other in this way would have known very well that such details were not 'historical,'" says historian James Carroll. "They would have known, say, that the 'seamless robe' had nothing to do with the robe Jesus wore but was an allusion-rich metaphor, since the only figure who wore such a robe was the high priest, and only upon entering the holy of holies. To that first circle, such details proved nothing. The point was not 'proof,' it was expression. The point was lament. The point was grief. The point was drawing order out of chaos, out of the worst thing that could have happened. The point was the story."

Yet if prophecy was historicized in this manner, there was also a strong element of self-fulfilling prophecy in the death of Jesus. Certainly Maryam can have been in little doubt that sooner or later, and probably sooner, she would see her son crucified. He was an activist preaching equality and justice; he had gathered a following, albeit only in the northern province of Galilee; now he was publicly baiting the powers-that-be on their own turf, Jerusalem. Every step he took seemed to be leading inexorably to Golgotha.

His message of the poor and the downtrodden reclaiming the kingdom was downright subversive in the ears of the wealthy elite.

To take this message to Jerusalem at Passover could only have been seen as a deliberate provocation. Since Passover celebrated the classic liberation tale of the exodus from Egypt, it was always a time of high political tension, with the Herodian military out in force and ultra-alert for any signs of disturbance. Overturning the money changers' tables in the temple forecourt could have only one result: arrest, and execution.

Maryam must have been steeling herself against this eventuality for months, if not years. She must have hoped against hope that it would never happen, even as she knew it was inevitable. But knowing it was coming would not have made it any easier to bear. On the contrary, it would have been all the harder. She was living her own nightmare, face to face with the worst thing that could possibly happen to a mother: the death of her child.

Strangely, Maryam never seems to age in all the great paintings of the *pietà*, where she cradles her dead son in her arms. She still looks as young and fresh-faced as at the Annunciation. Yet even by conventional reckoning, she was forty-six years old—old enough in her time for her hair to have turned gray and her face to be deeply lined with time and weather and experience.

Forty-six was indeed old by the standards of Palestinian peasant life two thousand years ago, and yet we know Maryam was in good health: how else could she have followed her son as he wandered around Galilee and trekked to Jerusalem? Far more likely, however, she was ten years younger: only thirty-six.

We know she was thirteen when she became pregnant. We also know—or think we know—that Jesus was thirty-three in 30 A.D., the year of his crucifixion. But this assumes that he was born in the year 4 B.C., and this assumption has been increasingly questioned by biblical historians. Most will now say only that Jesus was born somewhere between 4 B.C. and 6 A.D.

The earlier date was seized on for one major reason. If Jesus was born "in the days of Herod the king," as Matthew puts it, then it had to be by the year 4 B.C. at the latest, since that was the year Herod the Great died.

But there was more than one Herod who was king. After Herod the Great's death, the Romans divided his territory among his three surviving sons, making each one a client ruler with the title "Herod the king." The oldest, Herod Archelaus, got Judea, but only for ten years until the Romans banished him to Gaul and appointed a series of procurators, or sub-governors, to run the province under the direction of the Roman governor of Syria. (The most infamous of these procurators would be Pontius Pilate, who served from 26 A.D. 36 A.D.) The second son, Herod Philip, got Iturea, in what is now southern Lebanon and Syria. It was the youngest of the three—Herod Antipas—who got Galilee, and ruled it throughout Jesus' lifetime. And this is the Herod whom the gospels conflated with his father, Herod the Great.

The Matthew story of the massacre of the innocents at the birth of Jesus should surely peg the year to Herod the Great's reign, except that there is no historical evidence of his ever ordering all newborn males in the area of Bethlehem to be killed. The story, however, was almost bound to develop. Historian E. Mary Smallwood calls it "a typical tyrant-legend of the kind which readily grows up posthumously to blacken the memory of a hated despot." Matthew's account of Jesus' escape from the massacre—the unlikely flight all the way south into Egypt—was "typical of the stories of miraculous escapes from danger which cluster around the infancy of great men."

The only real indication of the year of Jesus' birth, in that case, is the census—the given reason for Mary and Joseph's journey to Bethlehem. In the gospel of Luke, this took place when "Herod, king of Judea" was in power, at the order of Quirinius, the Roman governor of Syria. But Quirinius (a.k.a. Cyrenius) was not governor in the reign of either Herod the Great or Herod Archelaus. He was only appointed in the year 6 A.D., after the Romans had deposed Archelaus. Josephus confirms in his *Antiquities of the Jews* that there was indeed a census that year, and certainly ordering a census for tax purposes would have been a logical first step for a new governor.

The Herod in question, then, had to be Antipas, the client king of Galilee. The year had to be 6 A.D., not 4 B.C., which makes Jesus twenty-one years old when he began preaching, and twenty-three when he was crucified.

There are thus no "missing years" in Jesus' life—no mysterious chronological gap in the gospel accounts such as has been assumed by those in constant search of the esoteric. There is no need for fanciful scenarios of Jesus learning the secrets of sorcery in India or China. In fact, such scenarios are self-defeating. In the reality of first-century Galilee, peasant villagers would have nothing to do with a thirty-one-year-old preacher and miracle worker who had suddenly appeared in foreign dress and with foreign notions. Jesus attracted followers because he was of his time and place, because he spoke to people's immediate concerns. He was one of their own, speaking in the Galilean peasant accent, in the language of the great Israelite prophets. And at twenty-one, he had all the energy, idealism, and audacity of his age—the very qualities so clearly in evidence in the gospels.

He would be executed two years later, and that means that Maryam was thirty-six years old when she stood at the foot of the cross. In modern terms, she was still a young woman; in the terms of her own time, she was the equivalent of a western woman in her early fifties today, with a sure sense of her own strength and power and ability. All of which she would need now.

How does a mother survive watching her child die in such a way? She survives, of course, in the most literal sense, but how does a large part of her not die with him when she sees him reduced to tortured helplessness? She feels his agony as her own even as she knows that hers can be only a fragment of his. And then she has to endure the almost greater agony of being unable to help. Forced into passivity, jeered at by soldiers, what can she do?

She rails, of course. Cries out and curses and protests until she is so hoarse the words stifle in her throat. She weeps, though her tear ducts have long dried up and she cries on empty. And those around her both encourage and expect her to do this. Crucifixion is the most public of deaths, and so her grief, whether she wants it or not, is the most public of griefs.

Anyone who has been close to a mother whose child is killed in war has seen how the personal is subsumed into the national. The sheer wrongness of a child dying before his parent is terrible enough, but then the mother has to deal with an extra level of horror: the onus of being the center of attention when all she wants to do is curl up in a ball and die herself.

You can see it happening at the funeral of an eighteen-year-old Israeli soldier. Or of teenage terror victims cut down doing something as normal as buying a slice of pizza or hanging out at the mall. Or of a young Palestinian olive farmer shot dead as he tried to harvest his trees, or a ten-year-old killed for throwing stones at a tank, or a five-year-old who stuck her head out the door during curfew only to encounter a bullet. The worst of all: the terrible pathos of the funeral of a very young child, the corpse tiny under the shroud used in both Moslem and Jewish burials.

You see the family gathered tight around the grave—the extended family, for every family at such times, even the most westernized one, becomes extended, ignoring degrees of removal and stretching out to encompass first cousins, second cousins, in-laws, great-aunts, all manner of relatives by marriage as well as by blood. And crowded in on the family are the human vultures—not just the media, but the hangers-on, the ones who are always there in times of tragedy and loss. They feed off it, pressing forward to get their faces in the photographer's lens, inflating their sense of self-importance by being part of the action and assuming someone else's tragedy as their own. Some do it for political reasons, some for pathological ones. For most, it's an odd mixture of the two. They are reacting, without necessarily knowing it, to a terrible truth: violent death brings people to life. It brings them together. It unites them in adversity.

And at the center, always, is the mother. Whether veiled and stoic, or beside herself with grief, the focus is on her.

The private is made unutterably, nakedly public. Even her tears are used to rouse the anger or compassion of others. She barely notices the cameras until later, when she sees the pictures of herself and is appalled. How could she not be? Being photographed as she mourns—her features distorted, her clothes disheveled, her whole body bent in pain—is surely one of the deepest invasions of privacy. It is as though the camera itself were trying to steal her grief.

In the days following the funeral, the flow of people coming to pay their respects is more disconcerting than comforting. Sometimes she doesn't even know their names. Total strangers hold her hand, hug her, stare deep into her eyes as though they understand. She knows they don't, knows they can't, but mourning has weakened her, and she hasn't the strength to rebuff them.

She realizes that they are merely trying to make her feel better. Or more likely, make themselves feel better. They mean well. Most of them, at any rate. But she also knows the simple, raw truth that is the province of every grieving mother: no consolation is possible. There is no such thing for the death of a child.

The comforters fall back on the repeated reassurance that this shall not be for nothing. He died the doing right thing, they tell her. He died for his country. For honor. For freedom. For justice. He is in heaven along with the martyrs or the saints or the angels. Rest assured that he will be revenged.

Yet she does not rest assured. She does not rest at all. Her son has suddenly been elevated into some kind of superior being, and she feels now as if he has been taken from her a second time—first by death, and then again by all those who claim her grief as their own. She tries to tell the comforters that revenge is pointless. That nothing anyone can do will bring her child back to life. It is all in vain. Every violent death of every human being. Each one an affront to justice, to freedom, to humanity itself. She feels that terrifying, primordial wail rising up again within her, from a place so deep it seems as though the whole earth is crying out in protest and despair. As it takes hold of her, she has no illusions of grace under pressure. She knows only one thing for sure, and that is that this death is wrong, wrong, wrong.

That artistic image of a calm and composed Maryam cradling her dead son with a look of infinite compassion may be well-intentioned, but it has the effect of a cruel lie. To think of her as stoic and accepting in her grief is not just to deprive her of the capacity to mourn; it is to deny her humanity.

Let us at least allow her to feel and express real grief. Let us give her the relief of being able to cry out loud, to rail against the forces who committed this crime, against the fates or the gods or Yahweh or the Romans or Herod or the temple, whomever she chooses—all of them guilty in her eyes. Let us hear her loud and long, in that animal wail so piercing that even if we cover our ears it still penetrates deep inside us, like an iron nail piercing the heart.

And then let us ask what she does with that grief.

IX

Several women push together to roll back the entrance stone, unsealing the mouth of the tomb. Big rounded stones like this one are essential: they stop jackals and hyenas from finding their way in and ripping the bodies apart. One woman wedges a rock under the stone to keep it in place, then two others stoop down and slip through the narrow entrance to the tomb. Those outside hand the body through to them.

They work well together; they've done this before, many times. Burial is women's work. The women who bring others into life, also escort them into death.

Inside, the dry smell of disintegrating bones mixes with the fusty dankness of decomposing flesh. The women pull their shawls over their mouths and noses. The flames of their oil lamps flicker in the close, dense air, giving just enough light to scan the deep niches carved into the rock walls, seeking out an empty one.

This is how burial is done in an arid land. Soil is too precious to waste on the dead. Bodies are placed in the coffin-sized niches for the first year, until the flesh has dried to dust. Then the bones are removed from the niches—or if the family is wealthy, placed in a small stone box—leaving the spaces free for the next occupants.

Bones are stacked high against the far wall, where they glimmer whitely in the faint light. They have been neatly sorted and arranged, like to like, the better to save space. Piled arm bones and leg bones and skulls each make their own separate patterns, as though order can be retrieved in the vast disorder of death.

The women have already prepared the body. They have sponged away the blood and the dirt, straightened the arms and legs, combed the hair. They have anointed him with herbal balms and spices—anointed him in death as they anointed him in life, with myrrh and aloe and the purest olive oil—then wrapped him in a linen shroud, leaving only his head bare. They have intoned psalms, and wept, and keened. Now there are no tears left.

Working in silence, they lift the body feet first onto the stone slab of an empty niche, then push it slowly in. As she watches them, it seems to Maryam that they are returning her son to the womb, only now the womb is made not of her own live flesh, but of unforgiving, unyielding stone.

The other women stand back. They take shallow breaths, as one does in tombs, fearful of breathing in the dust of others. But not Maryam. She breathes deep, closes her eyes a moment, prepares herself. Then steps forward.

Slowly, deliberately, she places her hands on her son's head: palms either side, thumbs towards the crown, fingers spread over his temples, his ears, the base of his skull. She cradles his head. And staring straight ahead into the blank darkness of rock, she lets the weight of her hands press down into him.

She feels the warmth and pulse of her own blood against his skull, and presses harder. Her whole world is in this moment, her whole being flowing down into her palms and her fingers. The flesh beneath her hands seems to drain the warmth out of them, soaking it up. If she can just press hard enough, surely the life in her can cross the seemingly impermeable barrier of death. She gave him life once; surely she can give him life again.

The veins jump in her arms. Her muscles tremble with the effort. Holding him like this, the weight of his head in her hands, it is as though she can be the midwife to her own son—as though with one deft twist of the wrists at just the right moment she can pull him out of this rock womb and back into the world. Her palms seem to vibrate with the power of it. Her whole body leans into its work. She closes her eyes and feels breath surging through him, blood flowing, life returning . . .

She feels a hand in the small of her back, the presence of the Magdalene behind her. Time to let go now, the hand says. She takes one more deep breath, and on the exhalation, lets go.

Christianity begins with these women. Not with Paul or with Peter or with any of the coming succession of saints and popes, but with these women in the tomb. They are the founding core of Christianity: the last to see the body of Jesus and the first to see him resurrected.

That they were even able to bury him is unusual. Burial of a crucified man was so rare that the only physical remnant is that one skeletal ankle of a crucified man found in Jerusalem, with the bent nail stuck in the bone. And this lack of burial was deliberate; it was part of the continuing horror of such a death.

The bodies were left to hang for days, even weeks. They rotted on the crossbeams, where anyone who entered or left the city could see them. If the wind turned to come from the west, those inside the city walls could smell them too. Even unseen, they were a constant presence.

The soldiers who had to take them down must have loathed the job. Up close, the stench was abominable, the sight truly ghastly. Eyes pecked out by vultures and buzzards, the bodies were crawling with maggots. Disposing of them was the lowest of duties, a means of disciplining the soldiers assigned to the task. They turned their resentment against the dead, mutilating them and urinating on them before finally tossing them into a nearby ravine for the jackals and hyenas to rip at. Anyone who tried to recover the corpses would themselves be crucified.

Once the bones were picked clean, they bleached in the summer sun and eroded in the winter wind and rain, and eventually, in the ancient biblical recognition of the fate of all life, disintegrated into dust.

This made no difference to the dead, of course, but it did to the living. It was believed that a body left unburied would doom the soul to wander restlessly for eternity. Throughout the Hebrew bible, a corpse eaten by birds and beasts of prey was a thing of horror—the fate of the faithless and of idolators. Even if all that remained was bones, they were carefully buried, as the bones of Joseph brought home from Egypt to Canaan. The king of Moab burned the bones of his enemy to drive home his vengeance, just as Josiah would exhume and burn the bones of idolators. Even today, small pebbles are still placed on Jewish graves so as to keep the spirit in and prevent it from wandering.

Jesus was saved from such a fate by one of the wealthiest of his followers—another Joseph stepping in to the rescue. It is unlikely that Joseph of Arimathea simply asked Pilate to give him the body, as the gospel accounts maintain. More likely, money worked two thousand years ago as it still does today; it made otherwise impossible things possible. The soldiers on crucifixion duty were as badly paid and as bribable as such guards anywhere, at any time. The right sum could ensure turned backs as the body was brought down from the cross, blind eyes as it was handed over to the women.

The women performed their traditional tasks, washing the body and rubbing it with olive oil from the tree that lived thousands of years, the tree they thought of as immortal. They called the perfumed oil *mishcha*, "anointing oil," for it was also used to anoint kings. The anointed man was thus the *mashiach*, the messiah, "he who is anointed." When translated into Greek, the term would retain its original meaning: *Christos* refers to the chrism, the oil used for anointing.

Once they'd prepared the body, the women wrapped it in a shroud and brought it to the tomb. Yet did they really want this soul to rest? They were wise, these women, as versed in matters of death as they were in matters of birth. They were surely aware of the paradox that a restless soul is one that lives on. They grieved over the body as Isis had done for Osiris, Ishtar for Tammuz, Anath for Baal, Cybele for Attis, knowing that in each of those instances, the dead had been resurrected by the power of a woman's grief.

At their center was Maryam. How not? That is only as it should be, for a grieving mother exerts a moral authority that even a grieving widow does not. She has known this child longer than any other person. She delivered him in pain, nursed and raised and loved him in steadfastness. Her own flesh and blood has died, and the tie of the womb is nearly always stronger than chosen ties of love when it comes to the status of grief. For there is indeed status in grief. It is the hardest won status of all, and any mother would give her own life to be free of it. But once the burden of it has been placed on her, if she is strong, she will find out how to use it for the best. She will fight for her child, even in death.

For her own sake, she has to do this, as well as for her child's. The alternative is to be reduced to grief and nightmares for the rest of her life. Maryam could not save her son. She could not offer herself up in his place. But she could still act. She could break free of the passive role of the witness, and make it into an active one.

"Do not let this pass unnoticed," she must have urged herself. "Do not be the quietly suffering one. Do not, above all, be silent."

And then, having determined what she would not do, decided on what she would: "Make your voice heard. Make this sacrifice count. Make it matter in the world."

In our own time, this is what the Mothers of the Disappeared did—those mothers who banded together during the "dirty war" waged by the Argentine junta against its own civilians from 1976 to 1983. Refusing to be cowed, defying the violent imperative to silence, they marched and demonstrated, demanding that the government be held to account for the disappearance of their children into torture cells and unmarked graves. They persisted, week after week, year after year. And though they couldn't bring their children back, they helped bring about what their children had died for: the downfall of the junta.

Such action takes strength, courage, and determination. It must seem easier by far to be passive—to retire into grief, hide from the public role of bereaved mother, and leave it to the comforters to go about their work. And there are certainly times when any activist mother may wish that is exactly what she had done, when the struggle seems too hard and long and even hopeless. Yet at the same time, she knows that to abandon the public role granted her at such a price would be to betray everything her child had stood for—and died for.

Maryam could not prevent her son's execution, but once it had happened, she would at least ensure that it not be in vain. She would accept the authority of her grief. She would help transform her loss. Through her son's death, she would give renewed meaning to life. In her own way, she would ensure his resurrection.

This is how we know it was, in our bones. Yet the gospels do not confirm it. Amazingly—shockingly—neither Matthew nor Mark nor Luke even places Maryam at the crucifixion, let alone at the burial or the resurrection. Instead, they show us what Marina Warner has aptly called "a muddle of Marys."

There is the Magdalene, of course, the only one who is given the honorific surname of the town she comes from, Magdala. Then there is Mary the mother of James and Joses, as well as Mary the wife of Cleopas, and finally the mysterious and utterly intriguing figure who appears in Matthew: "the other Mary."

The casualness of that phrase is stunning, and yet also somehow real. No fiction-writer would ever let it go at that; no editor would let it pass. A good story-teller would be sure to pin her down, even as a minor character. But not the Matthew author. It's as though we have tuned in to the story halfway through the narrative, and everyone already knows who "the other Mary" is. The author has forgotten that people will read this centuries on, in other languages and in other parts of the world—or rather, he is completely unaware of it—so he doesn't bother to say exactly which Mary he's referring to. The result is that she's been lost. Slipping through the mesh of history without any identifying mark, she's a poor relation, in a way, of Maryam herself.

She is certainly not the Magdalene Mary, for the Magdalene is already there, fully named. She could be the sister of Lazarus—the Mary, that is, of Mary and Martha—but then why not say so? She might be a Mary whose existence was gradually edited out of the gospels except for this one remaining reference in passing. Or perhaps "the other Mary" is a term of sexual significance, as in "the other woman." Or a term of insignificance, as in "that other one—you know, what's-her-name."

"The other Mary" couldn't, surely, be the Matthew author's way of referring to Maryam, to the mother of the man hanging on the cross? Surely she couldn't have been merely one of the "many women which came up with him into Jerusalem" in Mark? Yet what are we to think when she appears at the crucifixion only in John, the last of the four canonical gospels to be written and the one most removed from her in both time and place?

It seems an incredible omission. Almost an insult. And it becomes all the more incredible when you realize that the only named woman who appears at the crucifixion in all four canonical gospels is the Magdalene. Not the virgin, but the sinner.

This seems patently unjust. Maryam should be right there, at the center of the scene. She should have been there all along, instead of having to wait for John to place her there nearly seventy years later. How could this have happened? All those paintings of the *pietà*, all the images of the grieving mother cradling her dead son in her lap, do they show the wrong Maryam? Have we all, through the centuries, indulged in an act of collective unconscious wish fulfillment, and replaced what actually was with what we think should have been?

"Jezebel, Jezebel, fornicating under the walls of God's holy city!"

To be accosted this way by an irate stranger on an otherwise beautiful Jerusalem morning was not the best way to start the day. This middle-aged man seemed determined to denounce my imagined sins to both heaven and earth. He trailed me, ranting and raving all the while, as far as the walls of the Old City, when he finally gave up and turned back, doubtless to find another sinner.

He was mad, to be sure, but in a way that was entirely within the tradition of the place. What he saw was a woman with no shawl, no wig, no form of head-covering such as religious women wear: a secular woman walking alone. That could only mean that I was another Jezebel out to pollute holiness.

He might, however, have studied his bible a little closer. Fornication was not Jezebel's sin. She was neither an adulteress nor a prostitute, but a queen—an Israelite queen who had been devoted to pagan worship some twenty-seven centuries earlier, and for that reason was opposed and cursed by the prophet Elijah. Her sin was religious, not sexual. She had prostituted herself to false gods.

In the Middle East, calling someone a whore is a favored insult, whether they are male or female. It is a long tradition. The Hebrew prophets consistently use the harlot as the paradigm of unfaithfulness to Yahweh, accusing Israelites of "whoredom" with other gods. "Fornication," "harlotry," and "adultery" are all used interchangeably with "pagan worship," to the degree that if you read too literally, you might think of life at the time as one giant sexual orgy.

Using sexual metaphor as a means of denigration is a tradition that has persisted through the centuries. Accusations of being a whore—or the son or the daughter of one—are common slurs in today's Middle East, cast about with the same ease and relish as four-letter words in an American gang neighborhood. The difference is that in the Middle East, now as two thousand years ago, they also have strong political overtones. In the West Bank and Gaza, the radical Islamic group Hamas calls any woman who dares criticize its policies a prostitute. Her real crime is the same as it would have been in biblical times. It is a conceptual whoredom, as it were—a straying from the single path of righteous faith. It is the crime of possessing an independent mind in a world where politics is determined by claims of divine dictate.

The Magdalene is such a woman, the only one among Jesus'

followers who is not identified by her relationship to a man. She is no man's mother or sister or wife or daughter. As Susan Haskins has pointed out in her biography of her, she was probably a woman of some means—one of Jesus' less impoverished followers, that is, and a model for the many women Paul would later single out for honorable mention in his letters.

Yet three of the New Testament gospels first mention her only at the crucifixion. She makes no appearance until then, and there is no indication of how or why she would assume such a central role at this critical point in time. Only Luke identifies her earlier on as the woman ''from whom seven demons had gone out.'' Exorcized by Jesus? Luke does not say, though if it were so, he would presumably have shown the scene.

This is the only hint in the gospels of a troubled past for the Magdalene, and it is, to say the least, an ambiguous one. What were these demons? Had she been mad, or physically sick? Or perhaps heartbroken? The eastern Orthodox tradition reflected in Khiyr's re-telling of her story over the stone wall of Magdala has her driven to despair when her fiancé leaves her to follow Jesus. It sees the Magdalene not as a woman of abandon, but as an abandoned woman, sinned against as much as sinning.

Indeed, why would anyone assume from the meager gospel evidence that she had been a prostitute at all? The gospel writers were quite open about adultery and menstruation; there was no reason not to say that the Magdalene was a prostitute if it were so. On the contrary, it would be worth emphasizing as part of the message that the shunned would be welcomed and included, the sinful made pure.

In fact, the Magdalene's presumed sinfulness only developed as the church itself developed. True to Paul's dictum that ''in Christ there is neither male nor female,'' early Christian women preached, prophe-sized, baptized, and officiated as priests and bishops alongside men, free from any ''stain'' of sinful sexuality. They did so in a wide variety of Christian movements throughout the eastern Mediterranean. But as

orthodoxy was established, gaining both official recognition and political clout after the conversion of the emperor Constantine, the role of
women was severely curtailed. Religion might be a sphere for both men
and women, but politics was strictly for men.

In what theologian Harvey Cox calls "the most successful attempt by
any religious hierarchy in history to channel, defuse, and control
female religious symbolism," strong female images were cut down
to size. Latin theologians began to identify the Magdalene first with the
unnamed sinner who anointed Jesus' feet in Luke, then with the
adulteress in John, and finally with the many-husbanded Samaritan
woman in John. She became a kind of repository of sinful sexuality—
the mirror image of the Nazarene Maryam. As the one was restricted to
the now familiar image of the Madonna, so the other was straitjacketed
into the equally familiar one of the whore.

Any writings indicating a greater role were buried, burned, or simply
abandoned as orthodoxy imposed itself. The gospels we know as the
first four books of the New Testament are, as historian Keith Hopkins
puts it, "only a small fragment of early Christian history. In their time,
they had many competitors, nearly all of them now lost. There were
local traditions of teaching and practice, collective memories orally
transmitted, written sources such as those the gospel writers themselves used, and the ones they did not use."

But not all were lost. The gnostic gospels discovered in 1945 in
Nag Hammadi in Egypt, as well as a number of other early gospels
and writings, reveal at least some of the native Middle Eastern
traditions suppressed by the establishment of the universal Catholic
church in Rome. They are, as it were, alternative gospels, or to use
the title of one anthology, "the other Bible." And one of the most
striking things about them is the importance they accord the
Magdalene.

She is the one they state was closest and dearest to Jesus, the one he
loved better than all the other apostles and used to kiss on the mouth.
She is his consort, his lover. The gnostic gospel of Mary is her gospel,

not Maryam's, and as she passes on the special wisdom Jesus revealed to her, the male apostles can only listen and plead for more.

The gnostics honored the Magdalene as "the apostle to the apostles," since she was the first witness to the resurrection, and so it was she who brought the good news to the others. This makes her, in effect, the first Christian. For resurrection was essential to Christianity. It was the foundation stone. Divinity demanded it, as it was demanded in the immensely popular great mother religions throughout the Middle East.

Again and again, young male gods—Osiris, Tammuz, Attis—had to be sacrificed for the common good. All had to die so that both they and the earth could be born again. And all were given life again by the great female divine who defied human distinctions and was simultaneously virgin, mother, and lover. Simultaneously, that is, both the Nazarene Maryam and the Magdalene.

The two separate women gradually became one. Though the Greek-speaking writers of the gospels of Mark, Matthew, and Luke denied Maryam a presence at the crucifixion and the resurrection, those who wrote other gospels in Aramaic and Coptic and Armenian—the languages of the Middle East—placed her right there. They followed the logic of their hearts, and the spirit of their times. Who better to witness Jesus' resurrection than the woman who gave birth to him the first time? It would be inconceivably cruel to deny her that. Maryam does what they knew she should: she gives birth to her son, and buries her son.

"Mary received Jesus by conception, and saw an angel at his grave," wrote the lyrical fourth-century theologian Ephrem of Syria. An Armenian hymn from the same time was more specific: "It was she who bore the Son and gave him milk from her breast; it was she who sat at his feet and did him service by washing them; at the cross she was beside him, and in the resurrection she saw him."

She even becomes all possible Marys. In The Twentieth Discourse, a Coptic manuscript attributed to Cyril, archbishop of Jerusalem, Mary the virgin mother appears to the writer and declares: "I am Mary Magdalene, because I was born in Magdala. My name is Mary of Cleopas. I am Mary of James, the son of Joseph the carpenter."

And in what is possibly the ultimate melding of Marys, the gospel of Philip, recorded in the third century, says: "There were three who walked with the Lord at all times: Mary his mother and his sister, and Magdalene, whom they called his consort. For Mary was his sister and his mother and his consort."

The modern mind balks at such inclusiveness. "It is notorious that the early Christian world was in a state of inextricable confusion on the subject of the Marys in the gospels," says church scholar Robert Murray. But is it confusion or fusion? A muddle of Marys or a multiplicity of Marys? If we insist on reading the gospels as history, we end up bewildered. But if we can accept that the gospels were written as theology, then meanings emerge far beyond the literal ones.

Anthropologists may have the edge on historians here. Exploring a wide range of mythologies, Claude Lévi-Strauss identified a pattern he called "myth-splitting," in which a legendary figure gets divided into mirror images or twins. The same dynamic seems to be built into the structure of conceptual thought. The madonna and the whore, Eros and Thanatos, animus and anima, yin and yang, lightness and darkness, innocence and experience—all are dyads in which each part only gains its full meaning by being paired with its opposite. Perhaps it was inevitable, then, that as Christianity developed, it would obey this dynamic. The maternal would be separated from the sexual, the Nazarene played off against the Magdalene.

Two thousand years later, with their respective legends firmly developed, it may be shocking to even imagine that the mother and the lover could ever have been thought of as the same woman. We have internalized the separation of the maternal and the sexual to such a degree that it seems incredible they could coexist. And yet of course they do. To be a mother does not mean giving up one's sexuality. The maternal and the sexual are not mutually exclusive; they are different aspects of a woman's life.

Should we see the Magdalene as an aspect of Maryam herself or as another manifestation of her? As the complement to Maryam or as the antithesis? There can be no definitive answer, of course, but it seems to me that to even think in such dualities is to belittle both women—in fact, to belittle all women. The gnostics grasped a greater truth: in a very real sense, each and every one of the women at the tomb was Maryam, each one the loving, grieving mother, each one the wise woman gathering up her courage and her resolve, determined that this shall not be the end.

We will never know exactly what happened in the tomb, but we do know one thing for sure: it was the women who were there, and only the women. The male disciples had all fled.

The women placed Jesus in the tomb, kept watch, returned on the third day, and announced the resurrection. They, and only they, knew what had happened. It was their *gnosis*, their hidden knowledge. They would reveal part of it, at least, to the male disciples, but everyone else has had to accept the resurrection on faith—*in* faith, that is, and as an article of faith. Or, as some modern commentators have done, try to explain it with what suddenly seem the paltry tools of logic and speculation.

Logic says that the body did not simply disappear. And if not, it must have been taken away. But where to, and by whom?

The Matthew author provides an explanation of sorts. The high priests warn Pilate that since Jesus said he would rise again on the third day, the disciples might "come and steal him away and tell the people 'He has risen from the dead.'" So Pilate orders the tomb sealed and a guard placed over it to preclude this happening. When the resurrection happens nevertheless, the high priests bribe the guards to say that Jesus' followers have indeed stolen the body during the night. The guards keep their side of the deal and, Matthew says, "to this day that is the story among the Jews."

This certainly seems a workable explanation, not the least because it requires no faith, only a realistic sense of how things are in the corruptible human world. Stubborn non-believers such as "the Jews" would be bound to believe it, for what else could one expect of them? Matthew must have known that this explanation was current at the time, and so presents it as a false cover story. Even as he tells it, he makes sure it will not be believed; he forestalls the possibility of its being taken as truth by showing it to be a deliberate lie. And in the process, he makes the disappearance of the body all the more magical—Houdini-like, in fact—by adding the details of the seal and the guard on the tomb.

But the gospel of Mark, which scholars now agree was written earlier than that of Matthew, mentions no guard and no seal. Indeed, it is highly unlikely that Pilate would order such measures. Even if he was aware of Jesus' crucifixion, which is itself unlikely, he would have considered him merely another in a long line of minor nuisances—one more trouble-maker with delusions of grandeur. And we are still left with the puzzling question of why the women would come back to the tomb on the third day.

Mark shows three women—the Magdalene, Mary the mother of James, and Salome—bringing spices and oils to the tomb to anoint the body. But they would have done this before laying him there, not three days later, the intervening Sabbath notwithstanding. Later, John ignores the contradiction altogether; he simply states that the body was anointed with spices when it was laid in the shroud, and specifies no reason for the Magdalene coming to the tomb on the third day.

More basic still, why would anyone want to move the body at all? As in Jewish law today, bodies had to be buried the same day as death. The rock tomb donated by Joseph of Arimathea was as solid a resting ground as there could be. The image of Jesus' most devoted followers running around with his body under cover of night is close to desecration at best, grave-robbing at worst.

And yet this is what some of the more sensationalist explicators of the resurrection would have us believe. There seems to be an irresistible temptation for self-styled debunkers to turn historical detectives, coming up with reasoning so far-fetched as to make any self-respecting mystery writer blush. Among other things, we have been asked to believe that the authorities planned to steal the body to prevent any rumor of resurrection, and so the disciples broke in and stole it themselves, then sent the women to the tomb on the third day so that they would "discover" it empty. In various versions, the disciples hired a look-alike to act as the resurrected Jesus, or a total stranger as his messenger, or a fake medium through whom he could speak. One theory even ignores the gruesome horrors of crucifixion to argue that Jesus was not quite dead when placed in the tomb, that the herbs used to anoint him acted as medicine and the shroud as a bandage, and that he recovered.

There is a strong whiff of desperation in such extended reasoning. Certainly it reveals far more about those who make such arguments than about what actually happened. It makes the male disciples into a bunch of connivers, and the women into gullible dupes fooled into believing there has been a resurrection instead of a stolen body. The resurrection is seen at best as a hysterical misunderstanding, at worst as a scam.

This is what happens when we read the gospels as history instead of theology. We diminish the grandeur of metaphor, and find ourselves reduced from ultimate mystery to a poorly plotted detective story.

Of course literal resurrection is a physical impossibility. Therein lies the grandeur of the idea. But to say that it definitely did not happen makes no more sense than to say that it definitely did. For the real point of the resurrection is not literal, but metaphorical. Not physical, that is, but metaphysical.

Jesus' body may conceivably have been spirited away by his followers in the middle of the night. It may even have been taken away by temple guards sent to forestall a martyr's legend. Or it may simply never have disappeared in fact, but only in the telling. All these are possible, and in the end, none are relevant. For those who insist on the facts, there can be no resolution. The resurrection only makes sense on another level of knowledge, one that supersedes the factual and reaches deep into heart and soul.

When Isis sought out all the parts she could find of Osiris' body and brought him back to life, none of her worshippers took this literally. They instinctively grasped the power of metaphor. They took comfort in the idea that there is purpose in death—in the idea of death itself as part of life, part of the ongoing cycle of existence. But above all, they understood the power of grief to keep the dead alive.

As any newly bereaved spouse or parent knows, the absence of the dead person is as potent as their presence, perhaps even more so. The physical person is gone, but the hole he or she left in the world is undeniably there, its gaping emptiness an almost physical presence. And the survivors know that as long as they themselves live, so too will the ones who have died. They live on in the hearts and minds and dreams of those who mourn them. They live on in memory.

Maryam and the Magdalene and the "many other women" knew that the essence of resurrection lay not in the flesh, but in the spirit: the human spirit. "It was love that raised Jesus," declared the great nineteenth-century historian of religion Ernest Renan, and indeed it was. We mourn most deeply those we most deeply love. Whether Maryam's maternal love, the Magdalene's sensual love, or the loving faith of the other women, this was the force that would transform grief into joy, despair into hope, the end into the beginning.

It was not in grief, then, that Maryam and the women around her would resurrect the spirit of her son, but in love. This is how they would lead their lives from now on. This was their wisdom.

X

Maryam never ages in the New Testament gospels. She is never given a chance to age. After the crucifixion, she simply disappears, much as Joseph disappeared before her. There is just the sole point of reference at the end of John: "Woman, behold thy son," the dying Jesus tells Maryam. "Behold thy mother," he says to "the disciple standing by"— presumably John, though we already know that the male disciples have all fled. "And from that hour," the text continues, "the disciple took her into his own home."

The only other post-crucifixion reference to Maryam in the New Testament is a mere cameo appearance in the Acts of the Apostles. The disciples go back to the upper room where the Last Supper was held and pray "together with several women, including Mary the mother of Jesus." That word "including" seems amazingly casual; one would have thought Maryam would be at the center of such a gathering, not merely included as an afterthought.

But if we are not sure what to make of Jesus' last-minute passing off of his mother to John, at least the more traditional reader has the assurance that there is someone to look after her and provide a roof over her head. And indeed, over the next three centuries, one trend in apocryphal writing elaborated on John and his adoptive mother by placing them in Ephesus on the coast of what is now northwestern Turkey. That port city must have seemed a natural choice. It had been the center of worship of the great Diana of Ephesus, the many-breasted virgin fertility goddess whose temple would later be rededicated to Mary, and in the year 431 A.D. it would be the site of the Council of Ephesus, where Mary was declared *theotokos*: "mother of God." Modern pilgrims still visit the small stone house where she is said to have lived.

Other texts had Maryam living with John in Nazareth, and yet others, like The Twentieth Discourse, in Jerusalem, where she died at an unspecified date and was buried in the Vale of Jehoshaphat, below the towering walls of Herod's temple. The empty monument known as Mary's Tomb still stands there, curiously ignored by tourists and theologists alike.

But are we really to believe that the woman who raised as outspoken and revolutionary a man as Jesus would meekly disappear into the background after his death? Can we really conceive of her retreating to Nazareth to live out her days in the routine tasks of village life, as though nothing had happened? Or fleeing to Ephesus for no reason other than to live with John, as though she were incapable of looking after herself? In fact, how are we to believe that such a woman would retreat at all?

She has already left Nazareth, her ties to home and kinfolk weakened by the villagers' rejection of her son's preaching. For the past two years, she has traveled with her son and his followers on the road, from Capernaum at the northern tip of the Sea of Galilee all the way to the terrible destination of Golgotha. In this time, the followers, especially the women among them, have become her new family—an alternative, egalitarian family of the kind her son envisioned when he spoke of those who followed him as his true kin.

In this light, a number of apocryphal writers suggested what must be seen as far more realistic possibilities for Maryam than living out her days with John. For instance, the Discourse of Theodosius, archbishop of Alexandria, has her "living in Jerusalem with a number of virgins" as well as the apostles Peter and John, while the Homily of Evodius, archbishop of Rome, states that several disciples lived with Maryam after the crucifixion, "as did Salome and Joanna and the rest of the virgins who were with her."

"Living with a number of virgins" resonates with what we know of Maryam. These are certainly the women who stood vigil with her at Golgotha. They are the women who spread the word of the resurrection, and who, like Maryam herself, have come too far to turn back to so-called normal life. Deeply committed to the teachings of Jesus, it would make sense that they'd now gather in a new kind of community formed around the woman who raised and taught him. Led by Maryam, they will devote themselves to the principles of justice and wisdom, combine activism with contemplation, and offer shelter and healing to those in need: women and men, peasants and urban poor, rebels and outcasts. They will, in fact, create an early form of liberation theology.

In Jerusalem, as Theodosius has it? A few other apocryphal accounts are more specific, and have Maryam living and eventually dying on Mount Zion, just outside the Jerusalem city walls. This tradition led to the graceful Dormition Abbey being built there, its name deriving from the age-old euphemism for death—sleep—as in the Latin *dormit*, "she fell asleep."

But Maryam had a whole life yet to live before she was ready to "fall asleep." And Mount Zion was not the place to live it. Sheltering rebels right outside the city walls would be foolishly dangerous, but one of the many villages hidden in the hills around Jerusalem would be a very likely place—a village like Ein Kerem, for instance, whose name means "the spring of the vineyard." Just a couple of hours' walk due west from the Jerusalem city walls, its stone houses clung to the sides of a deep valley as they still do today, hidden from the world yet easily accessible to those in the know.

Let it be this village, with its spring and its vines, its fig and carob and olive trees, for this is a place that has meant renewal for me ever since a New Year's Eve many years ago. We were four women in an old stone house built into the hillside, talking and laughing through the night as children slept. We didn't even notice the passing of midnight. We realized we were tired only when we heard the first birds sing. Then, with dawn about to break, we went up to the large flat roof, glasses of strong sage tea cupped in our hands for warmth, and kept vigil as the first sun of the new year rose up in the east.

Ein Kerem, then, is where Maryam starts her life again after the crucifixion—not alone, and not with John or Peter or any of the male disciples, but with the other disciples: "the many women who went up with him to Jerusalem."

Maryam learns to laugh again. She plays hide and seek with the children between the rows of vines or along the stone-walled terraces planted with olive trees, and when she finds herself panting yet exhilarated with the effort of it, she grasps the lovely paradox that energy spent is energy created. That's when she knows that these children, born here to the women of her community, are the real resurrection of the flesh. For what is resurrection if not a matter of hope, of belief in the future? These women have given her new life.

Sometimes she goes out with the goats and the sheep, a switch of acacia in her hand, just as she did when she was still a girl. High on the hillside, she hitches up her smock once more to give her legs freedom to move, and urges the animals on with the familiar guttural "krrr." The Magdalene tells her she doesn't need to do this—it is young girls' work—but she replies that she does need to, for herself. She needs the sense of her muscles working, the feel of sweat on her forehead and in her armpits and trickling down her back: the physical signs of vitality, of life.

She watches every fall for the signs of renewal: anemones and cyclamens poking up between the rocks, ready to open into flower. She notes where artemisia and rue, sage and fennel grow thickest; when they're ready to harvest, she'll bring the young girls and teach them as her grandmother once taught her.

The herbs are harder to find here than in the greener, gentler hills of Galilee. Even the springs are different; they're set at the foot of steep slopes, instead of high up on the hillside. Yet there is something deeply satisfying about this Judean landscape. It may have the harshness of the desert, but it also has its cleanness. The cold winter nights are so sharp that Maryam's vision seems clearer than ever, while the searing heat of summer days burns clarity into her mind.

High up on the hillside, she turns and looks down on the community below, deep in the valley, and marvels at how much it has grown in the fifteen years they've been here. There were some twenty of them then, every one of them a refugee from Golgotha, every one feeling as though she'd aged a lifetime in the past few days. Now they are more than a hundred, and it's the spirit of her son's life that rules their days, not his death.

Maryam loves each of them like a daughter. They call her *amma*, "mother," in the same way that members of a family clan call the oldest man *abba*, "father," and she accepts the title gratefully, even as she says that like her, they are all daughters: the daughters of the Lady Wisdom. Through these women, the best of her son's teachings will bear fruit and bloom. In the spirit of Wisdom, they will keep him alive. And she knows they will carry on their work after she is gone.

She doesn't know how much longer she has left. Not long, for sure. She is fifty-one now, her face deeply etched by time and experience. Her hair has long turned gray, though in the summer it bleaches a silvery white in the sun. She still wears it in a single loose braid down her back, just as she still wears the thin linen smocks of her girlhood.

How strange it is to be old. She smiles as she remembers how incredible it once seemed that she would ever live to be as venerable as her grandmother. To a young peasant girl, the old seemed to exist in another country, one of infinite experience and wisdom. And only when she herself arrived in that country did she realize what she never could when she was younger—that there is no border, no barrier, between youth and age.

She feels as young now as she ever did, even if her muscles tire easier. Age, she has found, confers a different kind of strength. Call it mental, call it spiritual, no matter: it sustains her, as it sustains them all.

Yes, she's old enough now for the Magdalene to fuss over her, to try to stop her climbing up hillsides after the sheep and goats. Old enough to become venerable, though she adamantly refuses to be venerated. And the women respect this. To them, she is real, a flesh-and-blood woman like themselves. If she is an earthly manifestation of the Lady Wisdom, so too are they. She only wishes the male disciples could see this.

A few visit from time to time—Peter and James, Matthew and Luke—walking out to Ein Kerem from their small community inside the Jerusalem city walls. Always, they ask for stories of her son's life before they met him, but she can tell that they don't really listen. They have already formed the stories in their own minds, and if what she says does not fit, they barely hear her. In a way, she no longer exists for them. They come to pay their respects, yet they do not really respect Maryam the woman. She has become a figurehead for them, not a real person. "But I am here," she wants to say. "Touch me, I am real. Hear me speak, these words are mine." Then she looks into their eyes and sees the harshness of absolute conviction burning there, and she knows that nothing she can say will change them. They will place what they consider the right words in her mouth. And doubtless in her son's mouth too.

Where he preached renewal of the great Judaic tradition, they have begun to preach separation. They dream of a whole new tradition centered not on Yahweh but on her son. They talk of him almost as though he were divine. "We are all divine," she reminds them, "all children of God. If my son was the messenger of God, then so too are we. It is his message he would want you to honor, not his person." But they will not be content with a messenger, nor even with a prophet; like the Greeks, they seem to want the divine to have walked among them in human guise.

She places her faith where her son placed it. Wisdom will prevail.

Not in her lifetime, perhaps, nor even in the lifetime of the youngest of the children born in this community built around the spring of the vine. But eventually—she smiles to just think of it—a hundred years on perhaps, or a thousand, or two thousand or three . . .

Up on this stony hillside she sighs, and leans back against the rough, runneled trunk of an olive tree—"the tree of light," as they call it, whose oil dispels darkness. She remembers the smell and the smoke of burning olive trees when she was a child, when the Romans retook Sepphoris and vandalized the olive groves. Remembers the old men calmly telling her not to worry, that there is no destroying an olive tree. "Wait, little one," they said, "you'll see." And sure enough, by the same time the following year, new shoots had sprung up all around the burned-out stumps. The trees were coming back to life again. The villagers pruned the shoots carefully, leaving only the strongest and sturdiest ones to grow. By the time Maryam gave birth, they were large enough to bear their first fruit.

The Nazarenes knew what the Roman mercenaries did not: that olive trees live hundreds, if not thousands, of years. You can cut them down or burn them, neglect them or deliberately deprive them of water, and still, in time, they will come back to life. They cannot be killed. They are the ultimate symbol of resurrection.

Some of the trees on this hillside are ancient, like the one Maryam now rests against. Others are still young, grown from shoots transplanted by the women each time a child is born. At age five, the child is brought to pick the first fruit of the new tree, plucking the proof of renewal.

Many such rituals bind their community, along with songs to Miriam the prophet of exodus and freedom, offerings to Isis the greatest of virgins, celebrations of Eve the mother of all. But they are bound above all by their practice, for this community exists not only for those who are already here, but also for those who might one day want to come. It is a safe haven, a refuge for those in need of shelter, or of healing, or of a renewed sense of faith and life.

Maryam has handed on the art and science of healing, and the other women are now as skillful as she. Word has spread. People in pain or chronic sickness, city dwellers and peasants alike, make their way here to be cured. Wounded resistance fighters are brought here by kinfolk or fellow partisans to be nursed back to health, staying for weeks and sometimes months at a time until it is safe for them to move on. Women who have been beaten and raped, men who have been imprisoned and tortured, all find refuge here. Some never leave. They come to be healed, and stay on to heal others.

The years of hard work have left their mark on the faces and bodies of the small group of founding women—not just the Magdalene and Joanna and Maryam herself, but the prophetess Hanna and the seamstress Tabitha, emancipated slaves—*libertinae*—like Rhoda, and entrepreneurs like Lydia, who used to trade in lapis lazuli, the treasured pigment made from crushed azure stone from far to the east along the great Silk Road. And the other Maryams, of course: the wife of Cleopas, the mother of James and Zebedee, and Lazarus' sister Mary, together with Martha. They are all ageing now, yet their eyes shine like those of young girls, as alive and vital as ever.

Maryam admires them as much as she loves them, and has done ever since they refused to disband after the crucifixion. It was no longer possible, they said. After becoming so close to each other over the two years of Jesus' ministry, how could they now abandon everything he stood for? How return to conventional family and respectability? And so Joanna, who was married to a high official in the Herodian treasury and who managed all his estates as high-born women often did in Rome, led them to this land in Ein Kerem. "We shall be safe here," she said. "This now belongs to us all."

And in a way, Maryam admires those who have joined them over the years even more, for these younger women never saw or heard her son; they acted on faith alone. They had been prostitutes and courtesans, pampered urban wives and hard-working peasant women, women of the lowest social rank and of the highest too, like Caletha the daughter of Nicodemus, Neshra the daughter of the famed Pharisee sage Gamaliel, and Tabitha the daughter of the deposed king of Judea, Archelaus. Now they are all part of this discipleship of equals around Maryam. All are her sisters, all her daughters.

Shadows begin to lengthen on the hillside. The bright light of afternoon is deepening into the soft gold of early evening. Maryam hasn't meant to sit here so long. Perhaps she really is beginning to tire.

She stands and stretches her arms and her back. Becomes aware of voices calling for her from far below. Yes, she has been blessed with these women who love her. She thinks of the Essenes down in the desert fastness of the Dead Sea, "the sons of light," they call themselves, girding for an apocalyptic war with the sons of darkness. Here in Ein Kerem, the daughters of light follow a different path—the path of understanding, of healing both body and spirit. Where the Essenes dream of overthrowing the temple hierarchy and instituting a new, purer temple of their own, the women know that the true temple is not one of marble and gold, nor of any other physical material, but of the mind. It is the spirit of Wisdom. "Honor her in yourselves," Maryam will tell the women this evening, "and in each other. This is where renewal starts."

She smiles, and follows the sheep and goats down the hillside.

"Wise" is not a word much used any longer. One can be smart, one can be intelligent, one may even be a genius. But wise? That has an unreal feel to it, as though it were simultaneously too grand and too vague for practical people to wrap their heads around.

Yet in Maryam's time, there was nothing vague about wisdom. Quite the contrary. A great deal of contemporary Jewish theology was built around the divine female figure known as the Lady Wisdom. And she had a very distinct voice. She spoke directly, in quotation marks, in several books written by Judean gnostics living in Egypt from the third century B.C. on.

Her Hebrew name, Hochma, was the abstract form of *hachama*, "wise woman." Her earliest appearance—at least the earliest that we know of—is in the third-century B.C. Book of Proverbs, where she descends from the divine world to guide and save humanity. She was there when God created the world, she says, before anything else existed. She proclaims her greatness, gives dire warnings of the dangers of ignoring her, and demands and expects loyalty. As the manifestation of God's presence in the world, this is her due. She is the female aspect of God. And she is wise indeed.

In the Book of Wisdom, written in the first century B.C., her knowledge encompasses all the sciences of her time: physics, alchemy, astrology, biology, psychology, herbalism, and medicine. She knows:

the structure of the world and the properties of the elements,
the beginning, end and middle of times,
the alternation of the solstices and the succession of the seasons,
the revolution of the years and the position of the stars,
the natures of animals and the instincts of wild beasts,
the powers of spirits and the mental process of men,
the varieties of plants and the medical properties of roots.

The book goes on to praise Hochma in a list of twenty-one attributes—three times the magical number seven—that make her everything a woman and a goddess could be: "Intelligent, holy, unique, manifold, subtle, active, incisive, unsullied, lucid, invulnerable, benevolent, sharp, irresistible, beneficent, loving to man, steadfast, dependable, unperturbed, almighty, all-surveying, penetrating all intelligent, pure and most subtle spirits."

At times, her language reflects the grandeur of contemporary hymns to Isis; at others it seems very close to the sensuality of the Song of Songs. In the second-century B.C. Ecclesiasticus—often called The Wisdom of Ben Sirach to distinguish it from the better-known Ecclesiastes—she says she is like the finest vines, the sweetest blossoms, the most beautiful roses, the tallest and most graceful trees:

> I have exhaled a perfume like cinnamon and acacia, I have breathed out a scent like choice myrrh . . . Approach me, you who desire me, And take your fill of my fruits, For memories of me are sweeter than honey, Inheriting me is sweeter than the honeycomb. They who eat me will hunger for more, They who drink me will thirst for more . . .

And so they did. Two centuries later, Christian gnostics would expand the earlier Jewish writings and elevate the Lady Wisdom still further. Calling her by her Greek name, Sophia, they explicitly revered her as the great virgin mother. In The Apocryphon of John, she becomes "the invisible, virginal, perfect spirit." She impregnates herself and so is "the Mother of everything, for she existed before them all, the mother-father." She is the origin of all things; without her, the world would not exist.

Inevitably, gnostics hungering for divine knowledge identified Sophia with the first great biblical figure who hungered for knowledge: the mother of all humans, Eve. Where Adam was content to exist in ignorance, Eve dared to reach for more. She picked and ate the fruit of the Tree of Knowledge of Good and Evil. The gnostics saw this as reaching for knowledge of the divine. It was an act of courage and spiritual integrity, not of disobedience. Eve was Wisdom in action, to the extent that in the gospel On the Origin of the World, she becomes Sophia's daughter, sent by her mother to teach Adam, who has no soul, so that he might attain one.

But Sophia's main child in the gnostic gospels is Jesus, the teacher and mediator of Wisdom. He is shown as her son, her lover, and even, in The Sophia of Jesus Christ, as Sophia herself. "The earliest Palestinian theological remembrances and interpretations of Jesus' life and death understand him as Sophia's messenger and later as Sophia," says theologist Elizabeth Schüssler-Fiorenza. "The earliest Christian theology is sophialogy."

It would not be allowed to last. Sophia was dangerous to the powers-that-be. She challenged the status quo: the traditional vilification of Eve, the priestly lock on knowledge, and above all, the separation of human and divine.

As the gnostics saw it, to eat and drink of Wisdom was not just to partake of the divine; it was to assimilate it, and thus become divine oneself. This was the ultimate expression of Jesus' teaching that "the kingdom of God is within you." The gnostic gospel of Philip stated it explicitly: whoever achieves *gnosis* or true knowledge becomes "no longer a Christian, but Christ."

In this, the gnostics were part of a long mystical tradition. As John the Baptist had taught, and as the Kabbalists would elaborate more than a thousand years later, a spark of the divine exists within every human being. We are all thus potentially divine—a belief that posed a radical challenge to the developing institution of the church, just as it had done earlier to Herod when preached by John the Baptist. If the divine lay inside each person, what reason then to have intermediaries? What purpose could be served by bishops, creeds, canons, prescribed ritual?

In the ensuing power struggle, the anarchic mysticism of the gnostics was no match for the increasingly politicized and centralized church hierarchy. In 367 A.D. the powerful bishop of Alexandria, Athanasius, ordered a purge of all apocryphal books with "heretical" tendencies. Most of the Egyptian gnostic gospels and writings were destroyed. The remnants were hidden deep in the desert, where some would be uncovered by chance only sixteen centuries later. The vibrant, dynamic presence of Sophia was suppressed, and would not resurface until the kabbalists revived her as the Shechina, the powerful and compassionate female manifestation of the godhead.

In Maryam's time, however, a world without Wisdom, without

Hochma, must have been unimaginable. She was literally a proverbial presence, constantly invoked. Jesus had spoken of himself as the child of Wisdom—of them all as the children of Wisdom. And now here she was among them. For if ever there was a flesh-and-blood manifestation of Wisdom, it was Maryam herself: the healer, the mother, the wise woman.

XI

Amma, mother, they called her. If the title seems unusual for the leader of a spiritual community, that is because it survived only in its male form, *abba*, which in English would become "abbot." Even when women were finally allowed to enter Catholic monastic life, the senior one among them would be called the abbess—the feminine form of "abbott"—making her a kind of female father.

And yet *amma* was definitely a familiar term in the first century, for women played central roles in numerous faiths throughout the Mediterranean of the time. Just as the divine was often female, so too were those who mediated it.

High priestesses were familiar figures. They presided over the worship of great mother goddesses like Isis and Cybele; officiated in the imperial Roman cult of the emperor; ran the temples of goddesses like Demeter, Kore, and Athena. And these were not merely ceremonial positions. Like high church office today, they involved enormous worldly as well as spiritual power, not the least because they included control over immense amounts of donated money. This money could be lent or used as endowments; it could fund the building of temples and palaces; it could sponsor both religious festivals and secular ones such as athletic games. And money worked then as it does now. Like commercial lobbying and sponsorship in our own time, financial largesse created enormous influence in political life.

The most famed such priestesses of Maryam's time were the Vestal Virgins in Rome. The six who served at any one time were elite women consecrated to the service of Vesta, the goddess who guarded the hearth of Rome. The eternal flame in her honor symbolized not only the Roman people but also male virility.

This last detail seems somewhat ironic, since the Vestals were indeed physical virgins, at least in principle. But any comparison with convents and nuns should be put aside. These highly educated women were the most liberated in the world of their time. They wielded extensive legal powers, including the right to grant pardons, a right belonging to only one other person: the emperor himself. Their most influential role was as the executors of the emperors' wills and guardians of other important legal documents like treasury and military records. This made the Vestals vital to the smooth succession of power from one emperor to the next. It also ensured huge legacies for them as beneficiaries of the wills. They lived in sumptuous luxury, with the kind of perks—the best seats at the Coliseum, imperial-level bodyguards—familiar to chief executives of major corporations today.

At the other end of the scale, women were also active in the far more spartan form of contemplative life we now think of as monasticism. The best known such movement at the time was not the relatively small, men-only Essene group down on the shores of the Dead Sea, but the far more widespread and influential Therapeutics, a Jewish monastic movement whose largest community was in Egypt, on the shores of Lake Mareotis near Alexandria.

Therapeutic communities were made up of both women and men who lived, practiced, and worshipped on equal terms, calling each other "brother" and "sister." Begun in the first century B.C. by Greek-speaking Judeans who had fled the Hasmoneans and settled in Egypt, they had established communities throughout the Middle East by Maryam's time. The women among them were mainly widows or had left their husbands to take up the contemplative life. They were known as virgins and daughters of Miriam, and one of their main hymns was Miriam's exultant song of freedom after the crossing of the Red Sea in Exodus.

The movement's name was as suggestive two thousand years ago as it is today. These monastics were as famed for their skill in herbs and healing as were their counterparts in the cult of Isis. But the therapy was not just physical; it was also psychological, and above all spiritual.

The Therapeutics were gnostics—literate and philosophically sophisticated, with a highly developed sense of metaphor. They saw the mystical union of the soul with the divine as both a spiritual marriage and a form of rebirth: the soul was reborn through union with its divine mother Hochma, Wisdom, whom they called "The Eternal Virgin."

When Jesus called on his followers to abandon blood ties of family and see each other as brothers and sisters, he undoubtedly had the Therapeutic example in mind. And a community of sisters formed around Maryam in a village like Ein Kerem would have been very much in the Therapeutic tradition: both contemplative and activist, alongside the world rather than in retreat from it.

They would have had a strong core of founders: not only Maryam herself, but those other women who took the road to Golgotha, and who were, if all too briefly, acknowledged as apostles. The gnostic text Pistis Sophia for example—literally, Faith Wisdom—which shows Jesus teaching the apostles as the child and messenger of Wisdom, has not twelve apostles present, but seventeen. Maryam, the Magdalene, Salome, and Martha and her sister Mary are gathered together on equal terms with the twelve men. And of course the gospel of Mary shows the Magdalene teaching the male apostles.

Like the Therapeutic women, the women in Maryam's community would have considered themselves daughters of Miriam—or rather, in the Aramaic, daughters of Maryam. For if Jesus was the spiritual child of Wisdom, he was also the earthly child of Maryam. He could be seen as having two mothers—or the two mothers, the spiritual and the earthly, could be seen as one.

Eventually, this is exactly what would happen. Maryam would be seen as the flesh-and-blood manifestation of the great female divine, and worshipped as such. But that would be long after her death, not in her own time or in her own community. Like her son, she would have thought of herself not as divine, but as living in the spirit of the divine: a child of Wisdom, not Wisdom herself. Spirit had not yet been fused with physical presence.

In those first years of what has since been called "the Jesus movement," to be a follower of Jesus was not to worship him, but to work for what he preached: a spiritual renewal among Jews, a return to a purer ethic and an end to the politicization of the temple. His followers were Jews who believed in him as a sage and a prophet of Jewish renewal. They were not Christians, for Christianity as a faith separate from Judaism did not yet exist. Paul had not yet begun his travels and his letters. He had not yet acted on his epiphany on the road to Damascus.

Read Paul's letters—really read them, that is, with a fresh mind—and you realize what a brilliant organizer he was. They could be the prototype for the correspondence of a modern political organizer, or even for a sales executive trying to motivate his staff. Most of them start by thanking those who have made outstanding efforts in the recent past, singling out the most active and the most financially generous for special mention. Next, the letters go on to outline how much work is still to be done. Then comes an account of Paul's own trials and tribulations. And finally, a Pauline sermon, clearly intended to inspire and rouse the troops to renewed effort.

But what is most notable for a modern reader is how many of those Paul singles out for special mention are women. There is Phoebe, the deacon of the congregation of Cenchrea, who carries Paul's letter to the Romans and whom he introduces as his patron. Junia in Rome is "foremost among the apostles." Prisca, Julia, Persis, Euodia, Synteche are all hailed as fellow workers, praised for their efforts in spreading the message. Prisca is the leader of a house church—all the early churches were inside private estates and homes—as are Lydia of Thyatira and

Nympha of Laodicea. In fact, of the twenty-eight people Paul specifically praises in his letters, ten are women.

Women took leading roles in early Christianity. And we have more than Paul's testimony. In the Acts of the Apostles, the head of the Ebionite church in Jerusalem—the main Palestinian Jewish group that saw Jesus as the messiah—is Mary the mother of John Mark, and it is to her that Peter comes to announce that he's been freed from prison by an angel. Later, in the Acts of Paul and Thecla, a popular collection of Pauline stories, Paul is outshone by the aristocratic Thecla, who renounces the wealth and security of an arranged marriage for the far riskier life—at that time, at any rate—of an evangelist.

"In Christ there is no male or female," Paul wrote in his letter to the Galatians, and throughout the first, second, and third centuries, early Christian women took him at his word. They became priests, prophets, preachers, deacons, and even bishops, on a par with and often outdoing their male counterparts.

Despite themselves, theologians like Tertullian seemed stunned into admiration. "These heretical women, how audacious they are!" he wrote. "They have no modesty. They are bold enough to teach, to engage in argument, to enact exorcisms, to undertake cures, and even to baptize!"

Among the most audacious were the trio of renowned prophets at the forefront of the widespread Montanist movement, which began in Asia Minor—now Turkey—in the second century. Their names, lyrically beguiling, were Priscilla, Quintilla, and Maximilla. Under their leadership, the movement focused on ecstatic prophecy and healing, nourishing such charismatic women that Tertullian's barely concealed admiration eventually got the better of him. He joined the Montanist group in the north African city of Carthage, where he wrote: "We have among us a sister who has been favored with gifts of revelation, which she experiences in the Spirit by ecstatic vision amidst the sacred rites of the Lord's day in church. She converses with angels, and sometimes even with the Lord. She both sees and hears mysterious communications. Some men's hearts she discerns, and she obtains directions for healing for such as need them."

Like the Therapeutics before them, the Montanists honored Eve as a seeker after knowledge, Miriam as a prophet, and Sophia as the feminine divine; in one of their oracles, Jesus appears to Priscilla in the form of a woman and "puts Wisdom"—Sophia—inside her. But other charismatic movements like the Valentinians and the Carpocratians focused as much on Jesus' earthly mother as on his spiritual one, gradually fusing Maryam and Sophia into the feminine divine. When the main teacher of the Carpocratian group, Marcellina, began to reveal secret teachings she had received from Maryam, Salome, and Martha, it would be only a small step to singling out Maryam not just for veneration, but for worship.

Men could not participate in the rites and rituals of the Kolyridian movement, which formed in the early third century and rapidly spread throughout the eastern Mediterranean. Only women could do so. This fact alone would make the Kolyridians perhaps the most intriguing of all the early Christian groups. But there was far more.

Their name came from the Greek word *kolyris*, a small flatbread or barley cake baked and eaten as an offering in a ritual as old as civilization itself. Bread still plays a central sacramental role both in Judaism, with the Sabbath challah and the Passover matzo, and in Christianity, with the Eucharist wafer, but in ancient societies, its meaning was far more down to earth. It was offered to the great virgin goddesses of fertility—fruitfulness offered in the hope of more.

Sometimes, ritual breads or cakes were made in the shapes of human genitalia, both female and male, in a clear linkage of fertility of the earth and human fertility. If this seems exotic, consider that some such rituals still survive as customs. *Haman-taschen*, for instance—"Haman's ears" in Yiddish—are the triangular poppy seed pastries eaten at Purim, the feast that celebrates Esther saving the Israelite people from the Persian king Ahasureus and his evil advisor Haman. One look at the dark seeds bursting out of their pastry envelope and you need no

Freud to figure out the sexual symbolism. The name Esther, after all, is the Hebrew form of Ishtar. It seems appropriate, then, that Ishtar is one of the "guests" featured in a vivid modern expression of this ancient fertility rite: artist Judy Chicago's room-size installation *The Dinner Party*. First shown in 1979, the large triangular dinner table has thirty-nine flamboyantly sexual ceramic place settings, each named for a celebrated woman.

We know that the Kolyridian breads were not erotically shaped, or critics like Epiphanius, the fourth-century bishop of Salamis who took it on himself to catalog all the known "heresies" of his time, would have leaped gleefully all over the fact. "But bread it was," says classical scholar Stephen Benko, "the 'fruit of Demeter,' sacred to Artemis, Minerva, Juno, and all the great fertility goddesses of the ancient world. For bread has an awesome relationship to Gaia, earth, in whose 'womb' the seed is planted to multiply, grow, and become a life-giving element. In the sacred mystery of bread, every woman could view herself as possessing a portion of the creative power of the gods, for in every act of intercourse, conception, and birth, the sowing of the seed, the miracle of life and death, is repeated."

The Kolyridian goddess was no longer Artemis or Juno, however, nor Isis or Ishtar or Cybele. It was Maryam. They had taken the logical next step in the progression from Isis to Hochma to Sophia, and closed the gap between the earthly and spiritual mothers. Maryam was the mother of a divine son. She was thus the source of the divine, and had to be divine in her own right—the last and ultimate manifestation of the great mother.

As a result, the Kolyridians would play an ironic dual role in the development of Christianity. On the one hand, they made the new religion far more acceptable to people who worshipped other manifestations of the great mother, and who could not imagine a world without the presence of the female divine. On the other, their very success held the seed of their downfall. As the universal Catholic church gained power in Rome, it could not deny the power of the virgin goddess; it could, however, co-opt and limit it. Maryam and Sophia would be separated again—the fusion defused, as it were. Maryam would become holy but not divine, while an asexual version of Sophia, the Holy Spirit, would become the third element in what many gnostics had seen as the original trinity of mother, father, and son.

That gnostic view would be branded heresy and suppressed, which is almost certainly why we have no surviving gospel of Maryam, even though several were surely written. There were hundreds of apocryphal texts in circulation between the second and the fourth centuries. Many were the popular novels of their time, filling the gaps in the four New Testament gospels with vivid imagination. We can still read gospels named after minor New Testament characters like Nicodemus and Joseph of Arimathea, relating the life and death of Jesus from these characters' points of view. Even Pontius Pilate gets his apocryphal say in numerous texts of his own. And of course the Magdalene stars in the gnostic gospel of Mary. It is hard to imagine, then, that Maryam did not get to shine in her own right.

Is it really conceivable that a community of women living with her—anyone living with her, in fact, even if it was John—would not record her memories and thoughts? They would have been hungry for the kind of detail of Jesus' childhood that only his mother could provide, let alone for the teachings of the woman who taught him as she now taught them. They would have heard her voice as that of Wisdom. Her words would have been memorized, passed on to others, and eventually recorded in writing, albeit filtered through the dual lens of reverence and legend, to become sacred texts for movements such as the Carpocratians and the Kolyridians.

Some scholars have speculated that traces of Maryam gospels do appear here and there: in the passages of Matthew and Luke that feature her, for instance, and in gnostic "infancy gospels" like those of James and Thomas. But if so, they are indeed mere traces. One can barely hear the voice of the real woman behind them, the woman long dead by the time these accounts were written.

But that doesn't mean her voice did not survive.

We can still hear it, not in a gospel of Maryam, but in the surviving gnostic gospels, several of which were very likely written by women, given their active role in the early church. In fact it is all but impossible to imagine that one text in particular could have been written by anyone but a woman.

"Thunder, Perfect Mind" is written in a woman's voice. It is the voice of the female divine in all its wondrous and awesome paradox. Some read it as the voice of Wisdom, others of Eve, yet others as the voice of Maryam herself. I suspect it is better read as all three, for that is the point. The speaker transcends division to create a harmonious, dynamic interplay of opposites. She is, she seems to be saying, all women, all experience.

"Hear me," she insists. And since her words are an oracle rather than a gospel, they were originally intended to be recited out loud rather than read silently. Chant these extracts, even sing them if you dare, and it is almost as though you can see Maryam smiling in recognition:

Look upon me, you who reflect on me,
    and you hearers, hear me.
You who are waiting for me, take me unto yourselves
    and do not banish me from your sight . . .
Do not be ignorant of me anywhere or any time.
Do not be ignorant of me.

For I am the first and the last.
I am the honored one and the scorned one.
I am the whore and the holy one.
I am the wife and the virgin.
I am the mother and the daughter.
I am the members of my mother.
I am the barren one
    and many are her sons.

I am she whose wedding is great,
and I have not taken a husband.
I am the midwife and she who does not bear.
I am the solace of my labor pains.
I am the bride and the bridegroom,
and it is my husband who begot me.
I am the mother of my father
and the sister of my husband,
and he is my offspring . . .

I am the knowledge of my inquiry,
and the finding of those who seek after me,
and the command of those who ask of me,
and the power of the powers in my knowledge
of the angels sent at my word,
and of gods in their seasons by my counsel,
and of spirits of every man who exists with me,
and of women who dwell within me . . .

Hear me in gentleness, and learn of me in roughness.
I am she who cries out,
and I am cast out upon the face of the earth.
I prepare the bread and my mind within.
I am the knowledge of my name.
I am the one who cries out,
and I listen . . .

In a way, Maryam was fortunate to die when she did, some twenty years before the outbreak of the four-year uprising that would culminate in the Romans burning down the Jerusalem temple in 70 A.D. In that fire, the world she knew would be utterly consumed, and the new one that would come into being would certainly have dismayed her with its divisiveness. Faith would be separated from people, people from land, and perhaps most tragically, people from people. For if any single event can be said to lead directly to the establishment of Judaism and Christianity as two separate religions, it was the destruction of the temple.

Most of the priestly Sadducee elite were massacred, leaving the way clear for the Pharisee movement. Over the next two hundred years, first on the Mediterranean coast and then in Galilee, their descendants would lay the groundwork for the rabbinical Judaism we know today. In the lack of the physical temple or any chance that it would be rebuilt in the foreseeable future, the early rabbis internalized the idea of it, creating a vast philosophical structure of law and ethics in its place: the Mishna, and later, the Talmud.

The Palestinian followers of Jesus as a prophet of Jewish renewal were dispersed in the turmoil following the destruction, but Paul's organizational brilliance had by then created a rapidly growing non-Jewish Jesus movement throughout the rest of the Mediterranean. Already in the ascendance, this would now predominate. The Palestinian prophet would become the Christ, a divine being in the Hellenistic image. His Jewishness would be played down, and despite the fact that Paul himself was a Pharisee—and possibly Jesus too, as some scholars maintain—the gospel writers would severely distort the role of the Pharisees to avoid blaming Rome and thus antagonizing the authorities. Instead of the Romans, the Jews were set up as opponents.

It has always been this way when one group parts ways with the larger one within which it was born. Whether early Protestants separating from Catholicism, or American settlers separating from British rule, the parent group becomes the opponent. And just as the New World defined itself against the Old World even as it grew out of it, so too, sixteen hundred years earlier, the New Testament faith began to define itself against the Old. Jews were divided from Christians, and Christianity from its Jewish roots. Separation took the place of renewal, divisiveness the place of continuity.

It would surely have broken Maryam's heart, let alone that of her son.

But the spirit of continuity did not disappear altogether. It lives on quite vividly in the traditional accounts of Maryam's death.

In the apocryphal Twentieth Discourse, for instance, Maryam calls the women of her community to her as she lies dying, apparently peacefully, and of old age. When they have all gathered, she takes the hand of the Magdalene, and tells them: "Behold your mother from this time onwards."

It is a beautiful image. In that meeting of hands, the mother hands on to the chosen daughter. The daughter figure will become the new mother, the *amma*, continuing the line of wise women. The mantle is passed from one generation to the next, from the Nazarene to the Magdalene, the mother to the lover, one Maryam to another.

In that same spirit of continuity, the Discourse also reunites mother and son. It tells how when Jesus sees that Maryam is dying, he descends to earth with heavenly robes for her. She dies—"her soul leaped into the bosom of her own son, and he wrapped it in a garment of light"—and Jesus orders the apostles to take her body to the Vale of Jehoshaphat, where Mary's Tomb now stands. Three days later, he ascends to heaven and takes her with him: "There came a great choir of angels and caught away the body of the Virgin, and Peter and John and we looked on until she was carried to heaven, until we lost sight of it."

And lose sight of it we all did. Not just of Maryam's body, but of the woman herself—her spirit, her mind, her presence. The Mary who would come into being would be little more than a shadow of the real woman, so insubstantial that it would not be until 1950, under Pope Pius XII, that the Vatican would belatedly catch up with tradition and proclaim her bodily assumption into heaven.

What actually happened when she died? I think we can say that as with her son's resurrection, the spirit of the story carries more truth, and certainly more power, than the legendary details. In this spirit, Maryam dies, but in her own way, is resurrected. Not by Jesus himself, nor by choirs of angels, but by the women she loves. Her mantle is handed on to the next generation, and will continue to be handed on this way over the generations.

Each time a woman gives birth, each time a woman sits between another's legs and cradles the emerging newborn's head, each time a woman sings in joy or wails in mourning, seeks out knowledge or teaches it to others, works for justice or acts for peace or risks her life for freedom, the mantle of Maryam is handed on.

In the spirit of Maryam, we are all her.

NOTES

INTRODUCTION

2 *a name so common*: See, among others, Moltmann-Wendel, *Women Around Jesus*.

3 *the lingua franca*: C. Rabin, "Hebrew and Aramaic in the First Century," in Safrai and Stern, *Jewish People in the First Century*.

4 *C.E. and B.C.E.*: Since A.D. and B.C. are more commonly used, I have used them throughout this book.

4 *anxious at the temple*: Luke 2:48.

4 *the wedding at Cana*: John 2:3–4.

4 *at the foot of the cross*: John 19:25.

4 *legend accrued over the centuries*: Marina Warner's *Alone of All Her Sex* is a superb history of the development of the Marian legend.

5 *readers of Woolf's journals*: Lee, *Virginia Woolf*.

8 *olive tree can be a thousand years old*: Rosenblum, *Olives*.

10 *both empathy and imagination*: Collingwood, *Idea of History*.

I

15 *za'atar*: Still widely used throughout the Middle East. Often called hyssop or marjoram, it is in fact wild oregano mixed with sesame seeds and salt. It is sprinkled on bread before baking, used as a spice in stews and casseroles, and most commonly, mixed with olive oil into a paste used as a dip.

16 *tiny, dark rooms*: The modern visitor can get a sense of such rooms at Katzrin, in the Golan Heights, where archeologists have partially reconstructed a fourth-century village.

16 *during harvest times*: Granqvist, *Birth and Childhood Among the Arabs*. Hilma Granqvist was a young Swedish anthropologist whose

books, full of extraordinarily rich detail on Palestinian peasant life, were the result of three years spent in the village of Artas, just south of Bethlehem. She stayed with Louise Baldensperger, the daughter of an Alsatian missionary, who spent most of her life living in Artas and eventually coauthored *From Cedar to Hyssop* (Crowfoot and Baldensperger), a wonderful book on Palestinian plant lore.

17 *if you know astrology*: Astrology played a large role in temple practice, in Jerusalem as elsewhere. The Essene scrolls found at Qumran *(The Complete Dead Sea Scrolls)* contain astrological systems, zodiacal horoscopes, and even a brontologion, which interpreted the sounds of thunder (for instance, "If in Taurus it thunders, hard labor for the country and the sword . . . If in Gemini it thunders, terror and affliction will be brought by strangers"). The zodiac would later be a central decorative motif in many fourth-, fifth-, and sixth-century Palestinian synagogues.

18 *glimmer of an oil lamp*: Just a flat piece of clay folded and pinched into a triangle. A wick was placed in the mouth, and olive oil poured inside. You can find baskets full of such lamps outside tourist stores throughout the Middle East, selling for a dollar or fifty cents each, depending on your bargaining power. Take them home, fill them with olive oil, insert a wick, and they work—smokily.

18 *Not the Judean Bethlehem, near Jerusalem, but the Galilean one*: The consensus among biblical scholars and historians is that it is highly improbable that Jesus was born in Bethlehem, and he was most likely born in Nazareth (see for instance Shorto, *Gospel Truth*). They are apparently unaware of the existence of the Galilee Bethlehem. The author of the Gospel of Matthew may also have been unaware that it existed—like modern biblical scholars, he was not Palestinian. But his loose quote in Matthew 2:6 of Micah 5:2 ("For so it has been written by the prophets: And you O Bethlehem in the land of Judah . . .") makes it clear that he specified the Judean Bethlehem only because it accorded with established prophecy. Similarly, Luke 2:4 specifies the Judean Bethlehem, "the city of David," solely in order to establish Jesus' descent from David through Joseph.

20 *hard-packed fibrous pellets*: Sinai Beduin still use camel dung, and it is indeed a perfect fuel for cooking. Dense and dry, it burns smoothly for a long time, and with no odor.

21 *peculiar date of 4 B.C.*: When the Christian calendar was initiated in the seventh century, scribes miscalculated by about four years—

an understandable error since there was no universal calendar in use at the time.

21 *"the invention of childhood"*: Ariès, *Centuries of Childhood.*

21 *"the age of chasing stray sheep"*: Granqvist, *Birth and Childhood Among the Arabs.*

22 *The numbers are chilling*: Brydon and Chant, *Women in the Third World.*

22 *eighteenth-century London*: Jackson, *Doctors and Diseases.*

22 *ancient Rome*: Preston, *Mortality Trends*, and Jackson, *Doctors and Diseases.*

22 *nineteenth-century Massachusetts*: Preston, *Mortality Trends.*

23 *ancient Middle East*: Meyers, "Everyday Life."

23 *one out of three died in childbirth*: Jackson, *Doctors and Diseases.*

23 *effective birthrate was lower*: Ibid.

23 *number of siblings given*: Matthew 13:55–56.

25 *The few villages that have been excavated*: Most strikingly, Mordechai Aviam's excavations of Yodfat and Cana.

25 *elaborate mosaic-floored mansions*: See Netzer and Weiss, *Zippori.* Sepphoris is now an Israeli archeological park, with tourists drawn especially to the mosaic floors, in particular the one showing a smiling woman whom the archeologists dubbed "the Mona Lisa of the Galilee."

26 *"the salt of the earth"*: Matthew 5:13.

26 *a house was not stones, but people*: Throughout the Middle East and the Mediterranean and throughout the centuries, as in Le Roy Ladourie's account of fourteenth-century Montaillou in France.

27 *novelistic "infancy gospels"*: The father of all the infancy gospels was the Protevangelium of James (in *The Apocryphal New Testament*).

27 *bond between land and people*: See Qleibo, *Before the Mountains Disappear*; Benvenisti, *Sacred Landscapes*; and Khalidi, *All That Remains.*

28 *The name itself was foreign*: While it's often assumed that "Palestine" refers to the land of the Philistines, this is in fact highly unlikely. The Philistines had long disappeared from the historical record, back in the seventh century B.C., and even then their land was only the narrow coastal strip from Gaza to Jaffa. Moreover, the third-century B.C. Greek translation of Hebrew holy books, known as the Septuagint, used the word *Philistia* for that area, not *Palaestina*. One alternative theory (Jacobson, "When Palestine Meant Israel") has it that the name originated as a pun, a form much admired in Athens, where wordplay was elevated to a

sophisticated art. *Palaestina* may have worked off the Greek *palaistes*, meaning "wrestler," since the name Israel—*yisra-el* in Hebrew—means one who wrestled with God. The wrestler in question, of course, is Jacob, who fought through the night with the angel of God, and so had his name changed to Israel. Wrestling was so popular in Athens that this biblical story could well have caught the Greek imagination. It certainly appeals to any modern mind wrestling with matters of faith and doubt. And given the seemingly unending wrestling over the same land today, with the ever-growing religious fanaticism on both sides, it has a horribly literal relevance.

28 *always take place in the winter months*: Granqvist, *Birth and Childhood*. Also Norberg-Hodges on Ladakh, in *Ancient Futures*.

29 *the Galileans rose in rebellion*: 1 Kings 12.

30 *And so arose Elijah*: The story of Elijah in 1 Kings 17 and 18, and 2 Kings 1 and 2.

30 *the honey locust tree*: The account of the Baptist surviving on honey and locusts in Mark 1:6 undoubtedly comes from a mistranslation for the honey locust tree, also known as the carob. The Baptist could indeed have survived on carob pods.

30 *"And behold, the Lord passed by"*: 1 Kings 19:11.

31 *illiterate, as was everyone she knew*: For the elite monopoly on literacy, see Baumgarten, *Flourishing of Jewish Sects*.

31 *"without writing"*: Lévi-Strauss, *Myth and Meaning*.

32 *long narrative poems*: See, for instance, Clinton Bailey's translations of twentieth-century poems in *Bedouin Poetry*.

32 *rhythms, images, indeed whole phrases*: Excellent on the oral tradition are Niles, *Homo Narrans* on singers and poets as tradition bearers; Finnegan, *Oral Poetry* on memorization techniques and structure; and Whallon, *Formula, Character and Context*, on biblical and epic traditions.

32 *Mary conceiving through the ear*: A legend that began in the third century when Origen of Alexandria suggested that Mary was impregnated by the words of the angel. Within a century, the visual image of the angel talking into her ear had become the conceptual image of the angel impregnating her through the ear. For a more psychoanalytic take on the legend, see "The Madonna's Conception Through the Ear" in Jones, *Psycho-Myth, Psycho-History*.

32 *"the word was made flesh"*: John 1:14.

33 *"all part of the once undifferentiated collection"*: Whallon, *Formula, Character and Context*.

34 *"so he left Maria Magdalena"*: Up to this point, Khiyr's telling of the Magdalene's story follows the eastern Orthodox tradition, in which the Magdalene only despairs and/or turns to prostitution after being jilted by the man to whom she is betrothed. Only at the end does Khiyr give the story a unique twist of his own.

35 *"He who is without sin"*: John 8:7.

II

37 *raised from age three*: In The Protevangelium of James, a.k.a. The Infancy Gospel of James, in *The Apocryphal New Testament*.

39 *the woman in the gospels*: Luke 7:37–38.

39 *Sacrifice is a messy business*: For details of sacrifice and temple ritual in the following pages, see Klingaman, *First Century*, and Shmuel Safrai, "Religion in Everyday Life," in Safrai and Stern, *Jewish People*.

41 *Prayer was not part of the ritual*: "The contrast between sacrifice and prayer is the contrast between elitism and populism," says Shaye Cohen in *From the Maccabees to the Mishnah*.

41 *"whole families searching"*: Molly Moore, "Muslim Feat of Sacrifice Unsettles Modern Turkey," in *The Washington Post*, March 6, 2001.

41 *a vast array of activity*: see Horsley and Silberman, *Message and the Kingdom*.

43 *"a monumental institution"*: Ibid.

44 *the same slab of stone*: Kanan Makiya's book *The Rock* brilliantly incorporates the legends and history of this slab of stone.

46 *beliefs mirror those of legendary first-century Pharisee sages*: For instance, one of Jesus' most famous sayings, "Do unto others as you would have them do unto you, for this is the law and the prophets," mirrors Hillel's "Golden Rule" when asked the meaning of the Torah: "What is hateful to you, do not do to your fellow. This is the whole of the Torah. The rest is interpretation."

47 *exhibit on ancient goddesses*: "Local Goddesses: From Ancient Deities to Mythical Women of Today" was at the Tower of David Museum of the History of Jerusalem in spring 2001.

47 *A Jew—Yehudi*: "Jewish identity in antiquity was elusive and uncertain," says Shaye Cohen, who explores the issue in depth in *The Beginnings of Jewishness*. "Indeed," he continues, "the Greek word 'Ioudaios,' usually translated as 'Jew,' often is better translated as

'Judean.' " James Carroll *(Constantine's Sword)* notes the misleading assumption of a social-religious entity called "the Jews," as well as the powerful regional differences between Judeans and Galileans.

51 *mystical Judaism*: See Scholem, *Major Trends in Jewish Mysticism.*

51 *The gospel version*: Mark 6:17–28.

III

54 *Barabbas, the thief*: See Smallwood, *Jews Under Roman Rule.*

54 *"a notable prisoner"*: Matthew 27:16; Mark 15:7; Luke 23:19.

55 *"social banditry"*: Discussed at length by Horsley and Hanson in *Bandits, Prophets, and Messiahs.*

57 *"his" people never accepted him*: See Cohen, *Beginnings of Jewishness* for an excellent discussion of the Judean/Jewishness of Herod and the Idumeans.

57 *"an Arab from the southern Palestinian province of Idumea"*: Wilson, *Jesus.*

58 *Mark Antony in Rome*: The Mark Antony of Shakespeare's *Antony and Cleopatra.*

58 *"accidental death by drowning"*: There was nothing accidental about it, of course. The event is memorably portrayed in E. P. Cavafy's poem "Aristoboulus," which ends with the boy's mother longing "to go out and shout it to the Hebrews, to tell, to tell how the murder was done" (trans. Rae Daeven).

59 *Olympic Games*: Herod's long list of benefactions is detailed in Smallwood, *Jews Under Roman Rule.*

60–61 *Guile was needed too*: Smallwood gives an excellent account of the intricacies of Herodian politics, which could be said to have defined Byzantine three hundred years before the Byzantines came into being.

62 *tax burden was crippling*: See Richard Horsley's work on tax debt and its destructive effect on peasant society *(The Message and the Kingdom).* Le Roy Ladourie also records peasant hostility to tithes and resentment of the wealth of the church in fourteenth-century Montaillou, in southwestern France.

64 *"the bond with the land"*: Qleibo, *Before the Mountains Disappear.*

64 *"We are having to pledge our fields"*: Nehemiah 5:1–5.

65 *old Mosaic law*: Sabbatical release from debt mandated in Deuteronomy 15:1–2.

65 *The earliest version*: Matthew 6:12.

65 *lost partial sight of debt*: Luke 11:4.

67 *the still, humid days of summer*: On a single hot summer's day, the Sea of Galilee loses one whole centimeter of water level through evaporation.

68 *fishermen as exploited*: See Horsley and Silberman, *Message and the Kingdom*.

69 *many candidates*: See Horsley and Hanson, *Bandits, Prophets, and Messiahs*.

72 *"combined patriotism with moral purity"*: Schiff and Ya'ari, *Intifada*.

IV

77 *a stone on the floor*: As with many such details, in Granqvist, *Birth and Childhood*.

78 *"Come sister," she chants*: Ibid.

79 *"Give afflictions and enemies no power"*: Naveh and Shaked, *Magic Spells and Formulae*.

79 *to the earth we shall return*: Patai, *On Jewish Folklore*.

79 *dust to dust*: Genesis 3:19, Ecclesiastes 3:20.

81 *midwives and pharmacists*: Ehrenreich and English, *Witches, Midwives and Nurses*.

82 *Aristotle's wife Pythias*: Achterberg, *Woman as Healer*.

82 *Cleopoatra* Ibid.

82 *By Pliny's own admission*: Quoted in Jackson, *Doctors and Diseases*.

82 *art and science of herbal healing*: Historical sources include Jackson, *Doctors and Diseases in the Roman Empire*, and Preuss, *Biblical and Talmudic Medicine*. For specific Middle Eastern practices, see Crowfoot and Baldensperger, *From Cedar to Hyssop*, and Abu-Rabia, *Traditional Bedouin Medicine*. I am also indebted to Dr. Stephen Fulder of Klil for sharing his knowledge and expertise.

84 *raising the widow's son from the dead*: Luke 7:12–15.

87 *the visionary Wisdom of Solomon*: a.k.a. the Book of Wisdom, in *The Jerusalem Bible*.

87 *fourth-century B.C. bas-relief*: In the collection of the National Archaeological Museum, Athens. Photograph in Achterberg, *Woman as Healer*.

87 *"talitha kumi"*: Literally, "girl, arise." Mark 5:41.

88 *Jesus mixes spittle with clay*: John 9:6.

88 *more to clay and spittle*: See Hull, *Hellenistic Magic*.

88 *Isis kneads the spittle*: Witt, *Isis in the Graeco-Roman World*.

88 *call on the guardian deity*: Cumont, *Oriental Religions in Roman Paganism*.

88 *re-named with each new conqueror*: A practice that continued worldwide, into the twentieth century. For instance, the United States replaced Native American place names (e.g., Mount Tacoma became Mount Rainier), Australian settlers did the same with Aboriginal tribal names (e.g., Uluru became Ayer's Rock), and Israel replaced Arabic names with Hebrew ones (e.g., Saffuriya, once Sepphoris, became Zippori). In the Middle East, the succession of conquerors over the centuries means that one place can accumulate as many as six or seven names. Which name is used then becomes a kind of political statement in itself.

89 *commanding the demon to leave*: Smith, *Jesus the Magician*.

89 *"Adjured are you, spirit"*: In Naveh and Shaked, *Magic Spells and Formulae*.

89 *"I abjure you, fever and sickness"*: Ibid.

89 *lack of divine grace*: Discussed feelingly by Crossan in *The Historical Jesus*. See also Sontag, *Illness as Metaphor*.

90 *"Master, who sinned"*: John 9:2.

90 *the hemorrhaging woman*: Mark 5:25, Matthew 9:20, Luke 8:43.

90 *the leper as unclean*: Mark 1:40, Matthew 8:2, Luke 5:12.

91 *"eyes of the blind shall be opened"*: Isaiah 35:5–6.

91 *Messianic Apocalypse*: In *Complete Dead Sea Scrolls*.

92 *Book of Enoch*: In *Apocrypha and Pseudepigrapha of the Old Testament*.

93 *Contraception was widely used*: In the following discussion of contraception and abortion, I am particularly indebted to Riddle, *Contraception and Abortion from the Ancient World to the Renaissance*, and McLaren, *History of Contraception*.

94 *artemisia—wormwood*: The World Health Organization now recommends artemisinin, the active ingredient in artemisia, as the best long-term option for the treatment of malaria.

94 *chasteberry bush*: In 2001, German researchers reported in the *British Medical Journal* that a dried extract of chasteberry fruit *(Vitex agnus castus)* reduces most symptoms of premenstrual syndrome.

96 *women's fertility would be equated*: See Eliade, *Sacred and the Profane*, and Burkert, *Ancient Mystery Cults*.

97 *"God needed Mary's 'yes'"*: David M. Neuhaus sj of the Pontifical Biblical Institute in Jerusalem, in the sermon "Mary and the New Covenant," Easter 2001. Also Maeckelberghe, *Desperately Seeking Mary*. Michael Downey, the cardinal's theologian for the Archdiocese of Los Angeles, puts it this way in *The Cathedral at the Heart of*

Los Angeles: "The whole of her mystery rests in a word: fiat. 'Yes.' By it, she became the Mother of God. And us."

V

98 *makes offerings*: On paganism at the time, see Hopkins, *World Full of Gods*. Also Cumont, *Oriental Religions*, and Flusser, "Paganism in Palestine," in Safrai and Stern, *Jewish People*.

99 *the story of the Great Virgin*: See especially Witt, *Isis in the Graeco-Roman World*. Also Burkert, *Ancient Mystery Cults*, and Benko, *Virgin Goddess*.

100 *gnostic gospel of Philip*: In *The Nag Hammadi Labrary*.

101 *Isis suckling the infant Horus*: Photographic plates in Tran, *Isis Lactans*.

101 *a sense of the sacred*: Cioran, in *The New Gods*, notes that "in the eyes of the ancients, the more gods you recognize, the better you serve divinity, of which they are but aspects, or faces."

102 *more accessible gods*: As Shaye Cohen notes in *From the Maccabees to the Mishnah*, "monotheism is an ambiguous concept . . . The Jewish monotheism of antiquity did not exclude belief in many and diverse supernatural beings."

102 *A degree of polytheism*: See Hillman, "Psychology: Monotheistic, Polytheistic" in Miller, *New Polytheism*.

103 *"the rich native religious stew"*: Fredriksen, *From Jesus to Christ*.

103 *"In the pre-Christian epoch"*: Burkert, *Ancient Mystery Cults*.

103 *"no gods before me"*: Karen Armstrong discusses this excellently in *A History of God*.

104 *"Peer Gynt's famous onion"*: Cox, *Seduction of the Spirit*.

106 *"biologically insignificant tissues"*: Holtzman and Kulish, *Nevermore*.

107 *Hymen, the god of marriage*: Ibid.

107 *dire punishment*: Deuteronomy 22:20–21.

108 *"Behold, a virgin"*: Matthew 1:23 refers to Isaiah 7:14.

108 *the Greek word*: parthenos See Schaberg, *Illegitimacy of Jesus*.

109 *"virgin births"*: Hall, *Moon and the Virgin*.

109 *a widow became a "marriageable maiden"*: Leach, *Genesis as Myth*.

110 *a web of dualisms*: Lévi-Strauss, *Raw and the Cooked*.

113 *virgin goddesses*: I am deeply indebted to Stephen Benko's superb book *The Virgin Goddess* in the pages that follow.

113 *"the enigmatic virgin"*: Giulia Sissa's irresistibly titled *Greek Virginity* is an extended philosophical essay on virginity.

114 *"Nuth the mighty mother"*: Ashe, *Virgin*.

114 *"It is I alone"*: Ibid.

115 *Diana of Ephesus*: In the Museo Nazionale, Naples. Photograph in Neumann, *Great Mother*.

116 *Untamed, untouchable*: See Shinoda Bolen, *Goddesses in Everywoman*.

116 *the essence of fertility*: Benko discusses this in depth in *The Virgin Goddess*.

VI

120 *father provides the white stuff*: From the Talmud (Niddah 31a: Eccles. Rabah 5:10), quoted in Preuss, *Biblical and Talmudic Medicine*.

120 *"man lies with the woman"*: Granqvist, *Birth and Childhood*.

121 *the angel Gabriel kneads soil*: Ibid.

122 *"A biography may be considered complete"*: Virginia Woolf in *Orlando* (London, 1928). Interestingly quoted by Norman Mailer in his "speculative biography" of Marilyn Monroe.

123 *"No sooner have you grabbed hold"*: Calasso, *Marriage of Cadmus and Harmony*.

123 *Truth is an evolving idea*: James, *Pragmatism*.

124 *"so far as man stands for anything"*: James, *Will to Believe*.

124 *"Blessed be the Name"*: "The name" is used instead of "God" since Jewish tradition forbids uttering the name of God.

125 *"Blessed art thou"*: Luke 1:28.

125 *the Trobriand islanders*: Leach, *Genesis as Myth*.

127 *"daughter of a strange god"*: Malachi 2:11.

127 *apocalyptic battle*: "The War Scroll" in *Complete Dead Sea Scrolls*.

127 *"Leda and the Swan"*: In *Collected Poems of W. B. Yeats*, New York, 1956.

127 *the full version of the legend*: In Benko, *Virgin Goddess*.

128 *gods siring legendary humans*: See Graves, *Greek Myths*, and Phipps, *Sexuality of Jesus*.

128 *"Hatshepsut shall be the name"*: In Phipps, *Sexuality of Jesus*.

128 *"son of the living god"*: M. Smith, *Jesus the Magician*.

129 *the Holy Ghost "coming upon"*: *Maryam* Luke 1:35, "the Holy Ghost shall come upon thee."

130–31 *his first appearance*: Matthew 1:1–20.

131 *fetching him from the temple*: Luke 2:44–45.

131 *"Hail, holy Joseph, hail"*: In *The Westminster Hymnal*, London 1939.

132 *"the carpenter's son"*: Matthew 13:55.

133 *Wisdom of Solomon*: a.k.a. the Book of Wisdom, in *The Jerusalem Bible*.

NOTES

133 *Book of Enoch:* In *The Apocrypha and Pseudepigrapha of the Old Testament.*
133 *to establish Jesus' lineage:* Matthew 1:1–17, Luke 3:23–38.
133 *"the son of Mary":* Mark 6:3.
133 *"son of man":* An impassioned scholarly debate has developed on the possible messianic implications of this phrase. Particularly good on the subject are Lindars, *Jesus, Son of Man,* and Collins, *Apocalyptic Imagination.*
134 *a metaphorical beard:* In his novel *Fifth Business,* Robertson Davies has Père Blazon, an iconoclastic Jesuit priest of great age and greater learning, call Joseph "the world's most celebrated cuckold."

VII

137 *as a result of rape:* I am indebted to Jane Schaberg's courageous examination of this possibility in *The Illegitimacy of Jesus.*
137 *"cover you with its shadow":* This is the Jerusalem Bible translation of Luke 1:35. The King James version reads: "The Holy Ghost shall come upon thee, and the power of the Highest shall overshadow thee."
137 *"Behold the handmaid":* Luke 1:38. Mirrors 1 Samuel 1:18, where Hannah says "Let thine handmaid find grace in thy light."
137 *model rape victim:* Daly, *Church and the Second Sex.*
137 *the Magnificat:* Luke 1:46–55 and 1 Samuel 2:1–10.
138 *anti-Christian diatribes:* Panthera appears in pagan philosopher Celsus' work "True Doctrines." Writing in the year 178 A.D., Celsus probably drew on earlier sources. See Schüssler-Fiorenza, *Jesus,* and Schaberg, *Illegitimacy of Jesus.*
139 *revealed rape for what it is:* Brownmiller's book identified rape as an act of violence, not sexuality, and dispelled the notion that rape had anything to do with provocativeness on the woman's part.
140 *if a man rapes a betrothed girl:* Deuteronomy 22:23–27.
142 *Protevangelium of James:* a.k.a. the Infancy Gospel of James, in *The Apocryphal New Testament.*
142 *A ward of the temple:* See also the Gospel of Bartholomew, in *The New Testament Apocrypha,* where Mary, talking to the disciples, mentions living "in the temple of God" at age ten.
143 *Fathers did sell their daughters:* See Schüssler-Fiorenza, *In Memory of Her.*
144 *the law stated:* Deuteronomy 22:28–29.

144 *"about my father's business"*: Luke 2:49.

145 *"Blessed are the poor"*: Matthew 5:3, the first line of the Sermon on the Mount.

145 *"Is not this Joseph's son?"*: Luke 4:22.

145 *"Jesus, the son of Joseph"*: John 1:45, 6:42.

146 *"made of the seed of David"*: Romans 1:3.

146 *"woman," not "Mother"*: John 2:4, 19:26.

146 *"If anyone does not hate"*: Luke 14:26.

147 *"Call no man father"*: Matthew 23:9.

147 *"Unless a man is born again"*: John 3:3.

147 *Nearly a third of all births*: Sarah Lyall, "For Europeans, Love Yes, Marriage Maybe," in *The New York Times*, March 24, 2002.

VIII

153 *"was lost and now is found"*: Luke 15:32.

153 *"For many are called"*: Matthew 22:14.

154 *throwing dice:* Matthew 27:35, a reference to Psalm 22:18.

156 *They used iron nails:* See Hengel, *Crucifixion in the Ancient World* for details of crucifixion and its use.

157 *one detail that is rarely mentioned:* Noted by Catherine Clément in her correspondence with Julia Kristeva in *The Feminine and the Sacred*.

158 *"purest forms of governmental violence"*: Horsley and Silberman, *Message and the Kingdom*.

159 *The Temple Scroll:* In *Complete Dead Sea Scrolls*.

159 *"Anyone who was put to death"*: Wilson, *Paul*.

160 *"to fulfill the scripture"*: John 19:24, 19:28, 19:36, 19:37.

160 *"why hast thou forsaken me"*: Matthew 27:46, Psalm 22:1.

160 *"into thy hands"*: Luke 23:46, Psalm 31:5.

160 *"darkness over the land"*: Amos 8:9.

160 *"the foal of an ass"*: Zechariah 19:9.

160 *vinegar-soaked sponge:* Psalm 69:21.

160 *pierced hands and feet:* Psalm 22:16.

161 *"prophecy historicized"*: Crossan, *Historical Jesus*.

161 *earthquake . . . eclipse . . . rending:* Matthew 27:51, Mark 15:33.

161 *massacre of the innocents:* Matthew 2:16.

161 *flight into Egypt:* Matthew 2:15 refers to Hosea 11.1, where Yahweh calls his son out of Egypt. Jesus thus becomes a second Moses or Joseph.

161 *visits of the three magi:* Matthew 2:11.

161 *"adventure of the hero"*: Campbell, *Power of Myth*.
161 *"Those who told the story"*: Carroll, *Constantine's Sword*.
162 *Overturning the money changers' tables*: Mark 11:15, Matthew 21:12.
162 *somewhere between 4 B.C. and 6 A.D.*: Morton Smith *(Jesus the Magician)* estimates Jesus being born "probably within eight or ten years of the beginning of the current era." Hopkins *(World Full of Gods)* notes the census in 6 A.D. as a likely time.
163 *"in the days of Herod the king"*: Matthew 2:1.
163 *"a typical tyrant-legend"*: Smallwood, *Jews Under Roman Rule*.
163 *the census—the given reason*: Luke 2:1–5.

IX

170 *The bodies were left to hang*: Hengel, *Crucifixion in the Ancient World*, Horsley and Silberman, *Message and the Kingdom*.
170 *disintegrated into dust*: Genesis 3:19, Psalm 104:29, Ecclesiastes 3:20.
171 *a body left unburied*: Morgenstern, *Rites of Birth, Marriage, Death*.
171 *the bones of Joseph brought home*: Exodus 13:9, Joshua 24:32.
171 *burned the bones of his enemy*: Amos 2:1.
171 *exhume and burn the bones*: 2 Kings 12:14–20.
171 *asked Pilate to give him the body*: Mark 15:43.
172 *they marched and demonstrated*: See *Mothers of the Disappeared*, by Jo Fisher (Boston, 1989).
173 *"a muddle of Marys"*: Warner, *Alone of All Her Sex*.
173 *Mary the mother of James and Joses*: Matthew 27:56.
173 *Mary the wife of Cleopas*: John 19:25.
173 *"the other Mary"*: Matthew 28:1.
174 *"many women which came up with him"*: Mark 15:41.
174 *appears at the crucifixion*: John 19:25–26.
175 *devoted to pagan worship*: 1 Kings 18:4, 18:13. Jezebel's gruesome death is in 2 Kings 9:33–37.
175 *paradigm of unfaithfulness*: See Schüssler-Fiorenza, *In Memory of Her*.
175 *any woman who dares criticize*: Sabbagh, *Palestinian Women*.
176 *a woman of some means*: Haskins, *Mary Magdalen*.
176 *Only Luke identifies her*: Luke 8:2.
176 *"neither male nor female"*: Galatians 3:28.
177 *"the most successful attempt"*: Cox, *Seduction of the Spirit*.
177 *the unnamed sinner*: Luke 7:36–50.

177 *the adulteress in John*: John 8:3–7.

177 *the many-husbanded Samaritan*: John 4:18.

177 *repository of sinful sexuality*: In the sixth century, Pope Gregory the Great—he of the Gregorian chant—declared that the sinner, the adulteress, and the Samaritan woman were all Mary Magdalene.

177 *"only a small fragment"*: Hopkins, *World Full of Gods*.

177 *used to kiss on the mouth*: Gospel of Philip in *The Nag Hammadi Library*.

177 *gnostic gospel of Mary*: In *The Nag Hammadi Library*.

178 *"Mary received Jesus"*: In Murray, *Symbols of Church and Kingdom*.

178 *"It was she who bore the Son"*: Ibid.

178 *The Twentieth Discourse*: Full title "The Twentieth Discourse of Cyril of Jerusalem," in *The Apocryphal New Testament*. Also titled "The Discourse on Mary Theotokos by Cyril, Archbishop of Jerusalem," in F. Robinson, editor, *Coptic Apocryphal Gospels* (Cambridge, 1896). Cyril was indeed archbishop of Jerusalem in the late fourth century, but modern scholars doubt his authorship of this series of discourses, and refer to the author as Pseudo-Cyril of Jerusalem.

179 *"three who walked with the Lord"*: The Gospel of Philip in *The Nag Hammadi Library*.

179 *"a state of inextricable confusion"*: Murray, *Symbols of Church and Kingdom*. See also F. Jones, *Which Mary?*

179 *"myth-splitting"*: Lévi-Strauss, *Myth and Meaning*.

180 *an explanation of sorts*: Matthew 28:11–15.

181 *bringing spices and oils*: Mark 16:1.

181 *ignores the contradiction*: John 19:40.

182 *planned to steal the body*: Schonfield's *Passover Plot* keeps conspiracy theorists happy.

183 *"It was love that raised Jesus"*: Renan, *Life of Jesus*.

X

184 *"Woman, behold thy son"*: John 19:26.

184 *"including Mary the mother"*: Acts of the Apostles 1:14.

184 *one trend in apocryphal writing*: See Marina Warner's discussion of the Assumption in *Alone of All Her Sex*.

185 *Discourse of Theodosius*: Full title "The Discourse of Theodosius, Archbishop of Alexandria," in *The Apocryphal New Testament*.

185 *Homily of Evodius*: Full title "The Homily Attributed to Evodius, Archbishop of Rome," in *The Apocryphal New Testament*.

186 *a new kind of community*: Ashe, in *The Virgin*, speculates on such a community, centered on Mary as their prophet, and on a vernacular Gospel of Mary assembled from her prophecies and recollections.

186 *dormit, "she fell asleep"*: See for instance "The Discourse of St. John the Divine Concerning the Falling Asleep of the Holy Mother of God," in *The Apocryphal New Testament*.

190 *new shoots had sprung up*: See Rosenblum, *Olives*.

191 *the prophetess Hanna*: All the women in this paragraph appear in the New Testament gospels.

192 *Caletha the daughter of Nicodemus*: The "Syriac Narrative A" in *The Apocryphal New Testament* tells how Mary "left Jerusalem and went to Bethlehem with her three virgins, Caletha daughter of Nicodemus, Neshra daughter of Gamaliel, Tabitha daughter of Archelaus."

192 *divine female figure*: Elizabeth A. Johnson, *She Who Is*, and Schüssler-Fiorenza, *In Memory of Her* are particularly good on Wisdom/Hochma/Sophia.

193 *Her earliest appearance*: Proverbs 1:20–33, 8:1–36.

193 *the Book of Wisdom*: a.k.a the Wisdom of Solomon, in *The Jerusalem Bible*.

193 *"the structure of the world"*: Ibid., 7:17–20.

193 *twenty-one attributes*: Ibid., 7:22–23.

193–94 *Ecclesiasticus*: In *The Jerusalem Bible*.

194 *"I have exhaled a perfume"*: Ecclesiasticus 24:20–29. The whole of chapter 24 quotes Wisdom as she "speaks her own praises."

194 *Apocryphon of John*: In *The New Testament Apocrypha*.

194 *On the Origin of the World*: In *The Nag Hammadi Library*.

194 *Sophia of Jesus Christ*: Ibid.

194 *"earliest Christian theology is sophialogy"*: Schüssler-Fiorenza, *In Memory of Her*.

195 *gospel of Philip*: In *The Nag Hammadi Library*.

XI

197 *High priestesses*: Kraemer, *Her Share of the Blessings*. Kraemer is particularly good on women in sacramental roles.

198 *Jewish monastic movement*: Ibid.

198 *exultant song*: Exodus 15:20–21.
199 *abandon blood ties of family*: Matthew 10:35–37, 12:48–50
199 *Pistis Sophia*: In *The New Testament Apocrypha*.
200 *Phoebe the deacon*: Romans 16:1.
200 *Junia*: Romans 16:7.
201 *Acts of Paul and Thecla*: In *The New Testament Apocrypha*.
201 *"no male or female"*: Galatians 3:28.
201 *"These heretical women"*: Quoted in Pagels, *Gnostic Gospels*, an invaluable study of the history and philosophy of Christian gnosticism.
201 *widespread Montanist movement*: See especially Kraemer, *Her Share of the Blessings*.
201 *"We have among us"*: Ibid.
202 *the Kolyridian movement*: See especially Benko, *Virgin Goddess*, and Kraemer, *Her Share of the Blessings*.
203 *"But bread it was"*: Benko, *Virgin Goddess*.
204 *characters like Nicodemus* See "Gospel of Nicodemus," "The Narrative of Joseph of Arimathea," and "The Acts of Pilate" in *The Apocryphal New Testament*.
204 *gnostic gospel of Mary*: In *The Nag Hammadi Library*.
204 *"infancy gospels"*: See "The Protevangelium of James," "The Infancy Gospel of Thomas," and "The Gospel of Pseudo-Matthew" in *The New Testament Apocrypha*.
205 *very likely written by women*: See, for instance, Madeleine Scopello, "Jewish and Greek Heroines in the Nag Hammadi Library," in King, *Images of the Feminine in Gnosticism*.
205 *"Thunder, Perfect Mind"*: In *The Nag Hammadi Library*.
207 *the groundwork for rabbinical Judaism*: Neusner's *From Politics to Piety* is a superb account of this development.
208 *Twentieth Discourse*: In *The Apocryphal New Testament*.

SELECT BIBLIOGRAPHY

PRIMARY SOURCES

The Apocryphal New Testament: A Collection of Apocryphal Christian Literature in An English Translation. Edited by J. K. Elliot. New York: Oxford University Press, 1993.

The Apocrypha and Pseudepigrapha of the Old Testament. Edited by R. H. Charles. Oxford: Clarendon Press, 1912.

The Complete Dead Sea Scrolls in English. Edited by Geza Vermes. New York: Penguin, 1962.

The Holy Bible: King James Version. New York: New American Library, 1974.

The Jerusalem Bible: Reader's Edition. New York: Doubleday, 1968.

Josephus: The Essential Writings. Translated by Paul L. Maier. Grand Rapids Mich.: Kregel, 1988.

The Koran Interpreted. The Koran translated by A. J. Arberry. London: Allen and Unwin, 1955.

The Mishnah: A New Translation. Translated by Jacob Neusner. New Haven: Yale University Press, 1988.

The Nag Hammadi Library in English. Edited by James M. Robinson. San Francisco: HarperCollins, 1988.

The New Testament Apocrypha. Edited by Wilhelm Schneemelcher. Louisville, Ky.: Westminster/John Knox, 1991.

The Other Bible. Edited by Willis Barnstone. San Francisco: HarperCollins, 1984.

GENERAL

Abu-Rabia, Aref. *Traditional Bedouin Medicine* (in Hebrew). Tel Aviv: MOD, 1999.

Achterberg, Jeanne. *Woman as Healer*. Boston: Shambhala Publications, 1990.

Ackerman, Susan. *Warrior, Dancer, Seductress, Queen: Women in Judges and Biblical Israel*. New York: Doubleday, 1998.

Alain [Emile Chartier]. *The Gods* (Les Dieux). New York: New Directions, 1974.

Amiry, Suad, and Tamari, Vera. *The Palestinian Village Home*. London: British Museum Publications, 1989.

Ariès, Philippe. *Centuries of Childhood: A Social History of Family Life* (L'enfant et la vie familiale sous l'ancien régime). New York: Knopf, 1962.

Armstrong, Karen: *The Gospel According to Woman: Christianity's Creation of the Sex War in the West*. London: Hamish Hamilton, 1986.

—————. *A History of God: The 4,000-Year Quest of Judaism, Christianity, and Islam*. New York: Knopf, 1993.

Ashe, Geoffrey. *The Virgin*. London: Routledge and Paul, 1976.

Aviam, Mordechai. *Survey of Sites in the Galilee*. Jerusalem: Israel Exploration Society, 1995.

—————. "Tel Yodfat." In *Kadmaniot* (in Hebrew). Vol. 116, 1999.

Bailey, Clinton. *Bedouin Poetry from the Sinai and the Negev: Mirror of a Culture*. Oxford: Clarendon Press, 1991.

Baumgarten, Albert I. *The Flourishing of Jewish Sects in the Maccabean Era: An Interpretation*. Leiden: E. J. Brill, 1997.

Benko, Stephen. *The Virgin Goddess: Studies in the Pagan and Christian Roots of Mariology*. Leiden: E. J. Brill, 1993.

Benvenisti, Meron. *Sacred Landscape: The Buried History of the Holy Land Since 1948*. Berkeley: University of California Press, 2000.

Black, Matthew. *An Aramaic Approach to the Gospels and Acts*. Oxford: Clarendon Press, 1967.

Boer, Esther de. *Mary Magdalene: Beyond the Myth*. Harrisburg: Trinity Press International, 1997.

Bolen, Jean Shinoda. *Goddesses in Everywoman: A New Psychology of Women*. San Francisco: Harper and Row, 1984.

Boslooper, Thomas. *The Virgin Birth*. Philadelphia: Westminster Press, 1962.

Brooten, Bernadette. *Women Leaders in the Ancient Synagogue*. Chico, Calif.: Scholars Press, 1982.

Brown, Raymond E. *The Virginal Conception and Bodily Resurrection of Jesus*. New York: Paulist Press, 1973.

Brownmiller, Susan. *Against Our Will: Men, Women, and Rape*. New York: Simon and Schuster, 1975.

Brydon, Lynne, and Chant, Sylvia, eds. *Women in the Third World: Gender Issues in Rural and Urban Areas.* New Brunswick, N.J.: Rutgers University Press, 1989.

Burkert, Walter. *Ancient Mystery Cults.* Cambridge, Mass.: Harvard University Press, 1987.

Calasso, Roberto. *The Marriage of Cadmus and Harmony.* New York: Knopf, 1993.

Campbell, Joseph, and Moyers, Bill. *The Power of Myth.* New York: Doubleday, 1988.

Carroll, James. *Constantine's Sword: The Church and the Jews.* New York: Houghton Mifflin, 2001.

Certeau, Michel de. *The Writing of History* (L'ecriture de l'histoire). New York: Columbia University Press, 1988.

Charlesworth, James H. *Jesus and the Dead Sea Scrolls.* New York: Doubleday, 1992.

————, ed. *Jesus' Jewishness: Exploring the Place of Jesus in Early Judaism.* New York: Crossroad, 1991.

Chevallier, Andrew. *The Encyclopedia of Medicinal Plants.* New York: DK Publishing, 1996.

Christ, Carol, and Plaskow, Judith, eds. *Womanspirit Rising: A Feminist Reader in Religion.* San Francisco: Harper and Row, 1979.

Cioran, E. M. *The New Gods* (Mauvais démiurge). New York: Quadrangle, 1974.

Clark, Gillian. *Women in Late Antiquity: Pagan and Christian Lifestyles.* New York: Oxford University Press, 1993.

Clément, Catherine, and Kristeva, Julia. *The Feminine and the Sacred* (Le feminin and le sacré). New York: Columbia University Press, 2001.

Cohen, Shaye. *The Beginnings of Jewishness: Boundaries, Varieties, Uncertainties.* Berkeley: University of California Press, 1999.

————. *From the Maccabees to the Mishnah.* Philadelphia: Westminster, 1987.

Collingwood, R. G. *An Autobiography.* New York: Oxford University Press, 1939.

————. *Essays in the Philosophy of History.* Austin: University of Texas Press, 1965.

————. *The Idea of History.* Oxford: Clarendon Press, 1946.

Collins, John J. *The Apocalyptic Imagination: An Introduction to Jewish Apocalyptic Literature.* New York: Crossroad, 1984.

Cox, Harvey. *The Seduction of the Spirit: The Use and Misuse of People's Religion.* New York: Simon and Schuster, 1973.

Crossan, John Dominic. *The Historical Jesus: The Life of a Mediterranean Jewish Peasant*. San Francisco: HarperCollins, 1991.

————. *Jesus: A Revolutionary Biography*. San Francisco: HarperCollins, 1994.

Crowfoot, Grace M., and Baldensperger, Louise. *From Cedar to Hyssop: A Study of the Folklore of Plants in Palestine*. London: Sheldon Press, 1932.

Cumont, Franz. *The Oriental Religions in Roman Paganism*. Chicago: Open Court, 1911.

Daly, Mary. *The Church and the Second Sex*. New York: Harper and Row, 1975.

Davies, Stevan L. *Jesus the Healer: Possession, Trance, and the Origins of Christianity*. New York: Continuum, 1995.

Downey, Michael. *The Cathedral at the Heart of Los Angeles*. Los Angeles: Liturgical Press, 2002.

Ehrenreich, Barbara, and English, Deirdre. *Witches, Midwives and Nurses: A History of Women Healers*. Old Westbury, N.Y.: Feminist Press, 1973.

Eliade, Mircea. *Patterns in Comparative Religion*. New York: Sheed and Ward, 1972.

————. *The Sacred and the Profane: The Nature of Religion*. New York: Harcourt Brace, 1959.

Elliott, J. K., ed. *The Apocryphal Jesus: Legends of the Early Church*. New York: Oxford University Press, 1996.

Elon, Amos. *A Blood-Dimmed Tide: Dispatches from the Middle East*. New York: Columbia University Press, 1997.

Finnegan, Ruth H. *Oral Poetry: Its Nature, Significance, and Social Context*. New York: Cambridge University Press, 1977.

Flusser, David. *Jewish Sources in Early Christianity*. Tel Aviv: MOD Books, 1989.

————. *Judaism and the Origins of Christianity*. Jerusalem: Magnes Press, 1988.

————, and Notley, R. Steven. *Jesus*. Jerusalem: Magnes Press, 1998.

Frazer, James George. *The Golden Bough: A Study in Magic and Religion*. New York: Macmillan, 1922.

Fredriksen, Paula. *Jesus of Nazareth, King of the Jews: A Jewish Life and the Emergence of Christianity*. New York: Knopf, 1999.

————. *From Jesus to Christ: The Origins of the New Testament Images of Jesus*. New Haven: Yale University Press, 1988.

Geertz, Clifford. *Available Light: Anthropological Reflections on Philosophical Topics*. Princeton: Princeton University Press, 2000.

————. *The Interpretation of Cultures*. New York: Basic Books, 1973.

————. "Religion as a Cultural System" In *The Religious Situation*. Edited by Donald Cutler. Boston: Beacon Press, 1968.

Goodenough, Erwin R. *Jewish Symbols in the Greco-Roman Period*. New York: Pantheon, 1953.

Gordon, Mary. "Coming to Terms with Mary." *Commonweal*, January 15, 1982.

Granqvist, Hilma. *Birth and Childhood Among the Arabs: Studies in a Muhammadan Village in Palestine*. Helsingfors: Söderström, 1947.

————. *Portrait of a Palestinian Village: The Photographs of Hilma Granqvist*. Edited by Karen Seger. London: Third World Centre for Research, 1981.

Grant, Elihu. *The Peasantry of Palestine: The Life, Manners and Customs of the Village*. Boston: Pilgrim Press, 1907.

Graves, Robert. *The Greek Myths*. London: Pelican, 1955.

————. *King Jesus: A Novel*. New York: Farrar, Straus, Giroux, 1946.

————. *The White Goddess: A Historical Grammar of Poetic Myth*. New York: Farrar, Straus, Giroux, 1966.

Greeley, Andrew M. *The Mary Myth: On the Femininity of God*. New York: Seabury Press, 1977.

Grieve, M. (Maud): *A Modern Herbal*. New York: Harcourt Brace, 1931.

Haley, Jay. *The Power Tactics of Jesus Christ and Other Essays*. New York: Norton, 1986.

Hall, Nor. *The Moon and the Virgin: Reflections on the Archetypal Feminine*. New York: Harper and Row, 1980.

Hanauer, J. E. *Folklore of the Holy Land: Moslem, Christian, and Jewish*. Folcroft, Penn.: Folcroft Library, 1977.

Hanson, K. C., and Oakman, Douglas E. *Palestine in the Time of Jesus: Social Structures and Social Conflicts*. Minneapolis: Fortress Press, 1998.

Haskins, Susan. *Mary Magdalen: Myth and Metaphor*. New York: Harcourt Brace, 1993.

Hazleton, Lesley. *Jerusalem, Jerusalem: A Memoir of War and Peace, Passion and Politics*. New York: Atlantic Monthly Press, 1986.

————. "Magdala." In *Experimental Theology*. Edited by Rebecca Brown and Robert Corbett. Seattle: Seattle Research Institute, 2003.

————. *Where Mountains Roar: A Personal Report from the Sinai and Negev Desert*. New York: Holt, Rinehart and Winston, 1980.

Hengel, Martin. *Crucifixion in the Ancient World and the Folly of the Message of the Cross*. Philadelphia: Fortress Press, 1977.

————. *Judaism and Hellenism: Studies in Their Encounter in Palestine During the Early Hellenistic Period*. Philadelphia: Fortress Press, 1974.

Heyob, Sharon Kelly. *The Cult of Isis Among Women in the Greco-Roman World*. Leiden: E. J. Brill, 1975.

Himes, Norman E. *Medical History of Contraception*. New York: Gamut Press, 1963.

Hobsbawn, E. J.: *Social Bandits and Primitive Rebels: Studies in Archaic Forms of Social Movement in the 19th and 20th Centuries*. Glencoe, Ill.: Free Press, 1960.

Holmes, Richard. "Biography: Inventing the Truth." In *The Art of Literary Biography*. Edited by John Batchelor. New York: Oxford University Press, 1995.

Holtzman, Deanna, and Kulish, Nancy. *Nevermore: The Hymen and the Loss of Virginity*. Northvale, N.J.: J. Aronson, 1997.

Hooke, S. H. *Middle Eastern Mythology: From the Assyrians to the Hebrews*. London: Pelican, 1963.

Hopkins, Keith. *A World Full of Gods: The Strange Triumph of Christianity*. New York: Free Press, 2000.

Horsley, Richard A. *Archaeology, History and Society in Galilee: The Social Context of Jesus and the Rabbis*. Harrisburg, Penn.: Trinity Press, 1996.

————. *Galilee: History, Politics, People*. Valley Forge, Penn.: Trinity Press, 1995.

————. *Jesus and the Spiral of Violence: Popular Jewish Resistance in Roman Palestine*. Minneapolis: Fortress Press, 1987.

————. *Sociology and the Jesus Movement*. New York: Continuum, 1989.

———— and Hanson, John S. *Bandits, Prophets, and Messiahs: Popular Movements in the Time of Jesus*. Harrisburg, Penn.: Trinity Press, 1985.

———— and Silberman, Neil Asher. *The Message and the Kingdom: How Jesus and Paul Ignited a Revolution and Transformed the Ancient World*. New York: Grosset/Putnam, 1997.

Hull, John M. *Hellenistic Magic and the Synoptic Tradition*. Naperville, Ill.: A. R. Allenson, 1974.

Idel, Moshe. *Kabbalah: New Perspectives*. New Haven: Yale University Press, 1988.

Ilan, Tal. *Jewish Women in Greco-Roman Palestine*. Peabody, Mass.: Hendrickson, 1996.

Jackson, Ralph. *Doctors and Diseases in the Roman Empire*. Norman, Okl.: University of Oklahoma Press, 1988.

Jacobson, David. "When Palestine Meant Israel." In *Biblical Archaeology Review*, May 2001.

Jaffee, Martin S. *Early Judaism: Religious Worlds of the First Judaic Millennium*. Upper Saddle River, N.J.: Prentice Hall, 1997.

James, William. *The Meaning of Truth*. New York: Longmans, Green and Co., 1909.

————. *Pragmatism: A New Name for Some Old Ways of Thinking*. New York: Longmans, Green and Co., 1907.

————. *The Varieties of Religious Experience*. New York: Longmans, Green and Co., 1902.

————. *The Will to Believe and Other Essays in Popular Philosophy*. New York: Longmans, Green and Co., 1931.

Jay, Nancy, ed. *Throughout the Generations Forever: Sacrifice, Religion, and Paternity*. Chicago: University of Chicago Press, 1992.

Jeremias, Joachim. *Jerusalem in the Time of Jesus: An Investigation into Economic and Social Conditions During the New Testament Period*. Philadelphia: Fortress Press, 1969.

Johnson, Elizabeth A. *She Who Is: The Mystery of God in Feminist Theological Discourse*. New York: Crossroad, 1994.

————. *Women, Earth, and Creator Spirit*. New York: Paulist Press, 1993.

Johnson, Paul. *A History of the Jews*. New York: HarperCollins, 1987.

Jones, Ernest. *Psycho-Myth, Psycho-History: Essays in Applied Psychoanalysis*. New York: Hillstone, 1974.

Jones, F. Stanley, ed. *Which Mary?—The Marys of Early Christian Tradition*. Atlanta: Society of Biblical Literature, 2003.

Jung, C. G. [Carl Gustav]. *Psychology and Religion*. New Haven: Yale University Press, 1938.

Katz, Melissa R., ed. *Divine Mirrors: The Virgin Mary in the Visual Arts*. New York: Oxford University Press, 2001.

Kay, Margarita Artschwager, ed. *Anthropology of Human Birth*. Philadelphia: F. A. Davis, 1982.

Kazantzakis, Nikos. *The Last Temptation of Christ: A Novel*. New York: Simon and Schuster, 1960.

Khalidi, Walid, ed. *All That Remains: The Palestinian Villages Occupied and Depopulated by Israel in 1948*. Washington, D.C.: Institute for Palestine Studies, 1992.

King, Karen L., ed. *Images of the Feminine in Gnosticism*. Philadelphia: Fortress Press, 1988.

————, ed. *Women and Goddess Traditions: In Antiquity and Today*. Minneapolis: Fortress Press, 1997.

Klingaman, William H. *The First Century: Emperors, Gods, and Everyman*. New York: HarperCollins, 1990.

Kraemer, Ross Shepard. *Her Share of the Blessings: Women's Religions Among Pagans, Jews, and Christians in the Greco-Roman World*. New York: Oxford University Press, 1992.

————, ed. *Maenads, Martyrs, Matrons, Monastics: A Sourcebook on Women's Religions in the Greco-Roman World.* Philadelphia: Fortress Press, 1988.

Leach, Edmund. *Culture and Communication: The Logic by Which Symbols Are Connected.* New York: Cambridge University Press, 1976.

————. *Genesis as Myth and Other Essays.* London: Jonathan Cape, 1969.

Lee, Hermione. *Virginia Woolf.* London: Chatto and Windus, 1996.

Le Roy Ladurie, Emmanuel. *Montaillou: The Promised Land of Error* (Montaillou, village occitan de 1294 à 1324). New York: G. Braziller, 1978.

Lévi-Strauss, Claude. *Myth and Meaning.* New York: Schocken Books, 1995.

————. *The Raw and the Cooked* (Cru et le cuit). New York: Harper and Row, 1969.

Levine, Amy-Jill, ed. *"Women Like This": New Perspectives on Jewish Women in the Greco-Roman World.* Atlanta: Scholars Press, 1991.

Liebes, Yehuda. *Studies in Jewish Myth and Jewish Messianism.* Albany: State University of New York Press, 1993.

Lindars, Barnabas. *Jesus Son of Man: A Fresh Examination of the Son of Man Sayings in the Gospels.* London: SPCK, 1983.

Maeckelberghe, Els. *Desperately Seeking Mary: A Feminist Appropriation of a Traditional Religious Symbol.* The Hague: Pharos, 1991.

Mailer, Norman. *Marilyn.* New York: Grosset and Dunlap, 1974.

Makiya, Kanan. *The Rock: A Tale of Seventh-Century Jerusalem.* New York: Pantheon, 2001.

McLaren, Angus. *A History of Contraception: From Antiquity to the Present Day.* Cambridge, Mass.: B. Blackwell, 1990.

McNeill, William H. *Mythistory and Other Essays.* Chicago: University of Chicago Press, 1986.

Meier, John P. *A Marginal Jew: Rethinking the Historical Jesus.* New York: Doubleday, 1991.

Meyers, Carol. *Discovering Eve: Ancient Israelite Women in Context.* New York: Oxford University Press, 1988.

————. "Everyday Life: Average Lifespan for Women in Ancient Israel." In *The Women's Bible Commentary.* Edited by Carol A. Newsom and Sharon H. Ringe. London: SPCK, 1992.

Miller, David LeRoy. *The New Polytheism: Rebirth of the Gods and Goddesses.* New York: Harper and Row, 1974.

Moltmann-Wendel, Elizabeth. *The Women Around Jesus*. New York: Crossroad, 1992.

Morgenstern, Julian. *Rites of Birth, Marriage, Death and Kindred Occasions Among the Semites*. Cincinatti: Hebrew Union College Press, 1966.

Murphy, Cullen. *The Word According to Eve: Women and the Bible in Ancient Times and Our Own*. Boston: Houghton Mifflin, 1998.

Murray, Robert. *Symbols of Church and Kingdom: A Study in Early Syriac Tradition*. Cambridge: Cambridge University Press, 1975.

Naveh, Joseph, and Shaked, Shaul. *Magic Spells and Formulae: Aramaic Incantations of Late Antiquity*. Jerusalem: Magnes Press, 1993.

Netzer, Ehud, and Weiss, Ze'ev. *Zippori* (Sepphoris). Jerusalem: Israel Exploration Society, 1994.

Neumann, Erich. *The Great Mother: An Analysis of the Archetype*. Princeton: Princeton University Press, 1963.

Neusner, Jacob. *From Politics to Piety: The Emergence of Pharisaic Judaism*. New York: KTAV, 1979.

————. *Judaism in the Beginning of Christianity*. Philadelphia: Fortress Press, 1984.

————. Green, William S., and Frerichs, Ernest, eds. *Judaisms and their Messiahs at the Turn of the Christian Era*. Cambridge: Cambridge University Press, 1987.

————, and Kee, Howard Clark, eds. *The Social World of Formative Christianity and Judaism*. Philadelphia: Fortress Press, 1988.

Newman, Lucile F., ed. *Women's Medicine: A Cross-Cultural Study of Indigenous Fertility Regulation*. New Brunswick, N.J.: Rutgers University Press, 1985.

Niles, John D. *Homo Narrans: The Poetics and Anthropology of Oral Literature*. Philadelphia: University of Pennsylvania Press, 1999.

Norberg-Hodge, Helena. *Ancient Futures: Learning from Ladakh*. San Francisco: Sierra Club Books, 1991.

Pagels, Elaine. *Adam, Eve, and the Serpent*. New York: Random House, 1988.

————. *Beyond Belief: The Secret Gospel of Thomas*. New York: Random House, 2003.

————. *The Gnostic Gospels*. New York: Random House, 1979.

————. "What Became of God the Mother?" In *Womanspirit Rising*. Edited by Carol Christ and Judith Plaskow. San Francisco: HarperSanFrancisco, 1979.

Parke, H. W. *Sibyls and Sibylline Prophecy in Classical Antiquity*. London: Routledge, 1988.

Patai, Raphael. *The Hebrew Goddess*. New York: KTAV, 1967.

————. *On Jewish Folklore*. Detroit: Wayne State University Press, 1983.

Pelikan, Jaroslav Jan. *Mary Through the Centuries: Her Place in the History of Culture*. New Haven: Yale University Press, 1996.

Phillips, E. D. *Greek Medicine*. London: Thames and Hudson, 1973.

Phipps, William E. *The Sexuality of Jesus: Theological and Literary Perspectives*. Cleveland: Pilgrim Press, 1996.

Pomeroy, Sarah B. *Goddesses, Whores, Wives, and Slaves: Women in Classical Antiquity*. New York: Schocken Books, 1975.

————, ed. *Women's History, Ancient History*. Chapel Hill: University of North Carolina Press, 1991.

Potok, Chaim. *Wanderings: Chaim Potok's History of the Jews*. New York: Ballantine, 1978.

Preston, Samuel H. "Mortality Trends." In *Annual Review of Sociology* 3 (1977): 163–178.

Preuss, Julius. *Biblical and Talmudic Medicine*. New York: Sanhedrin Press, 1978.

Qleibo, Ali H. *Before the Mountains Disappear: An Ethnographic Chronicle of the Modern Palestinians*. Cairo: Kloreus, 1992.

Ranke-Heinemann, Uta. *Eunuchs and the Kingdom of Heaven: Women, Sexuality, and the Catholic Church*. New York: Doubleday, 1990.

Renan, Ernest. *The Life of Jesus* (Vie de Jésus). New York: Carleton, 1864.

Ricoeur, Paul. *Time and Narrative* (Temps et récit). Chicago: University of Chicago Press, 1984.

Riddle, John M. *Contraception and Abortion from the Ancient World to the Renaissance*. Cambridge: Harvard University Press, 1992.

Rosenblum, Mort. *Olives: The Life and Lore of a Noble Fruit*. New York: North Point Press, 1996.

Rougement, Denis de. *Love in the Western World* (L'amour et l'Occident). New York: Pantheon, 1956.

Ruether, Rosemary Radford, ed. *Religion and Sexism: Images of Women in the Jewish and Christian Traditions*. New York: Simon and Schuster, 1974.

————, ed. *Womanguides: Readings Toward a Feminist Theology*. Boston: Beacon Press, 1985.

————, and McLaughlin, Eleanor, eds. *Women of Spirit: Female Leadership in the Jewish and Christian Traditions*. New York: Simon and Schuster, 1979.

Sabbagh, Suha, ed. *Palestinian Women of Gaza and the West Bank*. Bloomington: Indiana University Press, 1998.

Safrai, Shmuel, and Stern, Menachem, eds. *The Jewish People in the First Century*. Philadelphia: Fortress Press, 1974.

Sanders, E. P. *The Historical Figure of Jesus*. London: Allen Lane, 1993.

———. *Jesus and Judaism*. Philadelphia: Fortress Press, 1985.

Saramago, José. *The Gospel According to Jesus Christ: A Novel*. New York: Harcourt Brace, 1994.

Schaberg, Jane. *The Illegitimacy of Jesus: A Feminist Theological Interpretation of the Infancy Narratives*. San Francisco: Harper and Row, 1987.

Schama, Simon. *Landscape and Memory*. New York: Knopf, 1995.

Schiff, Ze'ev, and Ehud Ya'ari. *Intifada: The Palestinian Uprising, Israel's Third Front*. New York: Simon and Schuster, 1990.

Schiller, Eli. *Landscape of the Land of Israel in the Nineteenth Century and Traditional Arab Agriculture* (in Hebrew). Jerusalem: Ariel, 1984.

Scholem, Gershon. *Jewish Gnosticism, Merkabah Mysticism, and Talmudic Tradition*. New York: Jewish Theological Seminary of America, 1960.

———. *Major Trends in Jewish Mysticism*. New York: Schocken Books, 1946.

———. *The Messianic Idea in Judaism*. New York: Schocken Books, 1971.

———. *On the Kabbalah and Its Symbolism*. New York: Schocken Books, 1965.

Schonfield, Hugh J. *The Passover Plot: A New Interpretation of the Life and Death of Jesus*. Rockport, Mass.: Element Books, 1965.

Schüssler-Fiorenza, Elizabeth. *In Memory of Her: A Feminist Reconstruction of Christian Origins*. New York: Crossroad, 1983.

———. *Jesus: Miriam's Child, Sophia's Prophet*. New York: Continuum, 1994.

Segal, Alan. *Rebecca's Children: Judaism and Christianity in the Roman World*. Cambridge: Harvard University Press, 1986.

Shanks, Hershel, ed. *Christianity and Rabbinic Judaism: A Parallel History of Their Origins and Early Development*. Washington, D.C.: Biblical Archaeological Society, 1992.

Shorto, Russell. *Gospel Truth*. New York: Riverhead Books, 1997.

Silberman, Neil Asher. *Heavenly Powers: Understanding the Secret History of the Kabbalah*. New York: Grosset/Putnam, 1998.

Sissa, Giulia. *Greek Virginity*. Cambridge: Harvard University Press, 1990.

Smallwood, E. Mary. *The Jews Under Roman Rule from Pompey to Diocletian: A Study in Political Relations*. Leiden: E. J. Brill, 1976.

Smith, Morton: *Jesus the Magician: Charlatan or Son of God?* San Francisco: Harper and Row, 1978.

Smith, W. Robertson. *Lectures on the Religion of the Semites*. London: A. and C. Black, 1894.

Sontag, Susan. *Illness as Metaphor*. New York: Farrar, Straus, Giroux, 1978.

Stone, Merlin. *When God Was a Woman*. New York: Dial Press, 1976.

Swan, Laura. *The Forgotten Desert Mothers: Sayings, Lives and Stories of Early Christian Women*. New York: Paulist Press, 2001.

Taylor, Timothy. *The Prehistory of Sex: Four Million Years of Human Sexual Culture*. New York: Bantam, 1996.

Torjesen, Karen Jo. *When Women Were Priests: Women's Leadership in the Early Church*. San Francisco: HarperSanFrancisco, 1993.

Toorn, Karel van der. *From Her Cradle to Her Grave: The Role of Religion in the Life of the Israelite and Babylonian Woman*. Sheffield: JSOT Press, 1994.

Tran, V. Tam Tinh. *Isis Lactans: Corpus des monuments Gréco-Romains d'Isis* (in French). Leiden: E. J. Brill, 1973.

Vermes, Geza. *The Changing Faces of Jesus*. New York: Fortress, 2001.

―――――. *The Religion of Jesus the Jew*. Minneapolis: Fortress, 1993.

Veyne, Paul, ed. *A History of Private Life, Volume 1: From Rome to Byzantium*. Cambridge: Harvard University Press, 1987.

Warner, Marina. *Alone of All Her Sex: The Myth and the Cult of the Virgin Mary*. New York: Knopf, 1976.

Whallon, William. *Formula, Character and Context: Studies in Homeric, Old English, and Old Testament Poetry*. Cambridge, Mass.: Harvard University Press, 1969.

Wilken, Robert L., ed. *Aspects of Wisdom in Judaism and Early Christianity*. Notre Dame: University of Notre Dame Press, 1975.

Wills, Gary. *Papal Sin: Structures of Deceit*. New York: Doubleday, 2000.

Wilson, A. N. *Jesus: A Life*. New York: Norton, 1992.

―――――. *Paul: The Mind of the Apostle*. London: Random House, 1997.

Witt, R. E. *Isis in the Greco-Roman World*. Ithaca, N.Y.: Cornell University Press, 1971.

Wroe, Ann. *Pontius Pilate*. New York: Random House, 1999.

ACKNOWLEDGMENTS

A book such as this cannot possibly exist without those whose expertise it draws upon: the historians, anthropologists, and biblical scholars whose work makes up the bulk of the bibliography. I am deeply indebted to them, and trust that they feel that their findings have been well used.

In the Middle East, particular thanks to Mordechai (Motti) Aviam, Galilee district archeologist for the Israel Antiquities Authority, who led the way unerringly through the thorns and broken cisterns of Yodfat and Cana; to Ali Qleibo, professor of the arts at Al Quds University in Jerusalem, who introduced me to the extraordinary work of Hilma Granqvist; to medical anthropologist Dr. Stephen Fulder of Klil, in the Galilee, who shared his immense knowledge on the local use of herbal medicines; to Melila Helner of the Hebrew University of Jerusalem and to David Neuhaus, SJ, of the Pontifical Biblical Institute in Jerusalem for their willingness to act as sounding boards; to Zvi and Devora Pantanowitz for their hospitality and unwavering friendship; and to Carol Ann Bernheim, who guided me thoughtfully through the Galilee and allowed me to work my way through her library.

In the United States, the University of Washington's permission to use the outstanding collections of the Suzallo and Allen libraries as an independent scholar was invaluable. I owe especially deep thanks to Richard Horsley, distinguished professor of liberal arts and the study of religion at the University of Massachusetts, Boston, for welcoming me into the research community and for sharing his expertise; to Olivier

D'hose, who acted as my sharp-eyed first reader and master of technology; and to Teresa Herriman, who insisted I write this book. At Bloomsbury USA, editor-in-chief Karen Rinaldi gave me the best things any writer could ask of an editor—unflagging support, enthusiasm, and encouragement—while Amanda Katz shepherded me through the publication process with admirable patience and understanding, as did Katherine Fausset at the Watkins-Loomis agency. And last but never least, deepest thanks to Gloria Loomis, president of Watkins-Loomis, my longtime friend and agent, and the wise woman to whom this book is dedicated.

INDEX

A NOTE ON THE AUTHOR

Lesley Hazleton is the award-winning author of eight books, including *Jerusalem, Jerusalem* and *Where Mountains Roar*. Her work has appeared in such publications as the *New York Times*, *Harper's*, *Parade*, *Esquire*, *Vanity Fair*, *Mirabella*, and *The Nation*. She lived in and reported from Jerusalem for thirteen years, and now lives in Seattle.

A NOTE ON THE TYPE

Guardi was designed by Reinhard Haus of Linotype in 1987. It was named after the Guardi brothers, Gianantonio and Francesco, the last famous artists from the Renaissance Venetian school of painting. It is based on the Venetian text styles of the fifteenth century. The influence of characters originally written with a feather can be seen in many aspects of this modern alphabet.